UNDERSTANDING STANDARD COSTING

UNDERSTANDING STANDARD COSTING

by
T. M. Walker, CA, ACMA

Published for
THE INSTITUTE OF CHARTERED
ACCOUNTANTS OF SCOTLAND
by
GEE & CO (PUBLISHERS) LIMITED
151 STRAND, LONDON WC2R 1JJ

FIRST PUBLISHED 1980
© T. M. Walker
SBN 85258 185 8

*Printed in Great Britain for Gee & Co (Publishers) Limited
by Tonbridge Printers Limited, Tonbridge, Kent*

INTRODUCTION

There is a great deal more to standard costing than the recitation of variance formulae and the light-fingered use of a calculator. The author lays the foundations of understanding by explaining the book-keeping steps involved in creating standard stock valuations, variances and other related nominal ledger accounts, and how the culmination is reached on profit and loss accounts and other performance reports. The effects of business transactions carried out by companies operating a system of standard costing on balance sheet figures are fully explored and illustrated.

While all of the basic standard costing variances are examined and illustrated in depth, the book also lays emphasis on the further analysis which is frequently vital in explaining causes and in suggesting remedial action: for example, there is detailed coverage of the capacity and productivity elements which constitute a fixed production overhead volume variance.

The strong relationship between variances and ratios is explored with illustrations. Extensive advice is provided on the preparation and presentation of the interpretative comments which form an essential supplement to figure-work statements.

This book will be useful to students studying for the examinations of accountancy and other professional bodies and to those at universities and colleges who are undertaking courses of study which feature costing or management accounting.

ACKNOWLEDGEMENTS

I would like to thank Mr W. J. H. Millar, CA, FCMA, JDipMA, and Mr D. G. Smith, BCom, CA, who read the book in typescript and made many helpful comments and criticisms, and whose suggestions for amplifications and amendments were based on experience and careful study. Thanks are also due to my colleagues in The Institute of Chartered Accountants of Scotland for their support and encouragement, and to Mrs Rona Johnston for her highly proficient secretarial and typing work.

I am grateful to The Institute of Chartered Accountants of Scotland for permission to include in this book certain examples, portions of narrative and questions which were first published in documentation for students or in examination papers of the Institute, and to The Institute of Chartered Accountants in England and Wales, The Institute of Cost and Management Accountants and The Association of Certified Accountants for allowing the reproduction of examination questions in an appendix.

CONTENTS

	Page
Introduction	v
Acknowledgements	vi
1. The Purposes of Standards, Standard Costing and Variance Accounting	1
2. The Creation of Variances: in at the Birth	15
3. Book-keeping, Nominal Ledgers and Trial Balances	25
4. Direct Material Variances	50
5. Scrapped Production and Production Yield Variances	73
6. Direct Labour Variances	81
7. Production and Administration Overhead Variances	95
8. Production and Administration Cost Ratios	115
9. Sales and Selling Cost Variances	125
10. Profit Statements	139
11. Causes of Variances	175
12. Ensuring Credibility	180
Glossary of Terms and Expressions Used	191
Further Reading	198
Selected Examination Questions	199
Index	205

CHAPTER 1

THE PURPOSES OF STANDARDS, STANDARD COSTING, AND VARIANCE ACCOUNTING

A Parallel in Sport

Those of you who are familiar with the game of golf will be well aware of the expression 'par for the course'. The par of a golf course is the number of strokes which a player should take to cover eighteen holes playing each shot in a thoroughly competent fashion. 'Par for the course' means 'just right' in terms of standard of performance.

However, if one looks a little closer at a golf course, and those floundering upon it at any time, 'par' is actually extremely challenging, indeed daunting, and needs to be adjusted by 'handicapping'. By a subtle change which recognises such factors as the overall length of a course, 'par' may be a stroke or two more or less than a course's 'standard scratch score', and it is upon the latter that a golfer's handicap is based. Each golfer becomes the proud possessor of his own standard or 'adjusted scratch score', at which he may aim with a greater chance of success. Thus, if I am in the habit of taking around 14 strokes more (on average) than the scratch score (SSS) for the course to which I belong, I will be given a handicap of 14 strokes; so my standard at which to 'shoot' is 84 if the course SSS is 70. I need to measure my *actual* performance thereafter against a standard performance of 84. If I take, say, 90 strokes in any particular round (quite a common occurrence), my 'variance' from standard is 6 strokes.

Each golfer has objectives; to become a better golfer, to straighten up his drives, to improve his putting, etc, in the same way that a business manager has objectives, to increase his staff's motivation, to become a better communicator, and so on; but, when all is said and done, there has to be an ultimate tangible test as to whether the golfer and the manager are successful. The golfer assesses his overall performance against his adjusted SSS for the course, the manager against his budget – the latter being adjusted to take account of conditions and circumstances.

If the manager can achieve enough business transactions which are related to saleable products and which are in line with expectations, the result is achievement of budgets. If the golfer can put enough individual shots together during any one round of golf – the result is achievement of his adjusted scratch score 'budget'. His adjusted score allows for 'wastage', deviation, etc, but if he has more than his normal number of bad shots, he will miss his budget. For example, he may be allowed to operate on the basis that three out of four drives from the tee ought to be straight, three out of four putts from within four feet ought to be successful, and so on.

In a production environment, management might assess that nine out of ten units produced ought to pass inspection, that nineteen out of twenty raw material portions ought to be usable/unbroken, fifty out of each sixty minutes operated ought to be directly productive, and so on. So, when an SSS is being worked out for a particular *product,* allowance is made for wastage, idle-time, occasional poor workmanship, etc, in the same way that an SSS is worked out for a particular golfer. If there are the right number of *good* product units at the end of the day, they will be able to absorb the effects of these deviations so that, overall, budgeted costs are not exceeded. If the golfer has enough good shots in a round of 18 holes he can meet his budget on the overall day by ultimately achieving his adjusted SSS.

A golfer has to face a moment of reckoning after 18 holes (one round). He may be in trouble against his own SSS at any time during the round, after say three or four holes, but it is the cumulative effect, aggregated over 18 holes, which really matters. Similarly, a manager in industry is assessed over a budget time-period. His moment of reckoning might be after a four-week period, or a month or a year. During day-to-day operations within the time period concerned there might be all manner of problems, but his performance is measured in aggregate over the whole period, and hopefully there may be enough plus points to cancel out the minuses. If, in the end, he has produced enough units of product, the aggregate costs of which are as expected, he will be on target for achieving his budget.

As a golf club formalises its SSS for the golf course concerned (a specific number of strokes over 18 holes) so management in industry and commerce will formalise a budget for a particular time period. Each manager studies a formal budget relating to his particular function . . . one might say 'The budget is 1,000 units of good production'; another 'The budget is 800 items to be sold'. The golfer relates to 18 holes, the manager to a time period.

What makes life interesting for the golfer and the manager is that the former's personal SSS and the latter's budget target leave plenty of scope as to *how* ultimate objectives are to be achieved. One golf stroke may be much better than the golfer could have reasonably expected, the next much worse; one batch of products may cost the manager much more than planned, the next correspondingly less. Standard costing provides the manager with a trail of tangible evidence during the time period in question, as to whether or not he is heading for budget achievement. It also provides clear-cut evidence at the close of the accounting period concerned as to why actual results overall have exceeded or fallen short of expectations.

Control of Detailed Transactions
There can be no doubt that the ultimate discipline is a comparison of overall total performance against a budget for the period, in the same way that the ultimate test of a golfer is not 'that twenty foot putt which went in

at the ninth hole' but the aggregate number of strokes taken over 18 holes. But standard costing is invaluable in relating overall budgets to more minute circumstances, narrowing concentration to the elements which need attention at individual transaction level: the cost per unit of a raw material part, the throughput in units per hour of a particular machine, the oil consumption per hour of a particular boiler, and so on. Any degree of deviation from expectation or standard for each of the above items triggers off a variance which may well have a bearing on the ultimate achievement of a budget. But at this level, the variance is *manageable:* it can be pinned down to specific causes and to specific people for attention, so that good deviations can be repeated and bad ones eliminated. To make his round manageable, the golfer, too, concentrates on achieving the detail within his budget for his round, step by step: 'This number 6 iron should take me 150 yards to somewhere on the green', or 'This drive should take me about 200 yards, just clear of that bunker': or 'This putt of 3 feet should go in the hole'.

At the close of a particular round, a golfer may actually have taken 86 shots against his own SSS of $70 + 13 = 83$. He has a *total* variance of 3 (unfavourable) against budget. Likewise, a manager may have agreed a budget of 1,000 units of production costing £40,000. His *actual* cost of the 1,000 units may be £43,000. By monitoring each element of the production process, standard costing gives clear indications as to why the unfavourable variance of £3,000 arose. There will doubtless have been several favourable deviations from plans for some cost elements and unfavourable ones for others, in the same way as the golfer will have had some particularly good shots and some very frustrating ones. The golfer may say 'It was that bunker shot at the twelfth'; the manager, 'It was that machine breakdown in Dept 2'.

Standard costing will spell out to the manager the monetary effect on costs of the machine breakdown in question, if the standard costing system has been planned and designed to achieve this end.

Standard costing therefore provides a vehicle for exception reporting. On the expenditure side, so long as the conversion of cash or credit expenditure into saleable stock gains is achieved on a 'pound for pound' basis, variances do not appear and reports to management advocate minimum action. As soon as the pound for pound conversion process breaks down, the deviation and its cause are reported for possible remedial action. A golfer may have his memory and his impressions to help him explain his variance of 3 strokes, but the manager has something rather more tangible: a set of detailed variances, analysed in ways which have been assessed in advance as likely to prove helpful, and the monetary evaluation of each variance should help him to ascertain whether it is significant (or 'material').

Balancing the Books
We should now relate to circumstances in which 'a system of standard costing and flexible budgetary control is in operation', to quote an endlessly recurring phrase from examination questions. Such questions usually contain a directive to 'value stock at standard cost, to include full (or total) works expenses'. This means 'value stock at standard *for balance sheet pur-*

poses'. For the purposes of the question concerned, you are therefore required to attribute to the actual balance sheet a cost of stock on hand which in all probability did not actually happen. You are required to assume that (1) the number of units of stock produced times their standard cost arithmetically balances precisely with (2) any consequent diminution of other assets such as raw materials or bank balances (or with any increase in creditors). The extent to which this principle provokes arithmetical imbalance in any given question is measured by a total variance. This variance represents the arithmetical shortfall of (2) below (1) (and in such cases is favourable), or the excess of (2) over (1) (an unfavourable variance). In any event, the amount of the total variance is needed to make the balance sheet square. Normally the total variance is transferred to the company's profit and loss account or earned surplus account, which remains open at the end of the accounting period concerned and is therefore shown on the balance sheet.

In simple terms, a company endeavours in using standard costing to achieve the following situation during the production process:

Balance Sheet

Sources of funds	
Earned surplus	NIL
Uses of funds	
Stock at standard cost	+£X
Cash: actual amount	−£X
	NIL

In a perfect world, in which standards could be anticipated with absolute certainty and accuracy, the above achievement might be just possible, but in reality, a company will find the following picture emerging:

Balance Sheet

Sources of funds	
Earned surplus	£Z
Uses of funds	
Stock at standard cost	+£X
Cash: actual amount	−£Y
	£Z

When actual cash spent is more than expected, Z will be a negative figure. In such cases the company will have converted a cash asset into stock of a lesser amount, giving a potential diminution in the strength of the company.

What can go awry in achieving a clean conversion from cash minus into stock plus?

  (1) Cost rates may in practice deviate from standard. Standards are built in advance of actual use, and staff involved need to anticipate a great deal of what may happen, not least the unit costs of raw material ingredients, and the wage rates of operatives. Each expense item which relates to products (ie which is part of the cost of bring-

ing production ultimately to a state of completion) involves crystal-ball gazing and it is easy to understand why actual cost rates may be different from plan.

(2) Efficiency may in practice deviate from expectations. For example, more units may be produced in an hour than anticipated. If each is valued at standard cost, stock valuation at standard will exceed the amount actually spent.

(3) Fixed (or static) costs, which do not rise or fall in sympathy with increases or decreases in the level of activity, may be spread over a smaller or greater number of units than budgeted. A 'set' unit rate is built in advance to convert fixed cost cash minus into the fixed cost element within stock plus. For example, if a company's budgeted fixed production costs are, say, £10,000 and budgeted production is, say, 10,000 units, a conversion rate of £1 per unit will be applied each time an actual unit is produced. If 12,000 units are made, they will each have £1 of value added to them in respect of fixed costs: so, all else being equal, the balance sheet will show (in respect of the fixed expenses situation only): stock plus £12,000, cash minus £10,000 and earned surplus (total variance) plus £2,000.

Categories of Variance

Standard costing therefore breaks down the total variance, which we have been discussing, into various segments, to provide a clearer picture of *why* cash minus and stock plus are not self-cancelling. Each reason is usually separated and dealt with by means of a constituent variance which has a meaningful title and can be of value to particular managers. When standard stock valuation is the basis for pricing policy, deviations represented by variances become important, lest customers be inadvertently over- or under-charged in relation to actual expenditure incurred.

Standard costing makes distinctions between controllable (manageable) and non-controllable deviations from plan: this is done by separating on output reports those individual variances which can be dealt with by specific people within an organisation from those which have been caused by external forces beyond the control of management. 'Of course it was the exceptionally strong wind' the golfer might say in his own defence, illustrating the latter. 'Of course it was the failure in supplies from our regular suppliers, which forced us to go elsewhere for more expensive raw materials' a manager might say, illustrating what, ostensibly at least, might be a non-controllable raw material price variance.

Whether variances are controllable or not usually depends upon the level of management to whom they are being reported. A variance which is con-trollable to a functional head such as a production manager may not be controllable to one of his foremen who wields lesser authority. Similarly, certain variances with which a production manager cannot cope may be readily controllable at board level. Lower levels of management are usually unable to exert strong or indeed any influence on certain cost elements which are affected by general company policy. In short, variances can therefore be controllable to one level of management but not to others. Standard costing systems, when properly designed, respect the various authority levels of the readership categories likely to receive performance reports. The reason, imagination and interest of appropriate management levels must be engaged.

The distinction of controllable from non-controllable variances highlights and quantifies individual management objectives, but confusion may arise when one department or location can exert undue influence, perhaps in intangible ways, on the performance of another, eg through production bottlenecks or varying standards of inspection of output.

In general terms, if someone can be found to accept responsibility for the control of specific *costs,* that person may acquiesce in assessing the significance of and reasons for the *variances* related to those costs.

Adverse non-controllable variances may need to be passed on to customers, but in some cases they may alternatively present a challenge to management to generate corresponding favourable controllable production variances elsewhere.

On the same theme of ensuring *optimum* rather than *maximum* management action, standard costing distinguishes between significant (or material) and trivial deviations from plan, offsets compensating variances, and presents aggregate (or cumulative) variances to avoid over-reactions to seasonal fluctuations or temporary problems. Enquiry time can then be properly weighted so that significant variances obtain a greater share. Significance (or 'materiality') may be measured by defining all cost variances above a specific percentage deviation from budgeted cost as material, or, alternatively, all variances above a defined monetary value may be classed as material. The *overall* effect of a single management action has to be evaluated. For example, a sales director could agree to an alteration to a selling price which would result in a sales price variance. However, the change in unit price could make the product more or less attractive on the market than anticipated (budgeted), and a compensating sales volume variance could emanate from the same root cause as the sales price variance, viz the decision not to use the standard selling price for actual sales. A favourable sales price variance caused by increasing actual selling prices above standard selling prices could be cancelled out by a compensating unfavourable sales volume variance, caused by selling fewer units than planned (budgeted). The whole result needs evaluation in monetary terms.

Harmonising Book-keeping and Physical Movements

Standard costing systems set out to achieve synchronisation between physical stock movements and supporting book-keeping entries. In the nominal (or general) ledger of a production (or manufacturing) company a monetary value of the various stock categories (raw materials, work in progress and finished goods) will be shown. The monetary amounts shown in these ledger accounts are supposed to reflect the amount and condition of physical goods visible for inspection. As there is continuous physical movement during production, through transfers from one stock category to another (eg raw materials to work in progress), and through continuous adding of value to production units and depletions through sales, life becomes very difficult for the accountant who has the job of ensuring that the books of account run smoothly in double harness with the physical stock situations apparent to the eye.

The nominal (or general) ledger entries which must be made involve transfers:

    (a) from Raw Material Stores (or Stock) Account
        to Work in Progress Account
    (b) from Work in Progress Account
        to Finished Goods Stock Account
    (c) from Finished Goods Stock Account
        to Cost of Sales Account.

During production various departments may be involved in which case there are accounting entries transferring what is (hopefully) an ever increasing stock valuation:

    (1) from Work in Progress subsidiary account for (say) Dept A
        to Work in Progress subsidiary account for (say) Dept B.
    (2) from Work in Progress subsidiary account for (say) Dept B
        to Work in Progress subsidiary account for (say) Dept C,

and so on.

The nominal ledger remains aloof from these subsidiary ledger transfers. Whether stock is held in Department A or B, the valuation is still 'Work in Progress'. In most accounting systems, each of the nominal ledger accounts named above has a subsidiary ledger in support, in which one account controls each separate stock item. Consequently, the full-bodied title of each nominal ledger account involved should have the word 'Control' within it, eg 'Raw Material Stores Control Account', the word 'control' implying the existence of detailed records in a separate subsidiary book, in the same way as a company maintains sales ledger detailed account records in support of its Sales Ledger Control Account.

Standard Product Specification Sheets

The linchpin of the accountant's defences in his battle to keep control of a very complex situation involves the creation of standard product specification sheets (SPSS) or standard cost specification sheets (SCSS), so that at any time of any physical movement to, on or from the factory shop floor, compatible accounting book entries can be based on measurement of the number of units concerned times the unit valuation shown on the SPSS concerned. In this way it is hoped that book applications and transfers of all the elements of cost (such as raw materials and labour) which ultimately form the cost of sales figure in the accounts are synchronised as much as possible with the physical evidence of growth and decline of raw material, work in progress and finished goods stock levels. Without this policy bookkeeping entries tracing physical movements would not keep pace with actual physical evidence, as analysis of actual costs attaching to each transfer, cost element by cost element, would cause serious delays.

By requiring management to prepare detailed product specification sheets as to standard contents and their costs under normal operating conditions, standard costing should assist in the making of effective decisions on product pricing, quoting, stock valuation and profit determination, by making sure that no costs incurred in 'bringing stock to its present condi-

tion and location' are overlooked. Standard contents, by the way, usually
include (within materials, labour and overheads) some reasonable additions
for scrap, labour inefficiency, machine downtime, and a portion of tool
costs which are to be spread over the useful life of the product concerned.

The creation of SPSS's breeds among management a familiarity with a
company's end-products, which activates constructive criticism of manufacturing, administrative and selling procedures. Each element of cost
attributed to a product is exposed for scrutiny and possible challenge. In
their wake, such challenges can bring improved efficiency and economies of
effort. Each cost line on a specification sheet shows a burden of cost which
will ultimately be passed on to a customer as part of the selling price of the
product concerned. Cost reduction can readily result either in sales price
reduction or in a wider profit margin. Specification sheets are therefore
useful discussion documents for future planning purposes.

Those of you who have been involved in the purchase of a house or flat
will no doubt remember reading 'specification sheets' for the properties
which interested you. When properties are handled by an estate agent or
lawyer their specifications can often be prefixed with a comment to the
effect that the writer is ... 'proud and privileged to present this property
which comprises ...'. There then follows a list of the property's constituent
parts, which, in total, must go some considerable way towards justifying the
price asked. By the same token, a well designed product specification sheet
can equip a company's sales force with useful information on a product's
contents, including the quality and type of raw material ingredients, labour
skills and time applied, machine time and power costs and the category of
machinery used, to enable staff concerned to speak knowledgeably and con-
fidently to potential customers. 'We use nothing but top quality ingredients
and skills' is a statement best made after obtaining the full facts of the case.

The Link between Budgets and Standards

While *budgets* certainly set targets to stretch management's potential and to
motivate them to greater effort, standards form the essential oil that greases
the works for anyone directly concerned with saleable products. Remember
that the budget (adjusted SSS for the course) reminds a golfer that he
should take (say) 83 strokes for his round. A standard, however, is perti-
nent to any more detailed situation within that round which has a bearing
on his final total performance. Finding himself in a bunker, he can relate an
actual recovery shot of thirty yards, sliced (to the right) into semi-rough
ground, to a standard for that situation of a forty yards shot 'punched'
straight towards the green. He *needs* such detailed standards to give
meaning to his ongoing performance. The manager can be well aware of a
budget requirement for a specific number of units of production, but he
needs detailed performance standards for each operational incident and
situation to help him concentrate on the many parts which go to make up a
successful whole.

In achieving overall objectives for a given time period, the interaction
between budgets and standards is critical. The next time you walk through
a pine wood you may care to draw a parallel.

The tree trunk is the 'functional budget', eg, to motivate the total production function of a business; the branches are individual production departmental budgets, and each pine needle represents one of the mass of product transactions within each department. Standards assess health and well-being at this latter detailed level. Each tree in turn belongs to the pine wood, which is necessary for whatever overall effect may be required, eg scenic attraction or timber, and in this sense the pine wood is like a company's 'master budget' which draws all the functional budgets together to achieve an overall effect or result.

Inter-relationships can also be illustrated, in rather less flamboyant fashion, by using a pyramid:

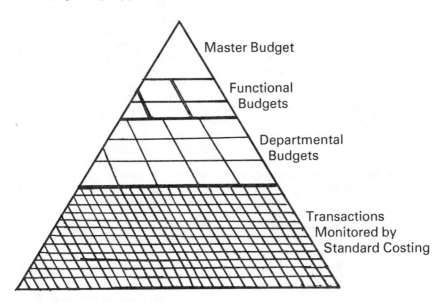

Controlling Unplanned Actions

Standard costing can also 'monitor' the effects of impulsive decisions, by, say, sales executives who offer unplanned discounts on certain product lines. Deviations in product price, mix or overall bulk quantity cause variances between actual and budgeted profits. Standard costing can evaluate these variances so that those concerned, realising that their spontaneous actions are being called to account, will take care and learn to consider the results which their actions may have on the broader canvas of their company's affairs. By 'Monitoring the Movements of the Mad Marketing Men' (MMMMM), the effects of their actions on other areas such as production (unexpected peaks and troughs in demand), cost recovery (greater or smaller number of products over which to spread fixed costs), stock levels (erosion of buffer stocks to meet customer service requirements or future sales promotions) and capital employed (higher or lower stockholdings or debtors than budgeted) can be quantified and kept under control.

Achieving Sensible Price Increases

Standard costing facilitates the calculation of realistic and prudent price increases, because of the distinctions which it makes between:

(a) controllable and non-controllable
(b) significant and insignificant, and
(c) temporary and permanent variances, and by setting off variances derived from a common cause against each other to ascertain a net result.

'Costs have risen alarmingly, so amend our quoted prices right away . . .' *may* be a correct course of action, but standard costing forces management to take a long, lingering look at all that is involved in the cost increases before passing them on to customers. For example, efficient management might firstly try to absorb cost increases of a controllable nature by internal efficiencies before saddling customers, realising that competitors could take advantage of any slackness in this field. Again, the costs which were allegedly rising might be easily identified and ostensibly alarming, but might in fact account for only a small percentage of total cost. Certain sharp cost increases could also be seasonal; many standard costs are built to operate over many months, so that over their useful lives periodic adverse variances cancel out against the favourable variances of other periods. If variances are intelligently analysed, they can help to avoid over-reaction by management who would otherwise need to operate on the basis of hunch and guess-work. In the case of new products, or where new production methods are initiated, a series of adverse variances may appear while operatives learn what is required; perhaps around the mid-term point of the standards which have been set, the unfavourable variances will become favourable ones, so that at the close of the time-span for which the standards are to operate, the speedy operating efficiency of later periods will compensate for the effects of the slower pace of earlier periods. Thus, if standards are built to last throughout periods of technological change or product development, management can expect to have variances: planned variances are indeed more than a possibility!

Pressures to Revise Standards

The above analyses also prove invaluable in forming conclusions as to when deviations from plan (variances) are indicative of a need to revise standards. Constantly recurring variances highlight the need for change: exact timing is a matter for good judgment. Frequently there is the temptation for favourable variances between actual and standard costs to be embedded in a new set of more demanding standards, a cause of some cynicism among executives on the 'front-line' who are therefore judged against increasingly demanding criteria for success as time passes, while a series of unfavourable variances will not produce a similar ready response in the form of alleviated standards. In most companies using a system of standard costing, there is constant pressure to improve on standards, in the face of increasing competition and narrow profit margins, so that actual performance is judged against ever increasing expectations. Each company concerned has to walk the narrow road between complacency caused by easy standards, and disillusionment caused by unattainable standards. The managements of many companies bend over backwards to prevent most forms of adverse cost variances from being classed as permanent, lest there be a formal, agreed deterioration in targets applicable for ensuing periods.

By careful planning, a company may segregate variances emanating from parts of the organisation using modern equipment from those resulting from use of older equipment. This can be done by having separate sets of performance standards so that whatever location was involved, variances have similar weight and significance.

The Weighting of Variances

Perhaps the most vital purpose of standards and standard costing is to quantify, with causes, deviations from plan in monetary terms, and to give each due weighting. At this stage you should remember that these deviations from plan represent an analysis of the total extent to which resources on the balance sheet such as raw material stocks and cash have not been converted *exactly* into other assets of like amount. The greater the number of *worthwhile* reasons for this total variance, the greater the range of variances which will be introduced into the standard costing system. Each of these afflictions must have full nominal ledger status, ie must form part of the company's trial balance, if the books of account and the balance sheet are to remain in balance. Each variance having appeared in the nominal ledger to reveal its story, a massive clearance of variance balances to the profit and loss account is likely to take place, so that variance accounts are squared off at nil value and the profit and loss account, which is merely another nominal ledger account, reflects the saga of actual expense and income and reveals actual profit or loss in due course.

Justifying Expenditure: the Acid Tests

Before turning to face (and disarm) the somewhat daunting Regiment of Variances, it is necessary, then, to affirm our faith in the value of all the elbow grease which has to be applied in setting up and operating a standard costing system in practice. There are many in a practical environment who baulk at the work load involved in setting, using and monitoring standards, and in such cases a cost justification exercise, comparing costs of the system with some financial evaluation of the benefits derived, can help. There are at least an equal number who are uneasy about the stringency which standards impose: standards represent control and discipline and lack of manoeuvrability. For most business managers, operating conditions are very volatile: standards tend to class together conditions, people, materials and machinery which produce dissimilar degrees of performance by the day if not by the minute. They tend to regard as identical, features of operations which are not identical. Moreover, standards are the satellites of budgets, in which cost rationing weighs heavily. The offering of allowances of cost appropriate to activity is the linchpin of cost control, and cost control is essential for the achievement of budgeted profit.

A company's potential for spending and its potential for earning are not locked together. They are governed by different rules, forces and influences. Damage will not be done if a willing buyer can readily be found to recompense a company for its outlays. A supplier's spending acceleration rate can, however, outpace the rate of growth of his customers' willingness to repay: and the longer the delay between spending by a supplier and recovery from a customer, the greater the need for cost control by the former, particularly if, for a proportion of this time lag, the customer remains uncommitted and the goods or services remain in stock. Cost control is a stepping stone or milestone control point between the spending of money and the attempt to recoup such expense from customers. It has much more to do with a company's survival than with petty disciplinary procedures against staff who have 'blown' a pound or two on a bottle of wine while on expenses. The control of costs is not founded on an attempt to impose moderation and restraint upon cavalier employees: it is based on the principle that actual expenditure should not exceed what the ultimate actual end products are capable of carrying to market. Thus the un-budgeted champagne bottle can be broken open when the unbudgeted sales order has been captured. The cost budget is not the ultimate resting place for the bill: only the penultimate. The final home for the bill will be a customer's invoice.

In a sense the amount of money which the staff of a company spends is the value which it places upon the goods or services which that company produces. But this value is subjective: potential customers of a company's output are not obliged to agree with the company's staff. Therefore those who prepare cost budgets, drawn from the company's ranks, disengage themselves for a moment from their company loyalties and personal opinions and try very hard to envisage what customers will select as a fair rate of cost outlay for a particular operation which will eventually. embed itself on sales invoices. The two criteria are:

(1)   there must be a product which can carry the *type* of expense in question in terms of common justice and relevancy;

(2)   the *amount* of the expense should be capable of standing scrutiny by customers in the clear light of day.

So managers who create budgets and who compare actual with budgeted costs are acting as scrutineers for the market place, simulating customer reaction to cost levels and measuring customers' willingness to have costs passed on to them for payment. The saving feature is that they do all this in advance: but it is then only worthwhile if a routine cost control system is used to winkle out unwanted costs. There must be acceptance of ostensibly excess spending when there are excess, unbudgeted increases in activity which have a market value. The skilful use of *flexible* budgetary control ensures the adjustment of cost spending entitlement in line with changing activity levels.

There are major steps which must be taken:

(1)   the collection in advance of acceptable cost specifications in view of what the company will have to offer;

(2)   the adjustment of acceptable cost levels in view of actual activity;

(3)   the monitoring of actual costs against predetermined acceptable levels.

Carelessness in the preparation of cost budgets at (1) betrays an insulting attitude to a company's future, for the company's future is placed at the mercy of a discerning and critical market, who may, or may not, acquiesce to the cost levels budgeted. Poor budgeting involves abdication by management from critical responsibilities. In effect, customers are advised: 'You tell *us* what our costs ought to be. Tell us when our goods go on offer, whether you think our chosen levels make sense'. If selling prices are derived from budgeted costs, a casual, uninformed approach to budgeting can be most unfortunate.

Much cost is incurred because it is in fashion to spend money in such ways: other people (companies) do it. Just as much is spent because employees' predecessors have been doing it for years beforehand. Neither of these reasons gives employees any right to spend a penny. Even common sense, or instincts of justice may cry out that particular expenses are needed, desirable or acceptable: cost control acts as a bulwark against such clarion calls, dampening down what instinct, 'gut feelings', personal or social satisfaction demand, and substituting one clear cut acid test: will the customer pay?

Effective Use of Standard Costing

If, therefore, we grudgingly accept that cost control involves 'the collection in advance of acceptable cost specifications . . .' (see (1) above), then we should set our minds to the task and use whatever techniques are available: these include standard costs. The point to stress is that standard costs must recognise the different cost elements which management identify in trying to control costs. Total cost is fragmented by management into elements or classifications and management concern is divided accordingly, often with different people directing attention to each element. Standard costing must slipstream behind this fundamental arrangement of cost control organisation, and as a result derives its somewhat lengthy list of variance categories. 'Adjustment of acceptable cost levels' (see (2)) *may* spike the guns of critics who complain that nothing should be artificially frozen as a standard in a far from standard environment. With this in mind, standard costing gallantly attempts to distinguish those costs which ought to vary in total with rises and falls in activity levels. Recognition of the principle of *flexible* budgetary control is vital, whereby actual costs are compared with what is acceptable (budgeted) not at budgeted activity but at actual activity. The penalty to be paid is a further lengthening of the list of variances: for example, some overheads are fixed by nature and others are variable, so separate variances are needed for both. 'The monitoring of actual costs against predetermined acceptable levels', at (3), should be regarded in a positive light. Upon budgeted profit a company's hopes will depend. Each time there is a deviation or variance from standard cost at business transaction level, the company takes one step away from budgeted profit. The size of the step, the direction in which it is taken and whether it is irretrievable are determined by preparation of variances. If a company's budgeted profit has an aura of credibility, if management believe it to be a valid goal and worth achieving, the large steps will be examined in more detail, the varying degrees of mischief caused will be analysed, and remedial action will be put in hand. Variances will be attributed to causes, which in turn will be classed as controllable and non-controllable. Some will be indicative of considerable malaise, and others regarded as trivial. Some deviations will be temporary, others threatening a complete change of route. For all of these reasons and more, the preparation of standard costing variances is a detailed, important but rewarding endeavour; for many companies, standard costing forms the soil in which their future health and strength are deeply rooted.

CHAPTER 2

THE CREATION OF VARIANCES:
IN AT THE BIRTH

A key objective of standard costing is to establish a cost recovery mechanism whereby 'CASH MINUS' sums are converted 'pound for pound' to 'STOCK PLUS', in a balance sheet environment. Pricing policies for finished goods for sale may be dependent upon the reliability of standard costing. Stock valuations made at standard cost are transferred within the books of account to COST OF SALES ACCOUNT in due course, when the products concerned are sold; hopefully, such amounts are recovered from customers via the SALES ACCOUNT with a little extra for profit. The balance sheet figures covering stock at standard cost are replaced at the time of sale by amounts for debtors in the case of credit sales, or cash or bank in the case of cash sales. The excess of the debtors amounts, which are for invoiced sales values, over the stock amounts being replaced on the balance sheet, which are at standard cost, represents profit. In book-keeping terms it is not possible to replace a stock figure 'A' with a debtors or bank figure 'B' and have a squared balance sheet. The thrill of a squared balance sheet is achieved by transferring (or posting) the difference mentioned above to the Profit and Loss Account figure in the balance sheet. For example if a company were to sell 100 units of product A for £700, the following situation would develop if the units had been held in the books of account at a standard cost of £500; assume that credit is allowed to customers, that selling prices are as expected and that the cost of the units is financed through a bank overdraft.

Extract from Balance Sheet

	Prior to Sale	After Sale
Source of funds		
Profit and loss account	—	200
Bank overdraft	500	500
Uses of funds		
Stock at standard cost	500	—
Debtors	—	700

From the balance sheet extract you will see that the size and strength of the company, or 'capital employed' has grown after the sale by £200 (£700–£500). This has been achieved through trading operations as the profit and loss account reveals.

Profit and Loss Account

	£ Prior to Sale	£ After Sale
Cost of production at standard	500	500
Less: closing stock at standard	500	—
Cost of sales	NIL	500
Sales for period at standard selling price	NIL	700
Balance on profit and loss account	NIL	200

When *standard* costs and *standard* selling prices are being used, there is nothing to prevent a company from trying to visualise *in advance* of production and sales activity, what is about to happen to the company's balance sheet image (and health and well-being). All that is needed is a very careful assessment of what activity levels are likely to be, what they are likely to cost, and what income is likely to be derived. Projections can then be made, plans laid for future deployment of resources, and everyone then goes to work to make it all happen. When the preceding profit and loss account and balance sheet are prepared on a hope and a prayer, the £200 balance on the profit and loss account becomes the BUDGETED PROFIT for the period concerned. After the production and selling wheels have begun to turn, an ACTUAL PROFIT exactly in line with budgeted profit would be a miracle. The extent to which actual profit differs from budgeted profit in due course is the basis for a TOTAL VARIANCE, the full title of which is TOTAL PROFIT VARIANCE.

Taking the preceding example, the actual cost of producing the 100 units might in practice be (say) £520. Suppose that the problem of the extra cost centred on that part of total costs which related to raw materials, and that within the £500, raw materials were expected to cost £200 but actually cost £220. Someone on the company's buying, accounting or stores staff would have a watching brief on raw material purchase invoices, and would notice an actual cost of £220 for particular items which should have been £200. With a system of standard costing in use, he would try to introduce standard costs for the raw materials involved at the earliest book-keeping stage and might well absorb the purchase transaction into the books as follows:

Raw Material Stock Account at standard   Debit £200
Raw Material Cost Variance Account   Debit £ 20
Sundry Creditors Control Account   Credit £220

In due course, when a foreman from an appropriate production department requisitioned the raw materials into production, the requisition would be priced at standard cost once more:

Work in Progress Account at standard   Debit £200
Raw Materials Stock Account   Credit £200

During the work in progress stage, labour and overhead value would of course be added as skill and effort were applied to make a saleable item, but for the time being let us confine our thoughts to raw materials.

After completion of production, when the 100 finished units containing the raw materials were complete, they would doubtless be removed from the shop floor and transferred physically to a finished goods store. The books of account would keep pace with this development, transferring the standard cost of the 100 units (including £200 for materials) as follows:

Finished Goods Stores Account at standard   Debit £200
   (raw material element only shown)
Work in Progress Account at standard   Credit £200

Then, in the happy event of a sale during the accounting period in question:

Cost of Sales Account at standard   Debit £200
Finished Goods Stores Account   Credit £200

Finally:

Profit and Loss Account   Debit £200
Cost of Sales Account at standard   Credit £200

This leaves the variance account open with a debit balance of £20. If the finished goods involved were sold, the company would have no choice but to 'write off' (transfer) the £20 to the Profit and Loss Account. The variance account balance would then be NIL.

Profit and Loss Account   Debit £ 20
Raw Material Cost Variance Account   Credit £ 20

Matters come to a head on the Profit and Loss Account. Comparisons are the essential oil that greases the works in management as well as in financial accounting.

Profit and Loss Account (all elements of cost included)

	Budget £	Actual £
Sales at standard selling prices	700	700
Less: cost of sales at standard	500	500
Budgeted profit	200	
Standard profit on actual sales quantities		200
Less: unfavourable cost variance:		
Raw materials		20
Actual profit		180

The company expected a profit of £200, but achieved £180. The profit variance of £20 is explained on the above report layout.

On the balance sheet, we have the following comparison to make:

Balance Sheet

	Budget £	Actual £
Source of Funds		
Profit and Loss Account	200	180
Bank Overdraft	500	520
	700	700
Uses of Funds		
Debtors	700	700

As you can imagine, actual costs can differ from budgeted costs for many reasons, some related to raw materials, some to labour, and others to overheads. Each of the cost categories or elements forming the ultimate cost of production total, and thereafter the cost of sales total, is likely to differ in practice from what was expected (ie from standard). In any event, standard costs are given their opportunity to 'speak' to management at the forefront of profit and loss or other performance report layouts: they are assumed initially to be correct, until proved faulty through the existence of balances on variance ledger accounts. On the immediately preceding profit and loss account, the standard profit on actual sales quantities was that profit which management were entitled to expect at actual sales quantity levels, had actual costs been in line with standard costs. £200 would have been not only the profit to expect but also the actual profit, had it not been for the fact that someone discovered an open debit balance of £20 waiting to be cleared to the Profit and Loss Account, bringing to rights a faulty profit of £200 which was not compatible with actual costs.

Had actual raw material costs been, say, £180 rather than in line with a standard of £200, the Profit and Loss Account would have shown:

Profit and Loss Account (all elements of cost included)

	Budget £	Actual £
Sales at standard selling prices	700	700
Less: cost of sales at standard	500	500
Budgeted profit	200	
Standard profit on actual sales quantities		200
Add: favourable cost variance:		
Raw materials		20
Actual profit		220

The company would have expected a profit of £200 but would have achieved £220.

On the balance sheet, the situation would have been:

Balance Sheet

	Budget £	Actual £
Sources of Funds		
Profit and Loss Account	200	220
Bank Overdraft	500	480
	700	480
Uses of Funds		
Debtors	700	700

This situation would have been initiated at the time of purchase invoice analysis:

Raw Material Stock Account at standard	Debit	£200
Sundry Creditors	Credit	£180

Raw Material Cost Variance Account   Credit £20
Then later:
Raw Material Cost Variance Account   Debit £20
Profit and Loss Account   Credit £20

At this stage we have ignored three probable features: (a) production and selling activity would actually be incompatible, ie taking place in differing accounting periods, (b) actual selling prices would vary from standard selling prices, (c) actual production and/or selling activity in physical unit terms would differ from budget. We can introduce these obvious complications one at a time.

In coming to terms with (a), ie producing and selling in different periods, let us assume that of the 100 units produced, one quarter unexpectedly remained unsold at the close of the accounting period. Building upon the previous situation, with actual costs of £480 the Profit and Loss Account would then be as follows:

Profit and Loss Account

Line ref.		Budget £	Actual £
1	Sales at standard selling prices	700	525
2	Cost of production at standard	500	500
3	Less: closing stock at standard	—	125
4	Cost of sales at standard	500	375
5	*Budgeted profit*	200	
6	Standard profit on actual sales		150
7	Less: sales volume variance (unfavourable)	50	—
8		150	150
9	Add: favourable production cost variance		20
10	*Actual profit*		170

A new variance has emerged at line 7. The SALES VOLUME VARIANCE measures the profit missed by the company through failing to sell 25 units which the budget specified would be sold. Before we aspire to master standard costing variance formulae (or descend into the dismal bog of variance formulae, depending on which way you look at things), try to realise that if 25 units unexpectedly fail to find their way onto sales invoices, the company will lose sales turnover to that extent. On the other side of the coin, it will not need to face up to the costs of these units on its profit and loss account; the costs will be lifted away as closing stock valuation. So actual sales on the profit and loss account are down £175 on budget, but cost of sales are also down on budget, by $25 \times £5 = £125$. So the sales volume variance is £50.

Now, the formula is:

Sales volume variance = (actual − budgeted) sales qty × profit per unit
$$= (75 - 100) \times £2$$
$$= -£50$$

There is a momentary reconciliation between the budget and actual columns at line 8. Notice that the sales volume variance is shown in the column containing faulty quantities. The budget column quantities are out of step with reality so it is this column which should take any volume correction.

The actual and budgeted balance sheets would be as follows:

Balance Sheet

	Budget £	Actual £
Sources of Funds		
Profit and Loss Account	200	170
Bank overdraft	500	480
	700	650
Uses of Funds		
Stock at standard cost	—	125
Debtors	700	525
	700	650

Notice that in this example, no attempt has been made to interfere with the valuation of closing stock. Strictly speaking, it is *not* being carried forward at the 'lower of cost or net realisable value'. However, for the most part, examination questions ask candidates to value any closing stock remaining at the close of an accounting period at standard cost: in such cases we have no choice but to comply with instructions. Secondly, cost may be standard cost when a company maintains its stock balances in the nominal ledger at standard cost, provided such standards are close to actual costs, ie provided there are no variances in the ledger disturbing enough to merit investigation with a view to spreading them equitably across closing stock balances.

Pursuing (b) (with actual selling prices varying from standard), in the context of this example let us suppose that the actual selling price per unit was £8, as compared with the standard of £7 recognised to this point (100 units × £7 = £700). We can expect an upsurge in actual profits against budgeted profits.

Profit and Loss Account

Line ref.		Budget £	Actual £
1	Sales at standard selling prices	700	525
2	Cost of production at standard	500	500
3	Less: closing stock at standard	—	125
4	Cost of sales at standard	500	375
5	*Budgeted profit*	200	
6	Standard profit on actual sales		150
7	Less: sales volume variance (unfavourable)	(50)	
8	Add: sales price variance (favourable)	75	75
9		225	225
10	Add: favourable production cost variance		20
11	*Actual profit*		245

The sales price variance at line 8 is:
Actual quantity sold × (actual − standard) unit price
$$= 75 \times £(8-7)$$
$$= \underline{\underline{£75}}$$

The preceding layout shows management, at line 6, the profit which they were entitled to expect for actual sales activity, if only standard selling prices and standard costs had been actually achieved. Line 11 less line 6 shows the total extent of the drift of actual profit away from revised standard profit of line 6. The fleeting reconciliation referred to earlier has now dropped to line 9. The sales price variance is shown in both budgeted and actual columns because each has wrongly presumed a selling price of £7 per unit. Lines 7 and 8 show the bearing which the selling function had on the drift of actual profits away from budgeted profit. Normally management would tend to set line 7 off against line 8 to show the net gain or loss resulting from a decision to alter the selling price of their finished product. In our example, there has been a consequent favourable profit variance of £(75−50) = £25.

The appropriate balance sheet entries are as follows:

Balance Sheet

	Budget £	Actual £
Sources of Funds		
Profit and Loss Account	200	245
Bank Overdraft	500	480
	700	725
Uses of Funds		
Stock at standard	—	125
Debtors	700	600
	700	725

If we are to pursue (c) (with actual production different from budget), the need for physical unit columns on the profit and loss account must be recognised. In fact, unit columns are a major feature on management accounting reports, and we shall need to keep this in mind from now on.

At (b), budgeted and actual production were identical, although actual sales were slower than planned. Let us now suppose that actual production was 120 units, of which 90 were sold in the accounting period for which the profit and loss account is being prepared. The actual costs of producing 120 units were, say, £612. Actual unit selling prices are as before (£8).

Profit and Loss Account

Line ref.		Budget Units	£	Actual Units	£
1	Sales at standard selling prices	100	700	90	630
2	Cost of production at standard	100	500	120	600
3	Less: closing stock at standard	—	—	30	150
4	Cost of sales at standard	100	500	90	450
5	*Budgeted profit*	100	200		
6	Standard profit on actual sales			90	180
7	Less: sales volume variance (unfavourable)		(20)		
8	Add: sales price variance (favourable)		90		90
9			270		270
10	Less: unfavourable production cost variance				12
11	*Actual profit*			90	258

The sales volume variance at line 7 is:
$(90 - 100) \times £2 = -£20$
The sales prices variance is: $90 \times £(8 - 7) = £90$
The production cost variance is:
actual quantity produced $\times$ (standard $-$ actual) unit cost
$= 120 \times £(5 - 5.10) = -£12$

It would do no harm to effect a simple proof reconciliation at this stage, of the profit derived using a profit and loss account based on standard costing procedures, and that achieved using basic financial accounting.

Profit and Loss Account (actual results)

	Units	£
Sales (actual selling price)	90	720
Actual production costs	120	612
Less: closing stock at standard	30	150
Actual cost of sales	90	462
Actual profit	90	258

The balance sheet reflecting the company's position after (c) would not normally include physical unit columns.

Balance Sheet

	Budget £	Actual £
Sources of Funds		
Profit and loss account	200	258
Bank overdraft	500	612
	700	870
Uses of Funds		
Stock at standard	—	150
Debtors	700	720
	700	870

The possibility of opening stock on hand must now be faced. So far it has been assumed that any sales achieved were the result of production activity of the current period. Let us suppose that there was, in addition to the immediately preceding situation, an opening stock of 10 finished units for sale, brought forward from the preceding accounting period.

When a system of standard costing is in use, there is no need to know the *actual* cost of production of the opening stock: the 10 units will be held, while unsold, at the standard cost in use in the previous accounting period, and this is the cost which the period now being dealt with will inherit. If the 10 units actually cost more to make than standard, the difference between actual and standard cost will already have been the basis for variances at an earlier date; the stock and profit and loss balances brought forward into the current period will reflect whatever tales of woe resulted from earlier management action. There is no need in our current period to re-open old wounds. All that is now needed is the standard cost of the 10 units. Some examination questions offer a unit standard cost for opening stock which differs from the current standard, while others assume consistency. Let us take the former, rather more complicated route and assume opening stock to be valued at £40. Let us also make things a little more mean and sneaky by assuming budgeted sales still to be 100 units at £7 each, and actual sales of 90 units at £8 each. In such situations we need to know whether finished units are sold on a 'first in, first out' basis (FIFO) whereby oldest stock was sold first, or on a 'last in, first out' basis (LIFO), with most recent production being first to reach customers. In many cases a mixture of old and new stock would be sold, but let us assume FIFO in this situation.

Profit and Loss Account

Line ref.		Budget Units	£	Actual Units	£
1	Sales at standard selling prices	100	700	90	630
2	Current cost of production at standard	100	500	120	600
3	Add: opening stock at standard	10	40	10	40
4	Total available for sale	110	540	130	640
5	Less: closing stock at standard	10	50	40	200
6	Cost of sales at standard	100	490	90	440
7	*Budgeted profit*	100	210		
8	Standard profit on actual sales			90	190
9	Less: sales volume variance (unfavourable)		(20)		
10	Add: sales price variance (favourable)		90		90
			280		280
12	Less: unfavourable production cost variance				12
13	*Actual profit*			90	268

There is a difference of £10 between the above actual profit of £268 and the preceding actual profit of £258. This is because in the more recent case, 10 of the units sold each carried £1 less cost in the books of account; the profit and loss account has been attacked above by old cost of 10 older units (£40) while in the earlier example there was nothing for sale at less than £5 unit cost.

In the next chapter, we shall pursue a set of business transactions into and across the books of account via relevant nominal ledger accounts, and ultimately into a profit and loss account. My quotation from Sir Winston Churchill's autobiography, 'My Early Life', may strike a few chords:

'We continued to toil every day, not only at letters but at words, and also at what was much worse, figures. Letters after all had only got to be known and when they stood together in a certain way one recognised their formation and that it meant a certain sound or word which one uttered when pressed sufficiently. But the figures were tied into all sorts of tangles and did things to one another which it was extremely difficult to forecast with complete accuracy. You had to say what they did each time they were tied up together, and the Governess apparently attached enormous importance to the answer being exact. If it was not right it was wrong. It was not any use being nearly right.'

CHAPTER 3

BOOK-KEEPING, NOMINAL LEDGERS AND TRIAL BALANCES

Cost Categories

COSTING depends on the identification of production or manufacturing departments (or cost centres), because it is there that COST OF PRODUCTION or WORK IN PROGRESS is built up. This build up is totalled in the WORK IN PROGRESS CONTROL ACCOUNT in the nominal ledger. The use of the word CONTROL implies that a subsidiary ledger is maintained, detailing separate subsidiary ledger accounts for each job, or process or product, in the same way that a subsidiary ledger is kept for Debtors' Control Account, to detail individual sales ledger accounts.

In addition to subsidiary records for jobs, processes or products, subsidiary records should also be kept for departments or cost centres handling the work. Thus, when Work-in-Progress Account is debited or credited in the nominal or general ledger, similar debits/credits should be made to subsidiary accounts for the product unit concerned *and* also the department concerned: obviously codes on prime documents such as purchase orders can become rather lengthy when they have to serve so many purposes.

Costing categorises each cost incurred throughout an organisation as: (1) DIRECT LABOUR. (2) DIRECT MATERIALS. (3) DIRECT EXPENSES. (4) VARIABLE WORKS OVERHEAD. (5) FIXED WORKS OVERHEAD. (6) ADMINISTRATION OVERHEAD. (7) VARIABLE SELLING OVERHEAD. (8) FIXED SELLING OVERHEAD.

From time to time, works overhead may not be split into variable and fixed categories. Similarly, administration and selling costs are sometimes regarded as one item. Moreover, a separate cost category may be used for DISTRIBUTION OVERHEADS – these are usually treated in the same way as (7) or (8).

(1) **Direct Labour**

Emanates from wages analyses: wages charged to specific jobs, processes or products are classified as direct.

Work in Progress Control Account	Dr
Wages Control Account	Cr

The appropriate job, process or product should also be debited in the work-in-progress subsidiary ledger. Outside the nominal or general ledger, a further subsidiary ledger should maintain records of departments (or cost centres) handling the work in progress activity, and this should be debited by way of a memorandum.

(2) **Direct Materials**
Emanates from analyses of stores requisitions and/or the purchase day book; the latter is more appropriate if materials are earmarked for work in progress as soon as the company concerned takes possession of the goods, eg when they are off-loaded at the goods inwards department and sent straight to production.

Work in Progress Control Account	Dr
Stores Control Account	Cr

OR

Work in Progress Control Account	Dr
Creditors Control Account	Cr

The same note as at the close of (1) above applies.

(3) **Direct Expenses**
Emanates from analyses of stores requisitions, purchase day book, and cash and petty cash books. Direct expenses usually constitute but a tiny fraction of total company expenditure, and indeed of work in progress. Perhaps the payment of professional fees when related directly to a specific end-product would serve as an illustration.

Work in Progress Control Account	Dr
Bank (or Creditors Control) Account	Cr

The same note as at the close of (1) applies.

(4) **Variable Works Overhead**
Emanates from analyses of stores requisitions, purchase day book, wages, cash book and petty cash book. The initial 'acid test' is whether the expense item has been incurred in 'bringing stock to its present condition and location'. Items passing the test are controlled through either (i) a general variable works overhead control account for the factory as a whole, or (ii) through departmental variable works overhead control accounts, depending on whether variable works overhead is charged to work in progress (i) at a blanket rate per unit of activity to recover all of the variable works overhead for the factory at one time or (ii) in stages.

(a) Variable Works Overhead Control Account — Dr

Stores Control Account — Cr
and/or
Creditors Control Account — Cr
and/or
Wages Control Account — Cr
and/or
Bank Account — Cr

} According to various analyses

Then separately,
(b) Work in progress Control Account   Dr
    Variable Works Overhead Control Account   Cr
    OR (when a separate account is opened for monitoring
    overheads charged or applied to work in progress):
    Variable Works Overhead Applied Account   Cr
Re (a), there has to be a subsidiary ledger in support of the Variable Works Overhead Control Account; examples of subsidiary ledger accounts could include factory overtime premium, idle time costs and machine running costs. Re (b), the same note as at the close of (1) applies.

(5) **Fixed Works Overhead or Production Fixed Overhead**
Emanates from the same analyses as at (4) above. It is unlikely that the analyses of stores requisitions, however, will yield much that can be classified as fixed expense. The 'acid test' referred to at (4) should also be applied.
(a) Fixed Works Overhead Control A/c   Dr
    Stores Control A/c   Cr ⎫
    or   ⎪ According
    Creditors Control A/c   Cr ⎬ to
    or   ⎪ various
    Wages Control A/c   Cr ⎥ analyses
    or   ⎪
    Bank A/c   Cr ⎭
Then separately,
(b) Work in Progress Control A/c   Dr
    OR, (when a separate account is opened for monitoring
    overheads charged or applied to work in progress):
    Fixed Works Overhead Applied A/c   Cr

Re (b), the same note as at the close of (1) applies.

(6) **Administration Overhead**
Depending on the nature of this category of overhead, which emanates from analyses of the purchase day book, cash book and wages, it may or may not be considered as having been incurred 'in bringing stock to its present condition and location'. For example, if much of a factory's accounting effort goes into the preparation of routine day-to-day reports on production achievement, costs and efficiency, it might be considered that the costs of running the accounting department, or a fair proportion thereof, could be included in the valuation of work in progress. In which case:
(a) Administration Overhead Control A/c   Dr
    Bank A/c   Cr
    or
    Creditors Control A/c   Cr
Then, separately,
(b)(i) Work in Progress Control A/c   Dr

Administration Overhead Control A/c	Cr
or	
Administration Overhead Applied A/c	Cr

However, in the event of administration overhead *not* being regarded as incurred in bringing stock to its present condition and location, substitute b(ii) below for (i):

(b)(ii) Cost of Sales A/c	Dr
Administration Overhead Control A/c	Cr
or	
Administration Overhead Applied A/c	Cr

Re (a), the rule about a subsidiary ledger applies.
Re (b)(i), the same note as at the close of (1) applies.

(7) **Variable Selling Overhead**
Emanates from analyses of the purchase day book, cash book, wages and petty cash book; employees' expenses claims analyses are presumed to be dealt with through the cash book or petty cash book. The total of such overhead rises or falls in sympathy with changes in the level of *selling activity.* As with production activity, some unit of measure has to be established for selling activity, eg £ of sales invoiced or number of physical units invoiced. The normal accounting entries would be:

(a) Variable Selling Overhead Control A/c	Dr
Bank A/c	Cr
or	
Creditors Control A/c	Cr

Then separately,

(b) Cost of Sales A/c	Dr
Variable Selling Overhead Control A/c	Cr
or	
Variable Selling Overhead Applied A/c	Cr

Work-in-Progress Control A/c should not, of course, be debited with this type of expense.
There is again a need for a subsidiary ledger at (a).

(8) **Fixed Selling Overhead**
Emanates from the same analyses as at (7) above. Such expense is regarded as insensitive to rises and falls in selling activity. The normal accounting entries would be:

(a) Fixed Selling Overhead Control A/c	Dr
Bank A/c	Cr
or	
Creditors Control A/c	Cr

Then separately,

(b) Cost of Sales A/c	Dr
Fixed Selling Overhead Control A/c	Cr
or	
Fixed Selling Overhead Applied A/c	Cr

Again, work in progress should not be debited with this type of expense. There is the usual need for a subsidiary ledger at (a).

The preceding book-keeping entries ring true whether or not a standard costing system is in operation.

Standard costing, however, maintains every STOCK account in the nominal ledger at standard, and also the ultimate COST OF SALES account (which is just another nominal ledger account). The basis for entries in stock accounts is as follows:

1. *Raw Material Stock Account:*
   (a) is debited with ACTUAL QUANTITY purchased (naturally) at STANDARD COST. As every debit must have a credit, the credit entry to creditors control A/c of ACTUAL QUANTITY purchased at ACTUAL COST creates an imbalance. Whatever the imbalance, it is entered in a RAW MATERIAL PRICE Variance Account; this account has full nominal ledger status and ensures a square trial balance.
   (b) is credited with ACTUAL QUANTITY issued (naturally) at STAN-DARD COST. As every debit must have a credit, the debit to Work in Progress A/c, of only the STANDARD QUANTITY allowed in view of what's going on in Work in Progress (ACTUAL AC-TIVITY), creates an imbalance. Whatever the imbalance, it is entered in a RAW MATERIAL USAGE Variance account; this account has full nominal ledger status and ensures a square trial balance.

2. *Work in Progress Stock Account*
   (a) is debited with standard raw material quantity at standard price, the quantity being based on the actual level of activity taking place in Work in Progress (see 1(b)).
   (b) is debited with standard wages cost for the actual work in progress level of activity, ie standard direct hours allowed at standard wage rates. As every debit must have a credit, the fact that the Wages Supervisor needs to clean out (credit) from the Wages Control A/c the actual hours paid for at the actual wage rate paid, creates an imbalance. The amount of the imbalance is entered in the Direct Labour Cost Variance Account, which has full nominal ledger status. This variance account is gross in that it can be analysed into Direct Labour Rate and Efficiency Variances. Sometimes this analysis is done while clearing out the Wages Control A/c, and the two more detailed variances accounts are opened when the standard posting to Work in Progress is done, rather than the Direct Wages Cost Variance Account.
   (c) is debited with the standard variable overhead cost for the actual work in progress level of activity. This is usually represented by:

   actual number of units of production activity

   $times$ $\dfrac{\text{Budgeted variable works overhead}}{\text{Budgeted production activity level}}$

   The corresponding credit for this debit to Work in Progress is made either to the Variable Works Overhead Control A/c or to the Variable Works Overhead Applied A/c. The fact that actual variable works overhead costs incurred are debited to the same account used for applied credits, does not in itself create an imbalance in the trial balance, as the credit to cash, or creditors (or whatever account is the source of the service received) is identical. The problem arises when the total of the debits for actual expense are matched against the total of the credits for the applied amounts. Any difference left over when this contra-cancellation takes place is transferred by journal entry to a Variable Works Overhead Variance A/c.

(d) is debited with the standard fixed cost for the actual work in progress level of activity. This is usually represented by:
actual number of units of production activity

$$times \ \frac{\text{Budgeted fixed works overhead}}{\text{Budgeted production activity level}}$$

The corresponding credit for this debit to Work in Progress is made either to the Fixed Works Overhead Control A/c or the Fixed Works Overhead Applied A/c. After that, the same pattern develops as at (c) above. The only caveat to debiting Work in Progress at all is that there must be a directive in the question that stock is valued at *full* cost (including fixed works cost).

(e) *may* be debited with the standard recovery rate for admin. costs × the number of units of activity in Work in Progress.

(f) is credited with the standard output cost per unit × the number of units finished. The debit goes to 3(a) below.

3. *Finished Goods Stock*
   (a) is debited with the standard unit cost of a finished unit × the number of units actually transferred from Work in Progress.
   (b) is credited with the standard cost of sales per unit × the number of units sold. The debit goes to 4(a) below.

4. *Cost of Sales at Standard*
   (a) is debited with the standard unit cost accumulated to the finished goods stock account level × the number of units sold.
   (b) may be debited also with standard variable selling cost per unit × the number of units sold. The other side of this entry is a credit to the Variable Selling Cost Applied Account (or to the Variable Selling Cost Control Account). Non-matching of the credit just mentioned, and the debit to Variable Selling Cost Control A/c for *actual* selling costs, causes the two to be set against each other so that when each is eliminated, only the variance remains. This variance is transferred to its own nominal ledger account.
   (c) may be debited with standard fixed selling cost. The credit in this case is to Fixed Selling Cost Control A/c. A variance emerges as at (b).

5. *Profit and Loss Account*
   To this account is transferred by journal entry the accumulated Cost of Sales at Standard account balance. In addition, any balances on any variance accounts are also transferred to the Profit and Loss A/c, where they meet the 'faulty' Cost of Sales at Standard figure, and correct it, so that an *actual* cost of sales is derived at last.

Full Nominal Ledger Status for Variances

A centre point in the 'raison d'être' of standard costing when applied to expenditure is to convert a decline of cash into an increase in stock. As indicated previously, if costs are anticipated entirely correctly when budgets are prepared, and levels of activity turn out to be exactly in line with budgeted expectations, then this conversion will be precisely achieved. Cash paid for materials, wages and overheads will cause a decline in the bank balance on the balance sheet, exactly counterbalanced by an increase in stockholdings elsewhere among current assets, remembering that stocks are valued at standard cost. It is when attempting this miraculous high wire act that you will first be menaced by Variances. For a sea of reasons actual costs can be at loggerheads with standard, and actual activity levels out of step with plan, so that the cash decline is not identical to the stock increase. The difference has been previously described as a Total Profit Variance, but in practice this monster is found by adding up all the variance account balances in the ledger which relate to expenditure, and transferring them by journal entry to another ledger account called (Costing) Profit and Loss Account, where they form a correcting influence upon the *standard* cost of sales already posted there.

The prefix 'costing' in brackets above can sometimes be omitted. Prior to their transfer to the Profit and Loss Account, variances become ledger accounts in their own right, and appear in the trial balance with the same status as any other nominal ledger accounts. They are essential if the balance sheet is to balance on any given day.

A simple illustration will help:

A. *Facts of the case*

   (1) 8 raw material units costing £2 each are used in production; looking at the production level achieved in practice, it is worth only 6 raw material units (ie it is incapable of carrying any more than the cost of 6 raw material units). It was also predetermined when setting standards that the unit price of raw materials would be £1.50.

   (2) 32 hours of direct labour are actually charged to the production concerned by operatives. In view of what has been achieved by way of output, it is considered that the production output is only worth 30 hours of direct labour. Each hour of direct labour was expected to cost £2, but in practice is found to cost £2.50.

   (3) Ignore overheads in this example.

   (4) The above efforts culminate in the credit sale of 6 finished products at £15 each.

B. *Solution of the problem*

   (1) *Raw Materials*

      There is no doubt about the company's legal liability to pay for 8 raw material units at £2 each. Let us suppose that a cheque is written (ie no credit is taken). In the first instance, the raw material stock is best described as 'RAW MATERIAL STOCK' rather than as part of the cost of production or WORK IN PROGRESS. At this early stage, we may:

Debit	Raw Material Stock	£16
Credit	Bank	£16

Thus, our balance sheet balances and we also show a true and fair view of the state of the company's affairs. However, the actual cost of £2 per unit is usually very late in being determined (eg from a supplier's invoice). We need to react by charging the storekeeper in charge of raw material stores with appropriate costs of 8 units as soon as they are delivered into his store from the incoming lorry; so we use the standard costs, and, instead of the entry shown in the previous paragraph, we

Debit	Raw Material Stock 8 × £1.50	£12
Debit	Raw Material Price Variance	£ 4
Credit	Bank	£16

When the raw material is requisitioned by a production foreman, we then:

Debit	Work-in-Progress
Credit	Stores

At this stage, however, we debit work-in-progress with a standard raw material cost entitlement in view of what the foreman is achieving by way of activity. At the same time, the raw material storekeeper must be credited with the actual number of units used, and at the same price at which he was originally debited (ie in this case at standard cost per unit.
Therefore:

Debit	Work-in-Progress 6 × £1.50	£ 9
Debit	Raw material Usage Variance	£ 3
Credit	Raw Material Stock	£12

(2) *Direct labour*

Actual wages cost incurred must be paid for: this is generally organised through a ledger account kept by the Wages Office:

Debit Wages Control Account 32 × £2.50	£80
Credit Bank A/c	£80

At this stage the Wages Control Account is analysed in total. In our simple example, all wage cost is known to be direct labour. We debit work-in-progress at what the production is worth in standard terms, but at all costs the wages supervisor needs to be credited with the full £80 so that his ledger account can be closed out.
Therefore:

Debit Work-in-Progress 30 hours × £2	£60
Debit Direct Wages Cost Variance Account	£20
Credit Wages Control Account 32 × £2.50	£80

When a trial balance containing all ledger accounts is prepared, the following situation is shown:

	Dr £	Cr £
Raw Material Stock A/c	—	—
Bank A/c (16 + 80)		96
Wages Control A/c		
Work-in-Progress A/c (9 + 60)	69	
Direct Material Price Variance A/c	4	
Direct Material Usage Variance A/c	3	
Direct Labour Cost Variance A/c	20	
	96	96

You will notice that all three variance accounts are showing debit balances. They illustrate the extent to which standard costing has failed to convert a cash decline of £96 into an equivalent stock gain. The three unfavourable variance account balances are in a sense showing stock valuation. The *real* cost of work-in-progress is £69 plus £27 = £96. In most examination questions you have to go ahead and 'value stock at standard cost', which in this case is £69.

When the green light shows to transfer work in progress to finished goods account, a journal entry will be made to this effect:

Finished Goods Stock Account (at standard)	Dr	£69
Work in Progress Account	Cr	£69

Not long after this step has been taken, a messenger may arrive hotfoot from the sales force with the inspiring news that a sale has been achieved. In conjunction with despatching the goods in question on a lorry, covered wagon or whatever seems most appropriate, the following journal entries will be made assuming a sales value of £90:

(1)	Cost of Sales Account (at standard)	Dr	£69
	Finished Goods Stock Account	Cr	£69
(2)	Debtors	Dr	£90
	Sales	Cr	£90

The final act prior to preparation of the Profit and Loss Account could be to prepare a trial balance, and then clear off all the open accounts relating to trading to the Profit and Loss Account which serves as a kind of marshalling yard at which a faulty standard cost of sales (£69) is confronted by variances which bring it into line with actual costs.

Trial Balance

	Dr £	Cr £
Bank A/c		96
Raw Material Price Variance A/c	4	
Raw Material Usage Variance A/c	3	
Direct Labour Cost Variance A/c	20	
Cost of Sales (at standard)	69	
Debtors	90	
Sales		90
	186	186

The following journal entries then apply: £

			£
(1) Profit and Loss Account – variances	Dr	27
Profit and Loss Account – cost of sales	Dr	69
Raw Material Price Variance	Cr	4
Raw Material Usage Variance	Cr	3
Direct Labour Cost Variance	Cr	20
Cost of Sales at Standard	Cr	69
(2) Sales	Dr	90
Profit and Loss Account	Cr	90

The profit and Loss Account can then be presented:

Profit and Loss Account

		£
Actual sales		90
Cost of Production at Standard		
Direct materials		9
Direct labour		60
Stock available for sale at standard		69
Less: closing stock at standard		—
Cost of sales at standard		69
Standard profit on actual sales		21
Less: unfavourable variances		
Direct material price	4	
Direct material usage	3	
Direct labour cost	20	
		27
Actual loss for period		6

The balance sheet will offer the following situation:

Balance Sheet

	£
Sources of Funds	
Earned surplus	(6)
Bank overdraft	96
	90
Uses of Funds	
Debtors	90

The embarrassment of losses must be faced stoically from time to time. Supposing all production had remained unfinished at the end of the accounting period; we would then have advanced from the position of the *first* trial balance shown previously, along the following alternative route:

(a) Debit Profit and Loss A/c	£69
Credit Work-in-Progress	£69

(b) Debit Profit and Loss A/c   £27
      Credit Raw Material Price Variance A/c   4
      Credit Raw Material Usage Variance A/c   3
      Credit Direct Labour Variance A/c   20
      With production being unsold, we need to remove the closing valuation from the Profit and Loss Account. We again use standard cost.
(c) Debit Work-in-Progress   £69
      Credit Profit and Loss Account   £69

For presentation purposes the Profit and Loss Account and Balance Sheet would then have shown:

Profit and Loss Account

		£
Costs of Production at Standard		
Materials		9
Labour		60
Total		69
Add: Unfavourable variances		
Material Price	4	
Material Usage	3	
Direct Labour Cost	20	27
Actual cost of production		96
Less: closing stock at standard		69
Loss for the period		27

Balance Sheet

	£	£
Sources of Funds		
Earned surplus (deficit)	(27)	
Bank overdraft	96	69
Application of Funds		
Stock on Hand (at standard)		69

Routine Book-Keeping for Ongoing Business Transactions

As the golfer must from time to time pursue his ball into impenetrable jungles of rough with a stout heart, so too must we now set our feet firmly in the inhospitable inner regions of variance accounting. With this in mind, a more comprehensive example, encompassing a list of typical business transactions and supporting background information, is shown below. On the basis that we will not be dealing with the first year of trading of the company concerned, we must bring forward a set of opening balances, which could in practice take many forms but which will now be established as follows:

Trial Balance

	Dr £	Cr £
Fixed Assets Account	20,000	
Raw Material Stock at standard	5,000	
Work in Progress stock at standard	18,000	
Finished Goods Stock at standard	74,800	
(17,000 units at £4.40 each)		
Debtors Control Account	3,000	
Sundry Creditors Control Account		14,000
Profit and Loss Account		27,800
Issued Share Capital		50,000
Bank Overdraft		29,000
	120,800	120,800

List of routine business transactions
1. Total actual wages paid, £50,000.
2. Raw materials bought on credit: 200 of part 62 at £5 each = £1,000.
   (The expected or standard price per part was £6.)
3. Actual factory rates paid: £3,000 (Credit had been taken).
4. Electricity account for machine power paid £11,000 (Credit had been taken).
5. The company's wages analysis shows:

	£
(a) Direct labour, 15,000 hours at £2	30,000
(b) Indirect labour (variable)	14,000
(c) Indirect labour (fixed)	6,000
	£50,000

   (The standard direct labour wage rate was £1.50 per hour.)
6. Raw materials: 120 of part 62 was requisitioned from the raw material store as direct material, using standard cost as the basis for pricing. (120 × £6 = £720.) In view of the actual production activity level achieved, only 100 of part 62 should have been requisitioned if standard usage was to be adhered to.
7. Current variable overheads (not previously accrued at the close of the previous period) were paid amounting to £11,000. By the same token, fixed overheads of £6,000 were paid. Assume no credit was taken by the company.
8. Work in progress completed during the period: 5,000 units at a standard cost of £4.40 each (to cover direct materials, direct labour, variable overheads and fixed overheads).
9. Sales invoice total for the period, £90,000, being 15,000 units at £6 each. The budgeted target was 10,000 units at £7 each.
10. Cash received from customers, £85,000.

Further information
    (a) A system of standard costing and flexible budgetary control is in operation.
    (b) The activity of the company is measured in MACHINE HOURS. For the period in question, budgeted activity was anticipated as 3,000 machine hours. The direct labour content of one machine hour was specified as 4 man hours, ie each machine hour would require direct manning by four operatives.
    (c) The budgeted fixed overheads for the period were £10,000.
    (d) Variable overheads were expected to be £18,000.
    (e) Actual production activity for the period was 3,300 machine hours.
    (f) For the sake of simplicity, ignore depreciation on fixed assets and also selling costs.

On the strength of the above information, the nominal ledger of the company can be written up and a profit and loss account and balance sheet prepared. You will see the treatment of each transaction on the ensuing 'T' accounts. 'O.B.' signifies opening balance; such entries emanate from the opening trial balance, 'C.B.' refers to closing balances. A bracketed number at the side of a 'T' account refers to the appropriate transaction number above. An un-bracketed number indicates the 'T' account number of the other side of the book-keeping double-entry.

Full explanatory notes supporting each step taken are offered immediately after 'T' Account No 23

1. Fixed Asset Account

	£			£
OB	20,000	CB		20,000

2. Raw Material Stock (at Standard)

		£		£	
OB		5,000	3 & 16 Requisitioned		
(2) 6 & 10	Purchases	1,200	(600 + 120)	720	(6)
			CB	5,480	
		6,200		6,200	

3. Work in Progress Stock (at Standard)

		£		£	
OB		18,000	4 Completed goods	22,000	(8)
(5) 9	3300 machine hours ×		CB	47,200	
	4 man hrs × £1.50	19,800			
(6) 2	Raw material				
	100 × £6	600			
18	Fixed overheads	11,000			
19	Variable overheads	19,800			
		69,200		69,200	

4. Finished Goods Stock (at Standard)

		£		£	
OB		74,800	22 Cost of Sales: 15,000 ×		
(8) 3	From W in P	22,000	£4.40	66,000	(9)
			CB	30,800	
		96,800		96,800	

5. Debtors Control Account

		£			£	
	OB	3,000	8	Cash received from		
(9)	16 Charged to customers			customers	85,000	(10)
	15,000 × £6	90,000		CB	8,000	
		93,000			93,000	

6. Sundry Creditors Control Account

		£			£	
(3)	8 Rates paid	3,000		OB	14,000	
(4)	8 Electricity paid	11,000	2	Raw materials	1,000	(2)
	CB	1,000				
		15,000			15,000	

7. Issued Share Capital

	£			£
CB	50,000	OB		50,000

8. Bank Overdraft

		£			£	
(10) 5	Cash from customers	85,000		OB	29,000	
	CB	25,000	9	Wages	50,000	(1)
			6	Rates	3,000	(3)
			6	Electricity	11,000	(4)
			13	Variable overheads	11,000	(7)
			14	Fixed overheads	6,000	(7)
		110,000			110,000	

9. Wages Control Account

		£			£	
(1)	8 Total wages	50,000	3	Direct wages (standard)	19,800	(5)
			11	15,000 hrs × £(1.50−2)	7,500	(5)
			12	1,800 hrs × £1.50	2,700	(5)
			13	Indirect labour (V)	14,000	(5)
			14	Indirect labour (F)	6,000	(5)
		50,000			50,000	

10. Raw Material Price Variance Account

	£			£	
23 To P & L A/c (J/Entry)	200	2	On 200 × Part R	200	(2)

11. Direct Wages Rate Variance Account

		£		£
(5)	9 15,000 hrs × 50p	7,500	23 to P & L A/c (J/Entry)	7,500

12. Direct Wages Efficiency Variance Account

		£		£
(5)	9 [(4 × 3,300)−15,000] hrs		23 Transfer to P & L A/c	
	× £1.50	2,700	(J/Entry)	2,700

13. Variable Production Overhead Control Account

		£		£
(5)	9 Indirect labour paid	14,000	J/Entry from Applied	
(7)	8 Payments	11,000	A/c 19	19,800
			J/Entry: Balance to Variance	
			A/c 7	5,200
		25,000		25,000

14. Fixed Production Overhead Control Account

			£		£
(5)	9	Indirect labour paid	6,000	J/Entry from Applied	
(7)	8	Payments	6,000	A/c 18	11,000
				J/Entry: Balance to Variance	
				A/c 21	1,000
			12,000		12,000

15. Raw Material Usage Variance Account

			£		£
(6)	2	20 excess units used		23 Transfer to P & L A/c	
		@ £6	120	(J/Entry)	120

16. Actual Sales at Standard Selling Prices

	£			£	
23 Transfer to P & L A/c		5 &	Sales invoiced at		
(J/Entry)	105,000	17	standard	105,000	(9)

17. Sales Price Variance

		£		£
(9) 16	15,000 units		23 Transfer to P & L A/c	
	× £(6-7)	15,000	(J/Entry)	15,000

18. Fixed Overhead Applied Account

	£		£	
14 J/Entry to Control a/c	11,000	3	$3,300 \times £\dfrac{10,000}{3,000}$ 11,000	(Notes (b) (c) & (e))

19. Variable Overhead Applied Account

	£		£	
13 J/Entry to Control a/c	19,800	3	$3,300 \times £\dfrac{18,000}{3,000}$ 19,800	(Notes (b) (d) & (e))

20. Variable Production Overhead Cost Variance

	£		£
		23 To P & L A/c	
J/Entry from A/c 13	5,200	(J/Entry)	£5,200

21. Fixed Production Overhead Cost Variance Account

	£		£
		23 Transfer to P & L A/c	
15 J/Entry from Control A/c	1,000	(J/Entry)	1,000

22. Cost of Sales at Standard

	£		£
(9) 4 From finished goods	66,000	23 To P & L A/c	66,000

23. Costing Profit and Loss Account

		£			£
22	Cost of sales at standard	66,000		OB	27,800
7	Var prod'n o/head cost var	5,200	10	Raw material price var	200
11	D Wages rate var	7,500	16	Sales at standard	
12	D Wages efficiency var	2,700		prices	105,000
15	R Mat'l usage var	120			
17	Sales price var	15,000			
21	Fixed prod'n o/head cost var	1,000			
	CB	35,480			
		133,000			133,000

Explanatory Notes

Transaction (1)
A Wages Control Account (No 9) is opened as a temporary measure to act as a form of suspense account until the analysis of payments made can be utilised to spread the cost of £50,000 to more appropriate accounts. In some examination questions, this account may be unnecessary, eg when question details include no separate transaction for a total payment. The Suspense Account is useful as the base from which to calculate variances, so that in effect it is a vetting point for costs before they are allowed to reach those ledger accounts where they may become part of product cost: the Suspense Account 'cleanses' actual costs so that only standard costs move forward to Work in Progress Account.

Transaction (2)
The company's legal liability to suppliers is shown at account No 6 (Sundry Creditors). However, the company presumably wishes to initiate its standard costing system at the earliest possible accounting point, so only the standard cost of raw materials bought is allowed to reach the raw material stock account. Notice that *actual* quantities bought or requisitioned are always the basis for entries in *any* stock account. The store-keeper concerned needs to keep the account in the ledger in line with the physical evidence of quantities coming and going – standard costing system or not. When raw materials are requisitioned, standard unit costs will again be used so that like value is compared with like on the debit and credit sides of the store-keeper's account, ie he will square both physically and financially.

Transaction (3)
This amount for factory rates must be kept well clear of any accounts which would route the £3,000 into costs of current production: £3,000 has already found its way to the debit side of the Profit and Loss Account in a previous accounting period. A simple financial accounting principle on the treatment of accrued charges is all that is involved.

Transaction (4)
Again, £11,000 is kept away from current charges.

Transaction (5)
This transaction must culminate in the clearance of the 'Suspense A/c' for wages (Account No 9). Ideally, £30,000 might have been transferred to the debit of Work in Progress, had standards been deadly accurate. As it is, the only charge to Work in Progress on a direct basis, ie for direct wages, can be for what the activity level is worth; in view of an output of 3,300 machine hours, a cost entitlement of $3,300 \times 4$ man hours $\times$ £1.50 per man hour can be charged to Work in Progress (Account No 3). The balance of £30,000 − £19,800 falls short of its Work in Progress target. There is simply not enough production achievement to justify expense of £30,000 on direct wages!

The problem of overspending has two constituents:
(a) only 3,300 × 4 = 13,200 hours ought to have been worked by operatives. In fact they worked (and needed paying) for 15,000 hours. This means that 1,800 hours were paid by the company with no production capable of sustaining the relevant cost (1,800 × £1.50). Note that the fact that £2 per hour was paid instead of £1.50 is *another* problem. We need to relate the *cost of lack of efficiency* to someone at this stage – all else being equal. To absorb a wage rate problem into this situation would involve challenging those responsible for production efficiency with a shortfall in cost recovery by work in progress of 1,800 hours × £2 = £3,600. This would be unfair as part of the £3,600 would be caused by faulty estimating of wage rates by some other management department such as personnel department.
(b) The rate variance comes to terms with the effect on the conversion of cash minus into stock plus of planning to charge work in progress at £1.50 per hour to recover what turned out to be a cost of £2 per hour. Management admit at this stage to an actual direct wages time sheet total of 15,000 hours, and say, 'Well, what should 15,000 hours have cost?' (£22,500). Then, 'What did they cost?' (£30,000). So for a cash minus of £30,000 we have a stock plus of £22,500, giving a direct wages rate variance of £7,500 (unfavourable).
The variable and fixed indirect labour of £14,000 and £6,000 respectively represents actual cost, which is debited to overhead control accounts (Nos 13 and 14 respectively). Such amounts cover cost which is as much a part of product cost as direct wages, yet it must be charged to Work-in-Progress via an intermediate stage. Whenever debits to these control accounts have been anticipated (budgeted), there will be a corresponding credit in the appropriate overhead applied accounts. The other side of these credits to the applied accounts are debits to Work in Progress. Thus, standard unit charge rates (recovery rates) for overheads absorb any anticipated normal cost; any unexpected extra cost, or any cost saving, will show up as an overhead variance when, at the close of an accounting period, control account debits and applied credits are set against each other by journal entry. In an ideal world, they would be an exact 'match' and there would be no overhead variances.

Transaction (6)
When, as in this case, raw material stock is being held at standard cost (in Account No 2), any requisitions should be debited to Work in Progress at standard, and credited to Raw Material Stores Account at standard. The opportunity should be taken to charge Work in Progress with what it is worth in standard terms. The question states that an entitlement of 100 of part 62 is appropriate, so Work in Progress Account cannot sustain any more. The 20 extra parts are therefore not catered for within the company's normal standard cost conversion procedures for converting cash minus to stock plus. A Raw Material Usage Variance of 20 × £6 = £120 appears therefore as a debit balance on a variance account, representing a potential charge for extra cost incurred in production: extra cost not included in the £66,000 standard cost of sales. In due course this £120 will penetrate the

'confrontation point' ie the Profit and Loss Account, and pare down the exaggerated profit derived from wrongly using £66,000. *After all, management want to know what actual profits were achieved.* Standard costing variances provide this information via an audit trail which shows *also* the profits which should have been achieved.

Transaction (7)
If these expenses were budgeted, the company should have nothing to fear from having to debit Variable Overhead Control A/c (No 13) and Fixed Overhead Control A/c (No 14) respectively: credits to those accounts (or to Overhead Applied Accounts if these have been opened in the nominal ledger) will exactly offset any debits at the time when Work in Progress Account is debited. However, if they are unbudgeted, the extent to which equilibrium is not achieved will form unfavourable variances.

Transaction (8)
Any transfers along the company's trading cycle, from Work in Progress Account to Finished Goods Account (No 4) should be at standard cost: this is yet another link in the chain, taking cost from the earliest trading cycle stages to the final reckoning on the Profit and Loss Account. Notice that the questioner in this case did not tell us to make this transfer of costs: a knowledge of basic accounting was presumed.

Transaction (9)
An essential measure is to recognise the extent of customer's liability for goods received. Therefore the amount of £90,000 is charged to Sundry Debtors' Account, as would be the case had there been no standard costing system. Management, however, are also offered information through a standard costing system of what the sales amount ought to have been if standard selling prices, presumably long discussed, had been utilised in practice. The difference between the credit to Actual Sales (Quantities) at Standard Selling Prices Account and the debit to Sundry Debtors is posted to a Sales Price Variance Account. Sales will wrongly appear at £105,000 in the Profit and Loss Account, but will be amended to a net (correct) figure of £90,000 when the Sales Price Variance balance of £15,000 is tranferred to the Profit and Loss Account. So management will be able not only to deduce actual sales on the Profit and Loss Account, but also to assess whether the results of pricing anomalies in practice were significant in comparison with budgeted turnover. In the basic 'T' account version of the nominal ledger accounts which are being prepared, there is no room for budget columns, but when the Profit and Loss Account (No 23) is prepared in fuller format for presentation purposes, as you will find on a later page, both budget and actual columns are shown.

Again, a transfer of the standard cost of the 15,000 items sold has to be made to Cost of Sales Account from Finished Goods, to keep the nominal ledger in line with the physical situation on the company's premises.

Transaction (10)
After expending so much money on the company's behalf, we find to our relief that it is not all one-way traffic on the cash front.

Notes re Utilisation of Further Information

(a) This note provides us with the justification for our entire modus operandi. To the wording of the note in the question we could add '...from beginning to end', ie '...from the earliest opportunity until final transfer of an amount from the Cost of Sales Account and the Sales Account to the Profit and Loss Account'.

(b) The budgeted activity of 3,000 machine hours must be divided into (1) £10,000 to derive the unit charging rate to Work in Progress for fixed overheads (see comment (c) in the question); (2) £18,000 to derive the unit rate for variable overheads (see comment (d) in the question). Each time the production manager signifies in due course that one machine hour's worth of production activity has actually been achieved, Work in Progress Account will be debited with (1) £10/3 for fixed overheads, and (2) £18/3 for variable overheads. This information is linked to recognition of the total activity achieved (see comment (e)) to provide the basis for the total debits to Work in Progress for fixed and variable costs.

(c) See above.

(d) The budgeted total for variable overheads was only £18,000 because the level of activity was expected to be 3,000 machine hours. The application rate of £6 resulting is used in due course 3,300 times, so an applied account credit of $3,300 \times £6 = £19,800$ will be measured against whatever has been debited to the control account for producing 3,300 machine hours of output.

(e) 3,300 machine hours is the actual activity level to be used: it forms the basis for any debits made to Work-in-Progress, albeit at standard cost per unit. Standard costing charges and physical transfers must be rooted in reality. Do *not* allow yourself to debit work-in-progress or credit work-in-progress at a standard cost rate times budgeted activity!

(f) In reality, machine depreciation would be an element of cost within either variable or fixed overheads. To the extent that a depreciation charge had been anticipated, the company would be covered within one of the overhead unit application rates. Selling costs are not incurred in 'bringing stock to its present condition and location' and therefore there is no question of debiting work-in-progress with such amounts. In simple terms, the Cost of Sales at standard account would often be debited with budgeted selling costs, and any difference between such cost and the necessary credit to Creditors or Bank would be posted to a Selling Cost Variance Account. The balance on such a variance account would be cleared to the Profit and Loss Account in due course.

While Account No. 23 shown earlier does provide some useful information in its present format to an aware reader, there is no doubt that it could be improved and thus become much more helpful. For example, the essential ingredient of comparison is notable for its absence. To make amends, and to capture further marks in an examination, a more comprehensive style of presentation is necessary. We can therefore build upon the work already done to re-design the Profit and Loss Account as follows:

PROFIT AND LOSS ACCOUNT

Line ref.		Budget £	Actual £
1	Sales at standard	70,000	105,000
2	Less: cost of sales at standard	44,000	66,000
3	Budgeted gross profit	26,000	
4	Standard profit on actual quantities		39,000
	Add/(deduct): favourable/(unfavourable)		
5	Sales variances:		
6	(1) price	(15,000)	(15,000)
7	(2) volume (Note 1)	13,000	
8		24,000	24,000
	Add/(deduct): favourable/(unfavourable)		
9	Cost variances:		
10	Raw material price		200
11	Raw material usage		(120)
12	Direct labour rate		(7,500)
13	Direct wages efficiency		(2,700)
14	Variable production overhead		(5,200)
15	Fixed production overhead		(1,000)
16	*Actual gross profit*		£7,680

Note 1   The sales volume variance is:
Standard profit per unit $\times$ (actual $-$ budgeted) quantity
$$= £(7 - 4.40) \times (15,000 - 10,000)$$
$$= £13,000 \text{ (favourable)}$$

Commentary
The actual profit of £7,680 must be compared with an original budgeted profit of £26,000 and a revised profit of £39,000 on line 4, the latter representing the new target which management could have achieved at actual activity levels if only all standards used had been exactly in line with reality. The influence of the sales function is shown as a net unfavourable profit variance of £2,000 (lines 6 and 7). The extent to which the company has misjudged cost levels when preparing budgets and standards is evident at lines 10 to 15.

The company's abbreviated balance sheet is shown below

BALANCE SHEET

	Previous period £	£	This period £	£
Sources of Funds				
Owners' Capital				
Share Capital	50,000		50,000	
Profit & Loss Account	27,800	77,800	35,480	85,480

Outsiders' Interest	£	£	£	£
Sundry Creditors	14,000		1,000	
Bank Overdraft	29,000		25,000	
		43,000		26,000
		120,800		111,480
Uses of Funds				
Fixed Assets		20,000		20,000
Current Assets				
Raw Materials stock	5,000		5,480	
Work in Progress stock	18,000		47,200	
Finished Goods stock	74,800		30,800	
Debtors	3,000		8,000	
		100,800		91,480
		120,800		111,480

It will soon be necessary to take a closer look at the full extent to which a Total Profit Variance can be analysed in depth.

In ensuing chapters we shall therefore examine the variances in common use. Each forms a part of any total profit variance which reflects the deviation between a company's intended or budgeted profit for a period and its actual profit. So when considering each variance, we will realise that it should be capable of bearing the prefix: 'Profit variance caused by . . .'. The description of the variance then follows. We will also expect that if Raw Material Stock Account, Work in Progress Stock Account, Finished Goods Stock Account and Cost of Sales Account are to be charged and balances held at standards related to actual physical quantities, any deviations between actual expenditure and standard will need to be reflected in nominal ledger accounts in their own right to make the trial balance square. A Profit and Loss Account is, after all, just another nominal ledger account; to it any balances on variance accounts are transferred by journal entry at the close of the appropriate period, provided that a policy of leaving standard stock valuations unaltered has been agreed by management and the auditors.

We should terminate this chapter, however, by eliminating certain pseudo-variances which sometimes masquerade in the ranks of text-book variances among the *genuine* variances which are capable of taking the prefix 'Profit variance caused by . . .'. These 'non-variances' are merely arithmetical flexing adjustments of variable costs.

To illustrate, suppose a company prepares budget expense levels based on a production activity of 1,000 units. At such an activity level, direct raw material costs are budgeted as £1,000, direct labour as £3,000, and variable overheads £2,000. In due course, actual costs are £1,400, £4,200 and £2,100 respectively. 'Aagh!', cries a shocked manager. 'No problem', responds the management accountant, soothingly. The reason? Actual activity is not 1,000 units, but 1,500 units. Flexible budgetary control adjusts the budgeted costs accordingly.

The flexing variances are shown in column (2) of the table overleaf. They are sometimes referred to as turnover variances. Certainly they represent a dramatic increase in actual expenditure over budgeted levels. However there will also be an increase in the level of stocks held, exactly equivalent to the

	(1) Original Budget		(2) Flexing because of activity change		(3) Revised budget for actual activity		(4) Actual costs for actual activity		(5) Variances affecting profits (a) Variable costs
	Units	£	Units	£	Units	£	Units	£	£
Production	1,000		500		1,500		1,500		
Direct material		1,000		500		1,500		1,400	100
Direct labour		3,000		1,500		4,500		4,200	300
Variable overhead		2,000		1,000		3,000		2,100	900
	1,000	6,000	500	3,000	1,500	9,000	1,500	7,700	1,300

upsurge in spending. So, by sanctioning more activity, the company authorised a further budget of £3,000 production cost, on the understanding that there was £3,000 worth of further stock on the balance sheet to show for it. A revision of targets of this kind can never constitute a profit variance: to take a simplified view of an extract from the balance sheet:–

	Original Budgeted Balance Sheet £	Revised Budgeted Balance Sheet £
Sources of Funds		
Profit and Loss Account	NIL	NIL
Uses of Funds		
Stock on hand at standard	6,000	9,000
Cash (decline)	(6,000)	(9,000)
Total	NIL	NIL

The total profit variance, for the purposes of this example is £1,300, because the company has produced £9,000 of stock at a cost of £7,700.

	Original Budgeted Balance Sheet £	Revised Budgeted Balance Sheet £	Actual Balance Sheet £
Sources of Funds			
Profit and Loss Account	NIL	NIL	1,300
Uses of Funds			
Stock on hand at standard	6,000	9,000	9,000
Cash (decline)	(6,000)	(9,000)	(7,700)
Total	NIL	NIL	1,300

In the same way, sales 'turnover' variances cannot be classed as full-status variances, and are excluded from membership of the Nominal Ledger Account Club; let us assume that the 1,000 budgeted units in the previous example were expected to sell for £15,000, and that the actual turnover (sales total) was £23,000, there being neither budgeted nor actual closing stock. Ignore selling costs and assume that fixed production overheads were budgeted as £6,000, and proved in practice to be £6,500.

Operating Statement

Line ref.	(1) Original Budget Units	(1) Original Budget £	(2) Flexing because of activity Change Units	(2) £	(3) Revised budget for actual activity Units	(3) £	(4) Actual costs for actual activity Units	(4) £	(5)(a) Sales Price	(5)(b) Cost	(5)(c) Expenditure	(5)(d) Fixed Cost Volume	(5)(e) Sales volume (col. 2)	(5)(f) Total
1 Sales	1,000	15,000	500	500	1,500	22,500	1,500	23,000	500(F)					500(F)
2 Cost of Production	1,000		500		1,500		1,500							
3 Direct Materials		1,000		500		1,500		1,400		100(F)				100(F)
4 Direct Labour		3,000		1,500		4,500		4,200		300(F)				300(F)
5 Variable Overheads		2,000		1,000		3,000		2,100		900(F)				900(F)
6 Fixed Production Overhead		6,000		3,000		9,000		6,500			500(U)	3,000(F)		2,500(F)
7 Total available for sale	1,000	12,000	500	6,000	1,500	18,000	1,500	14,200						
8 Less: closing stock	—	—	—	—	—	—	—	—						
9 Cost of Sales	1,000	12,000	500	6,000	1,500	18,000	1,500	14,200						
10 Profit	1,000	3,000	500	1,500	1,500	4,500	1,500	8,800						
11 Total Profit Variance													1,500(F)	5,800(F)

Explanation

The actual profit of £8,800 (col. (4)), represents a £5,800 (col. 5(f)) improvement against budgeted profit of £3,000 at col. (1). At actual selling and production activity levels, the actual profit of £8,800 would have been £4,500 (col. (3)) if actual selling prices and actual cost levels had been exactly in line with standards. Column (1) represents the targeted profit from the company's vital, original battle plan, but it must not be directly compared with column (4) which is based on entirely different activity levels. Cols. (2) and (3) show flexible budgetary control in action.

Notice how a sales turnover variance of £7,500 appears at line 1, but, this so-called variance represents the difference between original budgeted sales and actual sales quantitites at standard selling prices. To claim a £7,500 variance affecting profits merely as a result of revising sales invoice total expectations would be a nonsense. Consequently no accommodation can be found for this amount in column (5). In passing we can see a similar brush-off for £500 at line 3, £1,500 at line 4, and £1,000 at line 5: in these cases, the company has produced extra saleable stock which unexpectedly appears in the balance sheet: actual current assets are greater than budgeted current assets. Surely this is a case whereby unexpected asset gain should be balanced by profit gain! Such reasoning would be correct were it not for the fact that cash should have declined, all else being equal, by £3,000, in sympathy with the stock gain. So here we have an illustration to support the original contention that flexing adjustments to variable costs do not constitute variances in the proper sense: which brings us to line 6 on the statement.

At line 6, column (2), appears a flexing adjustment which, if you direct your gaze to column 5(d), assumes the role of a favourable variance. The reasoning is that with extra stock of 500 units being made, each unit should bear regular portions of standard cost for nominal ledger and balance sheet purposes. Such standard cost includes £6 per unit to absorb fixed expense.

The company budgeted for 1,000 units of production and, each time one unit was given clearance by the inspector, Cost of Production (Work-in-Progress) would be debited (charged) with £6 and Fixed Overhead Applied Account would be credited. After 1,000 units had been produced, the company would go on using the £6 rate another 500 times: at no extra cost, as fixed expenses, by their nature, do not cause cash declines fluctuating in sympathy with activity levels. So the company found themselves in a situation at production time of having £18,000 of stock for an expected outlay of £15,000 (£1,500 + £4,500 + £3,000 = £9,000 variable cost plus £6,000 fixed cost). This satisfactory situation was recognised, in the books of account, at production time. There was no need to wait until the point of sale.

At line 6, column (2), therefore, £3,000 is more than just a flexing adjustment. It represents a *Fixed Production Overhead Volume Variance,* necessary to bridge the gap between a stock plus which includes £9,000 for fixed expenses and a potential cash minus which ought to include £6,000 for fixed expenses.

Hopefully, you are not worrying about why I am 'flexing fixed costs'. Fixed costs are *not* being flexed! Stock valuation is being flexed, because there is more of it than planned. I can hardly point to 1,500 units of production on the shelves and claim that it is worth exactly the same as the originally intended 1,000 units. The rationale behind this assertion is of course that the company is valuing stock at *full cost,* ie to include fixed production overhead. Fixed cost is being absorbed into stock at a routine predetermined rate per unit, so that the more stock is made, the more it will be worth. It should also be stressed that the company's policy of using standard stock valuation on the balance sheet has to be acceptable to the auditors.

Now, if a profit variance of £3,000 is claimed at production time in the above way, the profit variance at the later stage of making unbudgeted sales of 500 units cannot in all fairness claim the £3,000 yet again. With £3,000 securely established at line 6, column (2), increasing the cost of sales figure at line 9 to £6,000, this double-claim is nipped in the bud: the *Sales Volume Variance* at line 10 is correctly diminished to £1,500. This figure represents the extra *profit* expected from selling not 1,000 units as planned, but 1,500 units. It shows an effect on profits, *all else being equal:* in other words, when actual profits are weighed against budgeted profits, the actual selling price used will not be the same as standard, and actual cost of sales will not be in line with standard, *but,* whatever the total profit variance happens to be, £1,500 of it will be as a direct, undistorted result of 'getting an extra 500 units away'. There is *another* variance to measure the effect of getting an extra 500 units away *at a non-standard price.* (*The Sales Price Variance* does this important job at line 1, column 5(a), measuring the effect of tampering with the standard selling price of the total quantity sold, *including* the 500 extra units.) There are yet further variances, derived at production time, for measuring the effect on profits of costs (calmly assumed as standard when calculating the sales volume variance) not actually being according to standard. (See col. 5(b) and column 5(c) for *Variable Cost Variances* and the *Fixed Overhead Expenditure Variance.*)

Supposing our examination question asked for the calculation of certain variances from a given set of figures, without requiring a performance report or a profit and loss account, and without regard to any book-keeping environment. The question would contain a list of standard costs, and a list of actual costs, and it would be necessary to utilise formulae for variance calculation, 'back of an envelope' style.

In determining specific variances, we ought to respect the split of total cost into various categories, direct materials, direct labour, (or wages), variable works (or production) overhead, fixed works (or production) overhead, administration overhead, variable selling costs (or overhead), and fixed selling costs (or overhead), for definitions of these terms refer to the glossary at the back of this book.

CHAPTER 4

DIRECT MATERIAL VARIANCES

A budgeted production activity for a given accounting period enables management to estimate or budget for an appropriate direct material cost for that activity level. As soon as the budgeted direct material cost at this level is divided by the budgeted number of production units, we derive the budgeted (or standard) direct material cost per unit. On occasion, examiners may provide standard unit costs without involving candidates in the above division sum. For the purposes of this text, *direct* materials and *raw* materials are interchangeable. The object is to compare actual direct material costs at the actual production level achieved, with what ought to have been incurred for direct materials at the actual activity level. From this comparison springs the *Direct Materials Cost Variance*. Consider the following example:

ABC Ltd has budgeted production of 100 units. Each unit has a standard direct material cost of £7.875 after deducting the sales value of scrapped materials. In practice 80 units are produced, and the direct material actually charged to production after deducting income from scrap material is £645. Direct materials are purchased from suppliers on credit.

Required: calculate the direct materials cost variance.

Solution:
As a starting point, we should find the *measure of activity* in the question. What is it that the company are making? Discovery of a measure for what is actually happening enables a direct material cost entitlement to be attributed, in this case £7.875 for each of 80 *units* actually produced. The measure of activity is *units* in this case. When management projected direct materials costs at the time of budget preparation, they had to guess at the precise level of activity which would be achieved. They would feel confident, however, that if their budgeted level of activity proved wrong, they would still be able to control direct material costs. They considered during budgeting that £7.875 was a fair

direct material cost entitlement for any one unit, and that multiplication of £7.875 by the number of units actually produced in due course would be a workable standard direct material cost of actual production, likely to be reflected in actual cash book expenditure. In this question, the fact that direct material cost is not £7.875 × 80 = £630 requires explanation. We have a direct materials cost variance of £(645−630) = £15. In balance sheet terms the company has created a finished goods asset which includes a standard direct materials cost of £630 and in so doing has incurred liabilities to creditors for direct materials amounting to £645.

An abbreviated balance sheet situation can be shown as follows:

	(a) Budgeted balance sheet in view of actual activity £	(b) Actual balance sheet for actual activity £
Sources of Funds		
Profit and loss account	NIL	(15) (loss)
Creditors		
(less debtors for scrap sales)	630	645
Uses of Funds		
Finished goods stock		
(at standard)	630	630

The actual profit and loss account line shows a deficit of £15 while the budgeted profit and loss account shows NIL. The balance sheet extracts above are a form of proof that a direct material cost variance is capable of taking the prefix 'Profit variance caused by ...'. There is a variance of £15 between the profit and loss account balance as it was envisaged and the balance actually appearing in the books of account, where the profit and loss account in the nominal ledger shows a debit balance of £15. The (a) column above is purely a memorandum, and plays no part in either the nominal ledger or the trial balance. This example assumes that a system of standard costing is in operation in the company and that stock on hand is held in nominal ledger control accounts at standard cost. Almost all costing or management accounting questions which probe understanding of standard costing support these assumptions.

Clearly there is a question mark hanging over the actual cost of £645. Was this cost incurred because the wrong price was paid to suppliers for direct material purchased, or did the quantity of direct materials issued to production deviate from the standard quantity entitlement for 80 units? Indeed, the £15 variance may emanate in part from each of these causes. Again, the allowed £7.875 unit is already known to be the net cost after deducting budgeted receipts receivable from sale of scrapped material; in practice there may have been less actual income from scrap either because the scrap quantity was not in line with the standard quantity, or because the sales price per portion of scrap was not what was expected. The direct materials cost variance can emanate from a *pot pourri* of causes. If causes can be particularised and evaluated, the 'coarse' direct materials cost variance may well be set aside in the nominal ledger in favour of other less ambiguous material variances, one for each cause, which even by their very titles, help management to understand more clearly why a profit variance caused by direct materials has been arising.

The most common initial step in 'breaking out' a cost variance is to compare direct material *prices* paid to suppliers with those expected, that is, to compare actual and standard direct material purchase price rates per unit of material purchased.

A *Direct Material Price Variance* is the end result of the above comparison. Let us assume in the above example that (1) only one raw material ingredient is needed in production, (2) it is measured in kilos, and (3) the standard buying price of a kilo is £1. In such cases management have a choice of methods of deriving the direct material price variance. Consider the following amplification of our previous example:

Actual production	80 units
Direct materials purchased	800 kilos
Direct materials used in production	600 kilos
Actual cost of materials purchased	£1.25 per kilo

The first and more popular method is to determine the price variance at time of purchase, as soon as ownership of the materials passes to ABC Ltd. The price variance in such cases is based on the buying department's total current purchasing activity, and any deviation between actual and expected prices negotiated by this department is reported as it happens (rather than after the delay of waiting for production departments to requisition material into work-in-progress). This early detection method adheres to the principle of reporting variances as quickly as possible to those who may be able to take appropriate action. The formula is: actual purchasing activity (in kilos) × (standard − actual) kilo price = direct material price variance. In the given example, the price variance is therefore $800 \times £(1 - 1.25) = £200$. As the actual cost exceeds the expected cost, the variance is unfavourable.

At time of purchase, the following journal entry would be typical:

Direct Material Stores Control Account	DR	£800
Direct Material Price Variance Account	DR	£200
Sundry Creditors Control Account	CR	£1,000

Notice that in the above scheme of things, there is no place for any Direct Materials Cost Variance of £15. Nevertheless, if we wish in due course to explain an aggregate profit variance of £15, our original figure, the sum of the analysis which we are hereby initiating with the price variance will need to be £15.

The company's storekeeper will maintain stock records at standard cost. Any requisitions to production will also be valued at standard material cost so that the only variance of interest at that time will result from quantities used deviating from plan, rather than purchase prices paid.

The alternative method of calculating a price variance is to wait until direct materials are requisitioned from stores to production, maintaining direct material stock in the nominal ledger at actual cost prices in the meantime. In the above example, the following situation would then accrue:

(a) Direct Material Stores Control Account (actual cost)   DR   £1,000

Sundry Creditors Control Account	CR	£1,000

Then, at time of issue to production:

(b) Work-in-Progress Control Account (at standard cost) DR £600
Direct Material Price Variance Account   DR £150
Direct Material Stores Control Account   CR £750
(being requisition of 600 kilos of material, at a
standard cost of £1 per kilo and an actual cost of
£1.25 per kilo).

Work in progress stock is held in the balance sheet at standard cost and direct materials at actual cost. The effects of what could be faulty buying practices are spread over the periods in which materials are actually used. If in our example we assume that the balance of direct materials is requisitioned in the subsequent period, the following entry would result at that time:

Work in Progress Control Account (at standard cost) DR £200
Direct Material Price Variance Account   DR £50
Direct Material Stores Control Account   CR £250
(being requisition of 200 kilos of material, at a
standard cost of £1 per kilo and an actual cost of
£1.25 per kilo).

If in an examination context, there is a clear direction that stock is to be valued at standard cost, the latter method involving postponement of price variances is out of bounds, as it necessitates a direct material stockholding at actual and not standard prices. In our efforts to reconcile to a total unfavourable variance of £15, let us assume that direct material stocks are held at standard and recognise a price variance of £200 (unfavourable) in the current period.

When an unfavourable price variance has been written off to cost of production in a company's profit and loss account, a proportion may relate to raw material which has not been used. In such cases, write off of the entire price variance may appear too harsh: at the same time, the raw material stockholding will be held at a standard cost which is below actual cost. In such cases, the company may feel inclined to debit stock accounts and credit the profit and loss account (usually via a price variance account) with the price variance which relates to unused raw materials. If this is done late in the accounting year, and suddenly, a very large 'profit' may arise in one of the last periods of the year, causing distortions (and long discussions with non-accounting management). Ideally in such circumstances the stock appreciation (which is the difference between the standard and actual cost of stock likely to be unused by the close of the year) should be phased in gradually over several periods. In general terms management are not happy about sudden significant charges or credits in periodic accounts which come dramatically 'out of a clear sky'.

Direct Material Usage Variance
The next possible source of a profit variance caused by direct materials arises from examination of the material quantities requisitioned into production (or work in progress). When building standard specifications of cost allowable in completing one unit of production, management would set a

target direct material weight per unit in kilos. In our example we have already assumed that raw materials comprise of only one ingredient. Multi-ingredient situations will be explored later in the chapter.

Let us further assume that the company's specification of contents of one production unit sets a stores issue allowance of 9 kilos per unit. The standard weight allowance for 80 units is therefore 720 kilos: as indicated previously, 600 kilos were actually issued to production. There is clearly a deviation or variance from plan of 120 kilos. In view of the actual activity achieved (80 units) the production department were entitled to use 720 kilos. The start-point in calculating a direct material usage variance is therefore to *find the measure of activity* (units), then the actual level of activity achieved (80 units), and then to evaluate those units at their standard direct material cost content (80 units × 9 kilos × £1 per kilo = £720). The price per kilo is the stores issue price used by the storekeeper in his records, and the price at which issues are credited to the Direct Material Stores Control Account: the price actually used, and the price at which direct material stock is actually valued in the balance sheet is the standard price of £1.

Against the above figure is set the actual number of kilos requisitioned, again valued at the actual issue price (the only unit price known to the storekeeper) of £1: 600 × £1 = £600. So for a depletion in direct material stock of £600, a new finished goods asset has been created of £720; the profit and loss account balance in the balance sheet will grow by £120 because of higher than standard efficiency in the *usage* of direct materials. The formula is:

Number of units produced × standard portion size of direct material allowed per unit × standard direct material price per portion, less actual direct material used × standard direct material price per portion.

Applying the formula:

(80 × 9 × £1) less (600 × £1) = £120

As the actual usage of material is less than could have been expected, the variance is favourable.

When we add the newly derived usage variance to the price variance, we fail to arrive at £15 (Unfavourable): £120 Favourable plus £200 (Unfavourable) = £80 (Unfavourable). So we need to continue our search for further variances until an aggregate of £15 (Unfavourable) is reached.

Direct Material Scrap Yield Variance

In many production departments, a certain proportion of the raw material issued from stores is likely to be scrapped. Much of this scrap can in practice be worth virtually nothing, ie it is written off to cost of sales at nil value. However, in some cases, scrap is in such a condition as to be of value to an outside purchaser or customer. Let us suppose in our example that management were led to expect that 1.5 kilos of saleable scrap material would emanate from each unit produced, but that in practice, 200 kilos of such material were 'rescued' while manufacturing the 80 units produced. The standard selling prices of such scrap was 75p per kilo. There is clearly a difference of 80 kilos (80 × 1.5 − 200) between the standard and actual scrap yields produced.

The variance formula is:
Number of units produced × standard weight of scrap expected per unit × standard selling price per kilo of scrap, *less* actual saleable scrap weight derived × standard selling price per kilo of scrap.
In this example:

$$(80 \times 1.5 \text{ kilos} \times 75p) \text{ less } (200 \text{ kilos} \times 75p) = £60$$

As the yield of saleable scrap is in excess of what could reasonably have been expected from a production level of 80 units, the variance is favourable.

The sum of our variances so far now comes much closer to the magic £15 unfavourable. (£200 unfavourable + £120 favourable + £60 favourable = £20 unfavourable.) However, there is clearly still a difference of £5 (favourable) to be explained and absorbed into the reconciliation.

Direct Material Scrap Price Variance

This variance arises when the sales price of scrapped material differs from the standard selling price. In our case let us assume that although the standard price was 75p per kilo, the actual price was 77.5p per kilo. The formula is:
Actual saleable scrap weight × standard selling price per kilo, *less* actual saleable scrap weight × actual selling price per kilo.
In this case:

(200 kilos × 75p) *less* (200 kilos × 77.5p) = £5

As the actual sales price per kilo is greater than the standard, the variance is favourable.

Summary

The situation is now as follows:

	£	
Direct Material Price Variance	200	(U)
Direct Material Usage Variance	120	(F)
Direct Material Scrap Yield Variance	60	(F)
Direct Material Scrap Price Variance	5	(F)
Direct Materials Cost Variance	£15	(U)

The formula for a Direct Materials Cost Variance in the above circumstances is therefore:

(1) (a) Actual production units achieved × standard direct material weight allowed per unit (in kilos) × standard purchase price per kilo
less:
(b) standard saleable scrap weight in view of actual production units achieved × standard sales price.
LESS

(2) (a) Actual direct material weight used × actual stores issue price (which is standard price)
less
(b) actual scrap material weight sold × actual sales price
add/(deduct)

(c) any unfavourable/(favourable) price variance covering all current purchases and taking the form of a debit/(credit) balance on the nominal ledger.

In the example of ABC Ltd:

		£	£
(1) (a) 80 × 9 kilos × £1 per kilo		720	
less:			
(b) 80 × 1.5 kilos × 75p per kilo		90	
Standard cost of actual production			630
LESS			
(2) (a) 600 kilos × £1		600	
less:			
200 kilos × 77.5p		155	
		445	
add:			
800 × £(1–1.25)		200	
			645
Unfavourable Direct Material Cost Variance			£15

So in view of an actual production activity of 80 units, the company was entitled to charge £630 to costs of production for direct materials: hopefully, the fact that an actual charge of £645 was felt necessary has been explained in the four-variance summary above. In cases where scrap has a nil value, and this has been recognised during the setting of standards, the Scrap Yield and Scrap Price Variances cannot exist: budgeted and actual scrap income in such cases are identical at NIL and there can be no profit variances caused by deviations in cash received from scrap.

Further Practical Examples of Direct Material Variances
Understanding of variances can be greatly reinforced by examining a series of practical examples.

Example One
XYZ Ltd budgeted to produce 1,000 units, but actually produced 1,200 units. The budgeted raw material cost at the original budgeted level of activity was £16,000. The actual raw material cost was £20,400.
Required: (i) calculate the Raw Material Cost Variance and provide (ii) appropriate profit statement and (iii) balance sheet extracts.

Solution

(i) *Calculation of Raw Material Cost Variance*   £

(a) Actual direct material costs chargeable to costs of production in respect of actual production levels: 20,400

(b) Standard raw material cost entitlement in view of actual production levels:
Actual production quantity × standard raw material cost per unit of production:

$$1{,}200 \text{ units} \times \frac{£16{,}000 \text{ original budgeted costs}}{1{,}000 \text{ original budgeted units}} \quad : \quad 19{,}200$$

As the actual charge at (a) exceeds management's expectation for 1,200 units, the variance of £1,200 is unfavourable.

(ii) *Profit Statement (extract showing situation on raw materials)*

((U) = Unfavourable)	(1) Original Budget		(2) Adjustment into line with actual activity		(3) Revised Standard charge		(4) Actual Profit & Loss A/C		(5) Variance affecting profit: (Raw Material Cost)	
	Units	£	Units	£	Units	£	Units	£	Units	£
Cost of Production	1,000		200		1,200		1,200			
Raw Material		16,000		3,200		19,200		20,400		1,200(U)

Note that in the event of the 1,200 units remaining unsold, they will feature on the balance sheet at standard cost which will include £19,200 for raw materials (col. (3). In achieving this situation, £20,400 will be charged to Cost of Production (col. (4)). Another format of the above statement would show (ignoring original budget figures):

Actual Profit and Loss Account

	Units	£
Costs of production at standard	1,200	
Raw materials		19,200
add: unfavourable cost variance		1,200
Actual cost		20,400
less: Closing stock at standard (only raw material constituent shown)		19,200
Loss for the period		£1,200

Extracts from Balance Sheets

(Brackets = loss)	Original budgeted balance sheet	Budgeted balance sheet in view of actual activity	Actual balance sheet for actual activity
	£	£	£
Sources of Funds			
Profit and Loss Account	NIL	NIL	(1,200)
Bank overdraft (Note 1)	16,000	19,200	20,400
Uses of Funds			
Finished goods stock	16,000	19,200	19,200

Note 1 It is assumed that creditors' accounts for raw materials have been paid using bank overdraft facilities.

Example Two

ABC Ltd, operating a system of standard costing and flexible budgetary control, have opening raw material stock at the beginning of period 5 of

5,000lbs, held in the books of account at £2 per lb. During period 5 they purchase a further 10,000lbs at £2.25 per lb. Budgeted production of finished units is 3,000, with a standard raw material content per unit of 4lbs at £2 per lb standard price. Actual production is 3,200. First-in, first-out (FIFO) requisitioning of raw materials is in use. Raw materials actually requisitioned to production totalled 13,000lbs.
Required: (i) calculate the Raw Material Cost Variance, and (ii) provide an appropriate profit statement extract.

Solution to Example Two

(i) *Calculation of Raw Material Cost Variance*	£	£
(a) Actual quantity of raw material used at actual *issue* price		
13,000lbs × £2 per lb	26,000	
Plus: unfavourable price variance on all current purchasing activity		
10,000lbs × 25p (price difference)	2,500	28,500
(b) 3,200 units of production × 4lbs × £2		25,600
Unfavourable Raw Material Cost Variance		£2,900

As a system of standard costing is in use, opening raw material stock of 5,000lbs, the first to be issued to production under FIFO, is assumed to be held at standard unit cost. Any difficulty on buying prices of this old stock will already have been faced in the accounts of preceding periods, when price variances were created and written off on any buying activity at that time. During period 5, new purchases were made which would be introduced into the nominal ledger as follows:

Raw Material Stores Control Account	DR	£20,000
Raw Material Price Variance Account	DR	£2,500
Sundry Creditors Account (actual cost)	CR	£22,500

The sum of £2,500 would be posted to the debit of Price Variance Account and after appropriate management enquiries and action to counter any unfavourable trend, this sum would be written off to Profit and Loss Account, provided there was agreement that raw material stocks should continue to be held at standard cost. At (i) (a) above we see the constitution of the actual profit and loss account charge for raw materials and that it includes the £2,500: section (ii) below shows the situation in profit statement format.

(ii) *Profit Statement (Extract showing situation on raw materials)*
((U) = Unfavourable)

	(1) Original budget		(2) Adjustment into line with actual activity		(3) Revised standard charge		(4) Actual Profit & Loss A/C		(5) Variances affecting profit: Raw Material Cost
	Units	£	Units	£	Units	£	Units	£	£
Cost of Production	3,000		200		3,200		3,200		
Raw Material		24,000		1,600		25,600		28,500	2,900(U)

Alternative simplified presentation	*Actual Profit and Loss Account*	
	Units	*£*
Costs of Production at standard	3,200	
Raw Materials		25,600
Add: unfavourable cost variance		2,900
Actual cost		28,500
Less: Closing stock at standard (only raw material constituent shown)		25,600
Loss for the period		£2,900

The difference between the Price Variance of £2,500 and the Cost Variance of £2,900 emanates from a Raw Material Usage Variance of £400 (unfavourable). (3,200 units × 4lbs × 2lbs (£25,600) less 13,000 × £2 (£26,000)). The book-keeping background would be:

Work-in-Progress Control Account	DR	£25,600
Raw Materials Usage Variance Account	DR	£400
Raw Materials Stores Control Account	CR	£26,000

Example Three

Budgeted purchases of raw materials	5,000lbs
Actual purchases of raw materials	4,000lbs
Opening raw material stock on hand	1,000lbs
Budgeted usage of raw materials	4,000lbs
Actual usage of raw materials	3,600lbs
Budgeted production	1,000 units
Actual production	800 units
Standard cost of raw materials	25p per lb
Actual cost of raw materials	£900

A system of standard costing is in operation: all stocks are held in the nominal ledger at standard cost.

Required: calculate raw material variances.

Solution to Example Three
  (1) *Calculation of Raw Material Cost Variance*
      Find the *measure* and *level* of activity
      Answer: *800 units*

	£	£
(a) Actual quantity of raw material used at actual *issue* price		
3,600lbs × 25p	900	
Less: favourable price variance on all current buying activity		
4,000lbs × 25p, less £900	100	800
(b) *800 units* × 4lbs per unit (standard allowance) × 25p per lb		800
Raw Material Cost Variance		NIL

(a) above would be shown at col.(4) of a profit statement, and (b) would appear at col. (3): see layout supporting previous example.

Analysis of Raw Material Cost Variance
  (2) *Raw Material Price Variance*
      Find current buying activity: 4,000lbs

	£
(a) Actual purchases at standard price: 4,000 × 25p	1,000
(b) Actual purchases at actual price	900
Favourable price variance	£100

  (3) *Raw Material Usage Variance*
      Find current production activity: 800 units

	£
(a) Actual quantity of raw material issued at actual *issue* price: 3,600 × 25p	900
(b) 800 units × 4lbs per unit × 25p	800
Unfavourable yield variance	£100

Notice how the information on budgeted purchases of raw materials and opening stock of raw materials has not been utilised.

Example Four

Production unit: steel blades
Raw material allowance: 5.5lbs per blade
Budgeted production: 100 blades
Actual production: 120 blades
Total purchases of materials: 800lbs
Actual usage of materials: 600lbs
Standard cost per lb of material: 50p
Actual cost per lb of material: 45p
Actual sales value of scrap material: 10p per lb
Budgeted sales value of scrap material: 20p per lb
Weight of each finished blade: 4.8lbs
A system of standard costing is in operation; stocks are valued at standard cost. There are no opening or closing balances on the Work in Progress Account.
Required: (i) calculate raw material variances and (ii) show the situation in profit statement format.

Solution to Example Four
  (i) *Calculation of Raw Material Cost Variance*
      Find the *measure* and *level* of activity: 120 blades

	£	£
(a) Actual quantity of raw material used × actual *issue* price (standard price) 600lbs × 50p	300	
less: favourable price variance on all current purchasing activity: 800lbs × 5p differential	40	
	260	
less: actual scrap income received (see note 1)	2.40	
Actual Profit and Loss Account charge: col.(4) at part (ii)		257.60

(b) Actual production × standard raw material weight
   entitlement × standard raw material price:
   120 blades × 5.5lbs × 50p   330
   less: standard weight of scrapped materials
      for 120 blades × standard scrap selling
      price: 120 × (5.5–4.8)lbs × 20p   16.80

Standard raw material cost of actual blades:
   col. (3) at part (ii)   313.20
Favourable Raw Material Cost Variance   £55.60

Note 1 Calculation of actual scrap quantity
Total material issued: 600lbs
Assume that this is all scrap, unless any material has clearly been used in
good blades: good blades worth 120 × 4.8lbs = 576lbs. Therefore 576lbs'
worth of material cannot have been scrapped. Therefore scrapped material
= (600 – 576) = 24lbs
Scrap income: 24lbs × 10p = £2.40.

As before, the Raw Material Cost Variance shows the aggregate profit
variance caused by all deviations from expected costs and performance as
regards raw materials. In view of more useful detailed variances which
would arise along the lines shown in the following analysis, the aggregate
cost variance above would rarely appear in its own right as a nominal
ledger account. The above calculation is an arithmetical exercise necessary
if one is to feel confident in the insertion of monetary amounts at columns
(3) and (4) of a profit statement.

Analysis of Raw Material Cost Variance

Raw Material Price Variance
Find the current purchasing activity: 800lbs
   800lbs × (standard–actual) price
   = 800lbs × (50–45)p = *£40 Favourable*

Raw Material Usage Variance   £
Find current production activity: *120 blades*
   (a) actual quantity of raw material issued at actual
      issue price: 600lbs × 50p   300
   (b) *120 blades* × 5.5lbs × 50p   330
      Favourable usage variance   £30

Raw Material Scrap Yield Variance   £
Find the current production activity: *120 blades*
   (a) Actual scrap yield: 600lbs – (120 × 4.8)
      = 24lbs × standard rate of 20p per lb =   4.80
   (b) *120 blades* × standard scrap yield per blade
      = 120 blades × (5.5 – 4.8)lbs × 20p =   16.80
      Unfavourable Raw Material Scrap Yield Variance £12.00

Raw Material Scrap Price Variance	£
Actual scrap weight: 24lbs	
(a) × standard selling price per lb (20p)	4.80
(b) × actual selling price per lb (10p)	2.40
Unfavourable Raw Material Scrap Price Variance	£2.40

Summary ((U) = Unfavourable, (F) = Favourable)	£	
Raw Material Price Variance	40	(F)
Raw Material Usage Variance	30	(F)
Raw Material Scrap Yield Variance	12	(U)
Raw Material Scrap Price Variance	2.40	(U)
Raw Material Cost Variance	£55.60	(F)

(ii) *Profit Statement (Extract showing situation on raw materials)*
    ((F) = Favourable)

	(1) Original Budget (See Note 1)		(2) Adjustment into line with actual activity (See Note 2)		(3) Revised standard charge		(4) Actual Profit & Loss A/C		(5) Variances affecting Profits: Raw Material Cost
	Units	£	Units	£	Units	£	Units	£	£
Costs of Production	100		20		120		120		
Raw Materials		261		52.20		313.20		257.60	55.60 (F)

Notice that no matter how complicated the question may be as regards detailed variance calculations, a single charge (£257.60) is all that is made at col. (4) on the raw materials line of the statement. In addition, the standard stock valuation at col. (3) may require working out, but when all is said and done, a single monetary stock valuation (£313.20) is all that appears. Poundage of raw materials should never be accommodated on such a statement. The company is in the business of making (and presumably selling) *steel blades,* and all other physical entities should be firmly denied any means of ingress to the units columns.

Note 1 Calculation of Column (1) figure	£
100 blades × standard raw material weight entitlement	
× standard raw material price: = 100 blades × 5.5lbs × 50p	275
less: standard weight of scrapped materials for 100 blades	
× standard scrap selling price: = 100 × .7lbs × 20p	14
Standard raw material cost of budgeted blades	£261

Note 2 Calculation of Column (2) figure	
	£
20 blades × standard raw material weight entitlement	
× standard raw material price:	
= 20 blades × 5.5lbs × 50p	55

	£
less: standard weight of scrapped materials for 20 blades × standard scrap selling price: = 20 × .7lbs × 20p	2.80
Standard raw material cost of 20 blades	£52.20

A full profit statement would, of course, show details of the other cost categories such as direct labour on additional lines. Those who present such statements have the option of showing a full analysis of variances at col. (5), or of restricting the reader to total variances, such as the £55.60(F) shown, and referring him to an appendix for details. In taking the former route, column (5) would be expanded: there is no hard and fast rule on presentation sequence, ie as to which variance should be represented at column 5(a):

(5)
Variances Affecting Profits

	Raw material price (a) £	Raw material usage (b) £	Raw material scrap yield (c) £	Raw material scrap price (d) £	Total (cost) (e) £
Raw Materials	40(F)	30(F)	12(U)	2.40(U)	55.60(F)

In deciding whether to show full details on a profit statement, the extent of variances on other cost categories should be anticipated. Paper size restrictions occasionally argue in favour of details on appendices. As has been implied earlier, detailed variances are created over a period as business transactions deviate from plan for a number of reasons. A direct material cost variance is usually the end result of several types of deviation; the effect in monetary terms of each type of deviation is monitored in the nominal ledger, with one variance account being opened for each type. In such cases a cost variance could only be created by journal entry if the balances on, say, price, usage, scrap yield and scrap price variances which might make up the detailed variances were written off by journal entry to a new variance which we have called Direct Material Cost Variance.

The creation of the four detailed variances in Example Four would take place along the following lines:

Raw Material Price Variance

Raw Material Stores Control Account (800 × 50p)	DR	£400
Raw Material Price Variance Account (800 × 5p)	CR	£40
Sundry Creditors (800 × 45p)	CR	£360

(To introduce 800lbs of purchased materials to the nominal ledger.)

Raw Material Usage Variance
  Cost of Production (or Work in Progress Account)
    (at standard): 120 × 5.5 = 660lbs × 50p   DR   £330
  Raw Material Usage Variance Account (660–600) × 50p CR   £30
  Raw Material Stores Control Account 600 × 50p   CR   £300
  (To recognise standard raw material content of actual production and to
transfer 600lbs from R.M. Store.)

Raw Material Scrap Yield Variance
  Finished Goods Stock Account at Standard:
    120 × ((5.5 × 50p) − (0.7 × 20p))   DR   £313.20
  Raw Material Scrap Stock Account: (24 × 20p)   DR   £4.80
  Raw Material Scrap Yield Variance Account
    ((120 × 0.7) − 24lbs × 20p)   DR   £12
  Cost of Production (or Work in Progress Account)
    at standard   CR   £330
  (To close out the Cost of Production (or Work in Progress Account)
upon completion of 120 blades.)

Raw Material Scrap Price Variance
  Debtors (or Cash) Account: (24lbs × 10p)   DR   £2.40
  Raw Materials Scrap Price Variance Account   DR   £2.40
  Raw Materials Scrap Stock Account   CR   £4.80
  (Upon sale of 24lbs of scrap material at 10p per lb which should have
realised 20p per lb.)
  Notice how the full debit to Cost of Production (£330) has been removed
at a later journal entry: this is essential as the work of production has
ceased and there is no closing stock of work-in-progress.

Further Analysis of Usage Variances
Most production processes involve the infusion of more than one raw
material ingredient. It then becomes possible for a usage variance to result
from one of two distinct causes.
  In exploring these causes, remember that actual production achieved is
shown in the appropriate nominal ledger account and in the company's
balance sheet at standard cost, which includes a valuation of an estimated
quantity of each of the raw material ingredients which *ought* to have been
used in producing one unit times the number of units produced. At the
same time declines in stockholdings of raw materials in the nominal ledger
and balance sheet are the result of recognising actual quantities requisitioned.
  In practice there are bound to be wide divergences between standard,
raw material-bearing potential of production on the one hand, and actual
material quantities issued from stores on the other. A usage variance
bridges the gap between the two sides so that the nominal ledger is maintained in a constantly 'balanced' condition. When production units achieved
are capable of carrying more material content (according to standard
specification sheets) than was actually needed in practice the journal entry
debiting Work-in-Progress (or Cost of Production) at standard, will exceed

the credit to Raw Material Stores Control Account at standard, not because of any raw material unit price deviation, but because of quantities of materials on the debit side exceeding actual requisition slip totals on the credit side. The usage variance is created at this juncture as a book-keeping device on the credit side of the journal entry to force reconciliation of the debit with the credit side.

Alternatively, when insufficient production is achieved to carry the full weight of actual raw materials used, the usage variance lies on the debit side as representing the extra raw material quantity which *ought not* to have been used because of the poor showing on production unit quantities. Debit (unfavourable) usage variances represent 'orphan' raw material cost which has become disengaged from the standard cost recovery system whereby, pound for pound, cost moves along a trading cycle from Raw Material Stock to Work in Progress to Finished Goods to Cost of Sales, all at standard. This latter figure is in such cases below actual cost and is up-lifted by the usage variance when the Profit and Loss Account stage is reached. Credit (favourable) variances represent the degree of over-statement of the cost of production at standard, so that in due course the Cost of Sales balance at standard, a figure in excess of real cost, is diminished after its transfer to the Profit and Loss Account, by the usage variance balance similarly transferred.

The two causes of a usage variance when more than one ingredient is re-quired are that (1) too much or too little total bulk of ingredients may be fed into production for the actual production units level reached, although the proportions of each raw material as regards share of bulk may be exactly in line with standard specifications; (2) the total bulk quantity of materials used may be exactly in line with standards, but too high or too low a proportion of the bulk issued may be of the more costly of the stan-dard ingredients. One can visualise the situation on the balance sheet of a baking company, where each fruit loaf in stock is supposed to contain a certain weight and proportion of more expensive additives such as sultanas, apart from basic dough, and is reckoned to justify issue of a certain total quantity of ingredients per loaf. Problems or carelessness with mixing, resulting in too rich a mixture of ingredients without a change to the stan-dard nominal ledger cost per loaf, plus unexpected wastage in handling of raw materials could result in an aggregate unfavourable usage variance which would be a hybrid of the two causes mentioned above.

The following examples illustrate the situation in which more than one raw material ingredient is used in the manufacture of a single finished product unit.

Example One
Production: budgeted 1,000 units; actual 1,250 units.
Standard raw material allowance per unit:
> 3lbs of raw material A
> 2lbs of raw material B

Actual requisitions: 3,900lbs of A; 2,600lbs of B
Standard prices of raw materials: 40p per lb of A; 60p per lb of B.
Required: calculate and analyse the Raw Materials Usage Variance.

Solution
  (1) *Calculation of Raw Material Usage Variance*
      Find current production activity: 1,250 units
      (a) Actual quantities of raw materials used at actual issue prices:
          A: 3,900lbs × 40p = £1,560
          B: 2,600lbs × 60p = £1,560
                                                              £3,120
      (b) 1,250 units × standard contents:
          A: 1,250 × 3lbs × 40p = £1,500
          B: 1,250 × 2lbs × 60p = £1,500
                                                              3,000
          Raw Materials Usage Variance (unfavourable)   £ 120

  (2) *Analysis of Raw Material Usage Variance*
      (a) *Caused by bulk deviation from plan*
          (i) Actual quantity used; assume that it is
              mixed in standard proportions   £   £
              A: 3/5 × 6,500lbs × 40p   1,560
              B: 2/5 × 6,500lbs × 60p   1,560
                                                                     3,120
          (ii) Standard quantity entitlement for actual production
              A: 1,250 × 3lbs × 40p   1,500
              B: 1,250 × 2lbs × 60p   1,500
                                                                     3,000
              Unfavourable Raw Material Yield Variance   £ 120

For the purposes of a yield variance, the actual aggregate or bulk quantity used is assumed to have been in the correct proportions of A and B. We wish at this stage to evaluate the damage caused by releasing 6,500lbs of raw materials from stores when all that the finished stock is capable of bearing is the cost of 1,250 × 5lbs = 6,250lbs. The problem at this stage is that *all else being equal,* ie assuming everything else is in line with standards, 6,500 − 6,250 = 250lbs of raw material stock has to be credited to the raw material nominal ledger but cannot be debited to Work in Progress, as there is insufficient activity there to justify the charge. We have the right at this stage to assume that the 250lbs is 'properly mixed' in terms of the mix formula. Therefore the 'orphan cost' involved is:

                                                              £
          3/5 × 250lbs × 40p   60
          2/5 × 250lbs × 60p   60

                                                            £120

  (b) *Caused by deviations from the standard mix of ingredients*
      (i) Actual quantity used, in actual proportions, valued at standard raw material unit prices: £   £
          A: 3,900 × 40p =   1,560
          B: 2,600 × 60p =   1,560
                                                                     3,120

(ii) Actual quantity used, in standard proportions, valued at standard raw material unit prices:

	£	£
A: 3/5 × 6,500 × 40p	1,560	
B: 2/5 × 6,500 × 60p	1,560	3,120
Raw Material Mix Variance		NIL

It is clear from the above that the problem of using the wrong total quantity (there was an excess of 250lbs), was not aggravated by issuing materials from stores in non-standard proportions.

Example Two

Production: budgeted 1,000 units; actual 1,250 units
Standard raw material allowance per unit:
      3lbs of raw material A; 2lbs of raw material B
Actual requisitions: 4,000lbs of A; 2,250lbs of B.
Standard prices of raw materials: 40p per lb of A; 60p per lb of B.
Required: calculate and analyse the Raw Materials Usage Variance.

Solution
(1) *Calculation of Raw Material Usage Variance*
    Find current production activity: 1,250 units
    (a) Actual quantities of raw materials used at actual issue prices:

	£	£
A: 4,000lbs of A × 40p =	1,600	
B: 2,250lbs of B × 60p =	1,350	2,950
(b) 1,250 units × standard contents:		
A: 1,250 × 3lbs × 40p =	1,500	
B: 1,250 × 2lbs × 60p =	1,500	3,000
Raw Material Usage Variance (Favourable)		£ 50

(2) *Analysis of Raw Material Usage Variance*
    (a) *Caused by bulk deviation from plan*
        (i) Actual quantity used; assume that it is mixed in standard proportions

	£	£
A: 3/5 × 6,250lbs × 40p	1,500	
B: 2/5 × 6,250lbs × 60p	1,500	3,000
(ii) Standard quantity entitlement for actual production:		
A: 1,250 × 3lbs × 40p	1,500	
B: 1,250 × 2lbs × 60p	1,500	3,000
Raw Material Yield Variance		NIL

    (b) *Caused by deviations from the standard mix of ingredients*
        (i) Actual quantity used, in actual proportions, valued at standard raw material unit prices:

	£	£
A: 4,000 × 40p	1,600	
B: 2,250 × 60p	1,350	2,950

(ii) Actual quantity used, in standard proportions, valued at
standard raw material unit prices:

	£	£
A: 3/5 × 6,250 × 40p	1,500	
B: 2/5 × 6,250 × 60p	1,500	
		3,000
Raw Material Mix Variance (Favourable)		£ 50

On this occasion the standard stock valuation of 1,250 units produced is
£3,000, and this is the figure which would appear on the balance sheet. To
achieve this level of production activity required the withdrawal and usage
of only £2,950 of raw material stock. The cause of this favourable variance
is a slight change of emphasis in the actual mix to ingredient A which is
cheaper than B. In theory and perhaps in practice, therefore, customers
would in due course be charged on invoices for proportions of A and B
which they did not actually receive. This gain, ie an opportunity to recover
costs from customers which did not in fact happen, is recognised under
standard costing at production time. Provided that management agreed that
the 1,250 units produced should continue to be valued at standard cost in
the nominal ledger and balance sheet, the £50 favourable variance balance
would be transferred by journal entry to the Profit and Loss Account and
would uplift the Profit and Loss Account balance on the balance sheet.

We can determine from the preceding examples that when more than one
ingredient is needed in production: Raw Material Usage Variance = Raw
Material Mix Variance + Raw Material Yield Variance.

Example Two can be used to illustrate what would take place in journal
entry format:

Work in Progress (or Cost of Production) Account	DR	£3,000
Raw Material Usage Variance Account	CR	£50
Raw Material Stores Control Account	CR	£2,950

Later, if analysis of the Usage Variance was considered useful and
practical, a further journal entry would result:

Raw Material Usage Variance Account	DR	£50
Raw Material Mix Variance Account	CR	£50

In due course, having agreed to hold the 1,250 units at a standard cost
which included £3,000 of materials, a closing journal entry would show
the following transfer:

Raw Material Mix Variance Account	DR	£50
Profit and Loss Account	CR	£50

Presentation layout of operating results could take either of the following
formats:

(a) *Profit Statement (Extract showing situation on raw materials)*
    ((F) = Favourable)

	(1) Original Budget		(2) Adjustments into line with actual activity		(3) Revised standard charge		(4) Actual Profit & Loss Account		(5) Variances affecting Profits: Raw Material Mix
	Units	£	Units	£	Units	£	Units	£	£
Costs of Production	1,000		250		1,250		1,250		
Raw Materials		2,400		600		3,000		2,950	50(F)

(b) *Profit Statement (extract showing situation on raw materials)*

	Budget		Actual	
	Units	£	Units	£
Cost of Production at standard	1,000	2,400	1,250	3,000
Less: favourable mix variance	—			50
Actual cost of production				2,950
Less: closing stock at standard		2,400		3,000
Surplus for period		NIL		£ 50

A more complex situation arises when more than one raw material in-gredient is used in the manufacture of two or more finished products. We can describe Example Three as illustrating a 'multi-input, multi-output' situation. This question has been taken from the Autumn 1978 Diet of the Management Accounting Examination of the Institute of Chartered Accountants of Scotland. It embraces price variances as well as mix and yield variances.

Example Three
Bright Walls Ltd prepares the pigments used for manufacturing paint by mixing zinc oxide with either chalk or limestone, depending on the quality of the paint.
The specifications of these products are:

	Standard cost per lb	Quality A	Quality B
Zinc oxide	40p	75lbs	80lbs
Chalk	10p	25lbs	
Limestone	8p		20lbs
Standard batch size		100lbs	100lbs

In addition, for both qualities there is a spillage allowance of 5%. For the four-week period ended 25th August 1978 the following information was made available:

Pigment produced	1,600 batches of quality A
	1,000 batches of quality B
Raw material input	Zinc oxide 224,000lbs at 45p per lb
	Chalk 47,000lbs at 11p per lb
	Limestone 28,000lbs at 8p per lb

Required:
Prepare a statement for the period to show the effect upon the standard cost of pigment of the –
  1. Materials price variance
  2. Materials mix variance
  3. Materials yield variance.

Solution
In attempting a solution to this question, notice that the company is making no effort to analyse total actual raw material input between quality A and quality B. This apparent shortcoming in cost control will be reflected in the lack of detail on the boxed statement of material cost which forms the initial part of the solution.

Bright Walls Limited: statement of materials cost for 4 weeks ended 25th August 1978
((F) = Favourable, (U) = Unfavourable)

Quality	Quantity (Batches)	Standard Cost (Note 1)	Materials Price Variance (Note 2)	Material Mix Variance (Note 3)	Materials Yield Variance (Note 4)	Total Variances	Actual Costs (Note 5)	Actual (+)/(−) Standard (%)
A	1,600	£54,600	11,670(U)	1,900(F)	8,560(U)	18,330(U)	108,210	20% (rounded)
B	1,000	£35,280						
		89,880						

Note 1 Standard material cost of Quality A

	St. cost per lb	No. of pounds	Batch Cost £	Cost of 1,600 Batches £	Spillage allowance 5%	Total Cost
Zinc oxide	40p	75	30	48,000	2,400	50,400
Chalk	10p	25	2.50	4,000	200	4,200
Limestone	8p	—	—	—	—	—
				52,000	2,600	54,600

Standard material cost of Quality B

	St. cost per lb	No. of pounds	Batch Cost £	Cost of 1,000 Batches £	Spillage allowance 5%	Total Cost
Zinc oxide	40p	80	32	32,000	1,600	33,600
Chalk	10p	20	1.60	1,600	80	1,680
Limestone	8p	—	—	—	—	—
				33,600	1,680	35,280

Again, there is some doubt about whether the spillage allowance is 5% of input or of output quantities. As the wording indicates a 5% allowance *in addition to* 100lbs of ingredients for each batch of paint, standard raw material cost entitlement per batch has been based on 105lbs of properly mixed ingredients per batch; that is, no finished product (paint) spillage has been recognised after a batch has been completed. The spillage has been of zinc oxide, chalk and limestone during the materials input stage.

Notice that current purchasing activity which would normally form the basis for the calculation of the materials price variance is not given. The question therefore necessitates the calculation of a materials price variance at the time of issue of materials from stores to work-in-progress, and it is actual issue quantities which must be used.

Note 2 Calculation of material price variance

	Actual input (lbs)	Standard cost per lb	Actual cost per lb	(F) = fav (U) = unfav. Variance
Zinc oxide	224,000	40p	45p	£11,200 (U)
Chalk	47,000	10p	11p	£470 (U)
Limestone	28,000	8p	8p	—
Total	299,000			£11,670 (U)

Note 3 Calculation of material mix variance
Standard mix of ingredients for actual batches produced

Batches	Zinc oxide	Chalk	Limestone	Totals
A 1,600	1,600 × 75lbs = 120,000 lbs + 5% 6,000 126,000	1,600 × 25lbs = 40,000 lbs + 5% 2,000 42,000		
B 1,000	1,000 × 80lbs = 80,000 lbs + 5% 4,000 84,000		1,000 × 20lbs = 20,000 lbs + 5% 1,000 21,000	
Totals	210,000	42,000	21,000	273,000
Proportions	10/13	2/13	1/13	100%
Actual input- actual mix	224,000	47,000	28,000	299,000
Standard mix	230,000	46,000	23,000	299,000
Difference (F)/(U)	6,000 (F)	1,000 (U)	5,000 (U)	—
At St. raw material prices	£2,400 (F)	£100 (U)	£400 (U)	£1,900 (F)

Note 4 Calculation of material yield variance

	Zinc oxide	Chalk	Limestone	Total
Actual input — standard mix	230,000 lbs	46,000 lbs	23,000 lbs	299,000 lbs
Standard input — standard mix	210,000 lbs	42,000 lbs	21,000 lbs	273,000 lbs
Difference (F)/(U)	20,000 lbs (U)	4,000 lbs (U)	2,000 lbs (U)	26,000 (U)
At St. raw material prices	£8,000 (U)	£400 (U)	£160 (U)	£8,560 (U)

Note 5 Calculation of actual cost

		£
Zinc oxide 224,000 lbs at 45p		100,800
Chalk 47,000 lbs at 11p		5,170
Limestone 28,000 lbs at 8p		2,240
		£108,210

A Raw Materials Usage Variance, which would show the combined effects of the Mix and Yield Variances, has not been calculated as this was not called for by the examiners.

In due course other examples will show direct material variances in the context of overall operating performances, where production and selling activity and actual and budgeted profits are compared.

An important principle established so far is that no matter how abstruse the detail in a question about one or other of the categories of cost such as direct materials, the presentation of results relating to that category should always be confined to a single line across the report (when the columns (1) to (5) format is utilised), against the narrative of the category concerned. In such cases column (5) will frequently show a "direct materials cost variance" which is capable of considerable analysis usually on an appendix. If space permits, however, candidates may exercise the option of showing variance analysis in separate sub-columns under column (5). In such cases, calculation details should feature on an appendix.

CHAPTER 5

SCRAPPED PRODUCTION AND PRODUCTION YIELD VARIANCES

Profit variances can often be caused by the failure of production units to pass inspection. Sometimes this involves straightforward scrapping of finished units, through breakage, etc. If the scrapping (or failure) of some of the total production is normal, and has been foreseen by management, arrangements can be made that the costs of making the gross quantity of units can be borne by the net, good units. Each good unit can be made to bear the cost of making itself, plus the cost of making a proportion of a 'lame duck' unit. Only when units are scrapped (or broken, etc) unexpectedly (or abnormally), does a profit variance emerge. The profit variance in such cases is the number of units or production abnormally scrapped times the standard output cost of a finished unit (unfavourable variance); or the number of units which, at that total production activity level, unexpectedly survived to go on for sale, times the standard output cost of a finished unit (favourable variance).

It must be emphasised that such variances are entirely separate from any *raw material* scrap variances. We are talking here of production units and their fate, not portions of raw material ingredients. Abnormally scrapped raw materials would be the subject of a raw material usage variance, whereas our present concern is for a possible PRODUCTION YIELD VARIANCE (or ABNORMAL SCRAPPED PRODUCTION VARIANCE). Abnormally scrapped units of production may or may not arise within the same question as some other aspect such as an unexpectedly high level of iron filings or shavings (scrap raw materials). In some questions, therefore, it is possible to have a Raw Materials Usage Variance when, say, materials are unexpectedly wasted, *and* a production yield variance when identifiable products are unexpectedly wasted.

Example One
The direct material cost of producing one unit of Alpha is £2. Direct labour and overhead costs, combined into 'time cost', total £4 per unit. The normal saleable (or good) yield from a gross batch of 100 units produced is 90% of the gross batch.

Required: If 15 of batch 7 are actually scrapped what is the Production Yield Variance?
Solution
Calculation of Production Yield Variance
Identify any production quantity deviation and evaluate it.
Physical reconciliation of production units

Batch 7 total production:		<u>100 units</u>
Whereof: good units	85	
normal scrap (10%)	10	
abnormal scrap	<u>5</u>	
Total accounted for		<u>100 units</u>

5 abnormally scrapped units form the basis for the variance.

These 5 units were expected to lend support in the struggle to recover the gross cost of making 100. 90 units were expected to be saleable, and to carry forward the cost of 100 to finished goods and in due course to customers' invoices. 85 units materialised. Therefore the company has lost 5 vital chances to recover costs. Each of the 5 units was expected to carry forward the cost of itself plus a portion of a budgeted scrapped unit. The ongoing standard unit cost is:

$$\frac{£(100 \times (4 + 2))}{100 - 10} = £6.66 \text{ (rounded)}$$

Had 90 good units been achieved, the cost incurred (£600) would have been duly carried forward as follows: 90 × £6.66 (rounded) = £600. However, the credit to Work in Progress and debit to Finished Goods is only 85 × £6.66 (rounded) = £566.66. £33.34 of cost incurred cannot be sustained in finished goods as there are simply not enough units. The Production Yield Variance is:

Number of units unexpectedly scrapped × standard (or normal) unit cost of output = 5 × £6.66 = £33.34 (rounded).

When a question merely asks for the calculation of a Production Yield or a Production Scrap Variance in the above context, the ideal solution route is to establish the number of units unexpectedly scrapped and multiply the standard (or normal) unit output cost by this number. However, when results have to be presented within a profit statement format, an appropriate presentation style is shown on page 75 (method (a)) and an alternative (method (b)) on page 76.

The units columns at (3) and (4) are *always* identical in any question dealt with in the above format. They both keep step with actual physical events on the production front. The monetary columns at (3) and (4), however, show costs kept rigidly in line with standards (3) and costs as they must be faced on the Profit and Loss Account in reality (4). From comparison of columns (3) and (4) at line 7 springs the Production Yield Variance. Line 6, column (3), shows the situation on transfers to Finished Goods that management expected from a batch of 100 units, but, as only 85 units were actually passed out of production, the deduction of £33.34 has to be made at line 7, column (3) so that line 8 column (3) shows the actual quantity transferred, at standard cost. (85 × £6.66 (rounded) = £566.66.) At column (4), on the other hand, while 85 units are featured at

Method (a)

Line Ref.	(1) Original budget (Note 1)		(2) Adjustment into line with actual activity		(3) Revised standard charge (Note 2)		(4) Actual Profit & Loss Account		(5) Variance Affecting Profit (a) Production Yield £	(b) Total £
	Units	£	Units	£	Units	£	Units	£		
1 Cost of Production	100				100		100			
2 Direct materials		200		—		200		200		
3 Time cost		400		—		400		400		
4 Total	100	600	—	—	100	600	100	600		
5 Less: normal scrap	10	—	—	—	10	—	10	—		
6 Standard good output	90	600	—	—	90	600	90	600		
7 Less: abnormal scrap	—	—	5	33.34	5	33.34	5	—	33.34(U)	33.34(U)
8 Good output	90	600	5	33.34	85	566.66	85	600	33.34(U)	33.34(U)

Note 1 It is assumed that a single batch of 100 units was the company's budgeted target for the period.
Note 2 It is assumed that actual materials, labour and overhead input to production was exactly in line with standards.

line 8, there can be no tampering with the monetary column amount of £600 brought down from line 6, merely because quantities are embarrassingly low. The company cannot pretend that cost, presumably established in the cash book at £600, did not take place; thus the difference of £33.34 between the two columns, posted out to column (5).

The balance sheet situation is as follows; assuming costs have been paid out of cash, along the lines of budgeted procedures:

Extracts from Balance Sheets

(Brackets = loss)	Original budgeted balance sheet £	Budgeted balance sheet in view of actual activity £	Actual balance sheet for actual activity £
Sources of Funds			
Profit and Loss Account	—	—	(33.34)
Bank Overdraft	600	600	600
Uses of Funds			
Finished goods stock	600	600	566.66

Profit statement method (b)	Budget Units	£	Actual Units	£
Cost of Production	100		100	
Direct materials		200		200
Time cost		400		400
Cost of aggregate production	100	600	100	600
Less normal scrap	10	—	10	—
Cost of standard good production	90	600	90	600
Less: abnormal scrap			5	
Cost of actual good production			85	600
Transferred at standard cost			85	566.66
Loss for period (being abnormal scrap cost)				£33.34

Note that a Direct Materials Usage Variance is inapplicable: as far as we know, the correct raw material quantity was requisitioned and used for the batch.

Example Two

£1,000 of direct materials and £2,000 of conversion cost (direct labour and overheads) is applied into a process, each at standard cost. 100 units are made in total, but good units which are saleable in due course are worth only £2,700 at standard cost. Normal scrap is 10% of total production units.

Required: calculate the Production Yield Variance.

Solution:

Standard (or normal) unit output cost: $\dfrac{£3,000}{100-10} = £33.33$ (rounded)

Therefore good output $= \dfrac{£2,700 \text{ (given)}}{£33.33} = 81$

Therefore physical reconciliation of production units is now possible

Total production:		100 units

Whereof:	good units	81
	normal scrap	10
	abnormal scrap	9

Total accounted for	100 units

Production Yield Variance = 9 units × £33.33 (rounded)	= £300
Good output is worth 81 × £33.33 (rounded)	= £2,700
Total cost accounted for	£3,000

Example Three

If a cook expects to derive 75% cooked meat from 4lbs of uncooked beef, what is the production yield variance if she achieves 3.5lbs? Her labour and overhead expenses are £2 and 40p respectively, and raw beef costs £1.50 per lb.

Solution:

Physical reconciliation:	total meat processed		4lbs
	whereof: cooked	3.5lbs	
	normal waste	1lb	
	favourable yield	(0.5)lb	
	Total accounted for		4lbs

Standard unit cost of cooked output: $\dfrac{£2 + 40p + (4 \times £1.50)}{4lbs - 25\% \text{ of } 4 lbs} = £2.80$ per lb

Therefore Production Yield Variance = 0.5lb × £2.80 = £1.40 (Fav.)

We could usefully pursue Example Three through the various journal entry stages which might be involved if our cook were prevailed upon to keep detailed book-keeping records:

(1) Work-in-Progress Control Account	DR	£8.40
Wages Control Account	CR	£2
Overhead Control Account	CR	40p
Raw Beef Stock Account	CR	£6
(at commencement of cooking process)		

(2) Cooked Beef Stock Account (at standard)	DR	£9.80
Production Yield Variance Account	CR	£1.40
Work in Progress Control Account	CR	£8.40
(upon transfer of 3.5lbs from cooking process)		

In due course, if the beef were actually sold, at, say, £4 per lb:

(3) Cost of Sales Account (at standard)	DR	£9.80
Cooked Beef Stock Account (at standard)	CR	£9.80

(4) Profit and Loss Account	DR	£9.80
Cost of Sales Account	CR	£9.80
(transfer of Cost of Sales Account balance to P & L A/c)		

(5) Production Yield Variance Account   DR   £1.40
     Profit and Loss Account   CR   £1.40

(6) Cash Account   DR   £14
     Sales Account   CR   £14
     (3.5lbs sold at £4 per lb)

(7) Sales Account   DR   £14
     Profit and Loss Account   CR   £14
     (transfer of Sales Account balance to P & L A/c)

Example Four
The budgeted expenses of XYZ Ltd for period 2 were:
     Direct materials   £50
     Direct labour   £100
     Variable overheads   £100
     Fixed overheads   £50
Total output was budgeted as 300 units, of which 10% would fail at inspection and be scrapped. The standard saleable value of a scrapped unit was 10p and this price was also realised in practice. The actual output was 300 units, but only 250 were saleable. Actual costs of production charged to Work in Progress were in line with budget.
Required: calculate the production yield variance and show the bookkeeping entries necessary to reflect the above situation in the nominal ledger.

Solution:
Physical reconciliation of production units
     Total output   300 units

     Whereof: good units   250
           normal scrap   30
           abnormal scrap   20

     Total accounted for   300 units

Normal (or standard) output cost per unit: $\dfrac{£(50 + 100 + 100 + 50) - (30 \times 10p)}{300 - 30}$

$$= £1.10$$

Production yield variance $= 20 \times £1.10 = £22$ (unfavourable)

Journal entries required
(1) Work in Progress Control Account   DR   £300
     Stores Control Account   CR   £50
     Wages Control Account   CR   £100
     Variable Overhead Control Account   CR   £100
     Fixed Overhead Control Account   CR   £50
     (to charge production with incurred costs)
(2) Finished Goods Control Account (250 × £1.10)   DR   £275
     Scrap Stock Account (30 × 10p)   DR   £3
     Production Yield Variance Account (20 × £1.10)   DR   £22
     Work in Progress Control Account   CR   £300
     (closing the Work in Progress Account after completion of production)

(3) Scrap Stock Account (20 × 10p)   DR £2
     Production Scrap Yield Variance Account   CR £2
     (unexpected extra scrap of 20 units, making a total of 50 units)
(4) Profit and Loss Account   DR £22
     Production Yield Variance Account   CR £22
     (to transfer the balance on latter account)
(5) Production Scrap Yield Variance Account   DR £2
     Profit and Loss Account   CR £2
     (to transfer the balance on latter account)

Notice how the net 'damage' to profits is £(22 − 2) = £20. Certainly if the company was successfully to carry forward a net cost of £297 from Work in Progress to Finished Goods, the full quota of 270 good units which they were entitled to expect from a production level of 300 was essential: (270 × £1.10 = £297). The unexpected loss of 20 units eliminated 20 × £1.10 = £22 from the carry-forward accounting procedure. However, the sum of £22 is net after receiving a fair proportion of the standard income of £3 from standard scrap quantities. The manager responsible for the unfortunate production yield variance has inadvertently been responsible for an extra £2 of income which was unbudgeted (20 × 10p). None of this £2 should be passed back to be included in good stock valuation. All of it should be attributed to the production manager holding the £22 production yield variance, as an offset to plane the damage caused by the whole affair down to £20.

An alternative treatment at journal entry (3) would be to credit the £2 to the Production Yield Variance Account to produce a net effect on that account of £20. Unexpected income from unbudgeted scrapped production would then be no longer shown as a separate item of information on the company's performance statement.

Example Five
This question illustrates a situation in which there is both raw material and production scrap:

The standard raw material allowance per unit of production in a factory is 5lbs, including a scrap allowance. In practice 5,024lbs are used to make 1,000 production units; of those units, 108 are scrapped although the standard good yield is 90% of total production. If the standard cost of raw materials is £2 per lb, and direct labour and variable overheads are allowed at standard rates of £3 and £4 respectively per unit produced, calculate any variances which are possible from the information provided. (Ignore any fixed overheads.)

Solution:
Calculation of Raw Material Usage Variance
Find the measure and level of activity: 1,000 units
    (a) Number of units produced × standard raw material weight allowance
       per unit × standard cost per lb of raw materials   £
       = 1,000 units × 5lbs × £2   10,000
    (b) Actual direct material used × standard cost per lb
       = 5,024 × £2   10,048
       Unfavourable Raw Material Usage Variance   £ 48

Calculation of Production Yield Variance
  Reconciliation of physical production units
    Total units produced   1,000 units

      Whereof: good units   892
               normal scrap   100
               abnormal scrap   8

    Total accounted for   1,000 units

Standard or normal unit cost of output: $\dfrac{1,000 \times £(10 + 3 + 4)}{(1,000 - 100) \text{ units}}$

                                     = £18.89 (rounded)
Unfavourable Production Yield Variance = 8 units × £18.89
                                     = £151.12 (rounded)

Notice that the unexpected scrapping of a percentage of production units
involves a company in a much more serious problem through breakdown of
the cost recovery procedures than unexpected loss of an equivalent percentage of raw materials. By the time the above 8 units were 'caught' they had
already attracted full portions of raw material, direct labour and variable
overheads; unexpected loss of one unit meant inability to find a place on
the balance sheet for £18.89 of incurred cost.

Notice again how a Raw Material Usage Variance is poles apart from a
Production Yield Variance in timing and in cause. The formula which was
provided earlier: (Raw Material Usage = Raw Material Mix + Raw
Material Yield) must *never* be misread as: Raw Material Usage = Raw
Material Mix + Production Yield. The problems of faulty raw material
stock usage and faulty production yield are quite distinct: they stem from
different causes and are frequently reported to different managers.

It is possible to analyse a Production Yield Variance: in Example Five,
the analysis can provide as many constituent parts as there are cost
categories. Thus of the £151.12 total variance:

8 units × $\dfrac{1,000 \times £10}{1,000 - 100}$ = £88.88 would be the measure of the company's

failure to recover *raw material* costs charged to the 8 'lost' units.
The amount for *direct labour* would be:

8 units × $\dfrac{1,000 \times £3}{1,000 - 100}$ = £26.66

The amount for *variable overheads*

8 units × $\dfrac{1,000 \times £4}{1,000 - 100}$ = £35.55

The difference in the total of £151.09 and £151.12 is due to rounding.

The above analysis would be helpful if management wished to highlight
the effects of unfavourable yields on the recovery of individual cost
categories.

CHAPTER 6

DIRECT LABOUR (OR DIRECT WAGES) VARIANCES

The two major variances in coping with direct materials (price and usage) have their exact counterparts in direct labour. The anticipatory powers of management can err on wage scales, and on the speed (ie efficiency) with which a particular piece of work is likely to be handled by the workforce: the results are a Direct Labour Rate Variance and a Direct Labour Efficiency Variance respectively. The above price and rate variances measure management's competence in reading tea leaves on what the future may hold on pay and prices. Usage and Efficiency Variances are a measure of skill in handling materials and production orders.

A budgeted production activity for a given accounting period enables management to estimate or budget for an appropriate direct labour cost for that activity level. As soon as the budgeted direct labour cost at this level is divided by the budgeted number of production units, we derive the budgeted (or standard) direct labour cost per unit. On occasion, examiners may provide standard unit costs without involving candidates in the above division sum.

As with direct material, the object is to compare actual direct labour costs at actual production levels achieved, with what ought to have been incurred for direct labour at the actual activity level. From this comparison springs the *Direct Labour Cost Variance*. Consider the following example:

The undernoted is available for Epsilon Ltd for accounting period 8:

	Budget	Actual
Production (units)	1,000	900
Direct labour cost	£8,000	£6,000

A system of standard costing is in operation: value stock at standard cost.
Required: calculate the Direct Labour Cost Variance.

Solution:
Find the measure and level of activity: 900 units

   (a) Actual production achieved × standard direct labour cost

      entitlement per unit: $900 \times \dfrac{£8,000}{1,000} =$ £7,200

(b) Actual direct labour cost chargeable to the
Profit and Loss Account   £6,000
Favourable Direct Labour Cost Variance   £1,200

Until the point at which the 900 units are sold, the Balance Sheet will show a stock valuation at standard cost which includes £7,200 for direct labour, although cash will have been depleted by only £6,000. Consequently, the Profit and Loss Account balance will be increased by £1,200 to ensure that the balance sheet actually balances.
Extracts from Balance Sheets (situation on direct labour only)

	Original budgeted balance sheet £	*Budgeted balance sheet in view of actual activity* £	*Actual balance sheet for actual activity* £
Sources of Funds			
Profit and Loss Account	NIL	NIL	1,200
Bank overdraft (Note 1)	8,000	7,200	6,000
Uses of Funds			
Finished Goods Stock	8,000	7,200	7,200

Note 1 It is assumed that wages have been paid out of bank overdraft.

Example Two
The following information is available for Zeta Ltd for accounting period 5:

	Budget	Actual
Production (units)	500	600
Production hours allowed per unit, 5		
Actual hours taken, 3,200		
Rate of pay per hour	£3	£3.25

A system of standard costing is in operation: value stock at standard cost.
Required: calculate the Direct Labour Cost Variance.

Solution:
Find the measure and level of activity: 600 units
  (a) Actual production achieved × standard direct labour
     cost entitlement per unit: 600 × 5 hours × £3   £9,000
  (b) Actual direct labour cost chargeable to the Profit
     and Loss Account: 3,200 × £3.25   10,400
     Unfavourable Direct Labour Cost Variance   £1,400

Although the question does not require the Cost Variance to be analysed, we can use it to serve as an introduction to Rate and Efficiency variances:
Analysis of Direct Labour Cost Variance
  (1) Calculation of Direct Labour Rate Variance
    (a) Actual hours charged as direct labour × standard
       wage rate per hour: 3,200 × £3   £9,600

(b) Actual hours charged as direct labour × actual
wage rate per hour: 3,200 × £3.25   £10,400
Unfavourable Direct Labour Rate Variance   £ 800

(2) Calculation of Direct Labour Efficiency Variance:
Recollect the measure and level of activity: 600 units

(a) Actual production achieved × standard direct
labour hours allowed per unit × standard rate
per hour: 600 × 5 hours × £3   £9,000

(b) Actual hours charged to direct labour ×
standard rate per hour: 3,200 × £3   £9,600
Unfavourable Direct Labour Efficiency Variance   £ 600

When direct material price variances were being calculated, we kept in
mind the ground rule: 'Tell the purchasing department (or the buyer)'. The
price variance was consequently preferably based on current actual
purchasing activity, so that the buyer could be advised as quickly as possible about the monetary implications of prices not running according to
plans. In the field of direct labour variances, we look for current actual
hours charged to direct labour; upon this total the size of wage rate deviations can be measured, often with a view to telling not the purchasing
department, but the personnel department who may well be responsible for
negotiating wage rates.

Example Three
Beta Ltd should take, according to the standard product specification sheet
concerned, 6 hours to produce one widget. The budgeted direct labour cost
of making the originally planned 1,000 widgets was £18,000, using a standard wage rate of £3 per hour. Actual production, which takes 8,000
hours, is 1,250 widgets. The actual wage rate is only £2.50 per hour.
Required: (1) Calculate the direct labour variances.
(2) Prepare an appropriate trial balance extract immediately
prior to write off of variances to the Profit and Loss
Account. Assume wages are paid from a bank overdraft.
(3) Show an appropriate profit statement extract.
(4) Show extracts from the original budgeted, revised budgeted
and actual balance sheets immediately after transfer of
variance balances to the Profit and Loss Account.

Solution:
(1) Calculation of Direct Labour Cost Variance.
Find the measure and level of activity: *1,250 widgets*
                                                            £
(a) Actual production achieved × standard direct
labour cost entitlement per unit: 1,250 × 6 hrs × £3   22,500
(b) Actual hours charged as direct labour × actual
wage rate per hour: 8,000 hours × £2.50   20,000
Favourable Direct Labour Cost Variance   £2,500

Analysis

(1) Direct Labour Efficiency Variance

		£
(a) Actual production achieved × standard direct labour hours allowed per unit × standard rate per hour: 1,250 × 6 hours × £3		22,500
(b) Actual hours charged to direct labour × standard rate per hour: 8,000 hours × £3		24,000
Unfavourable Direct Labour Efficiency Variance		£1,500

(2) Direct Labour Rate Variance

		£
(a) Actual hours charged as direct labour × standard wage rate per hour: 8,000 × £3		24,000
(b) Actual hours charged as direct labour × actual wage rate per hour: 8,000 × £2.50		20,000
Favourable Direct Labour Rate Variance		£4,000

(2) *Extract from Trial Balance*

	DR £	CR £
Bank Overdraft		20,000
Finished Goods Control Account – valued at standard	22,500	
Direct Labour Efficiency Variance	1,500	
Direct Labour Rate Variance		4,000
	24,000	24,000

(3) *Profit Statement (extract showing situation on direct labour)*

	(1) Original Budget		(2) Adjustment into line with actual activity		(3) Revised standard charge		(4) Actual Profit & Loss Account		(5) Variances affecting profits: Direct Labour (£)		
									Rate (a)	Effic. (b)	Total (c)
	Units	£	Units	£	Units	£	Units	£			
Cost of Production	1,000		250		1,250		1,250				
Direct labour		18,000		4,500		22,500		20,000	4,000 (F)	1,500 (U)	2,500 (F)

(4) *Extracts from Balance Sheets*

	Original budgeted balance sheet £	Budgeted balance sheet in view of actual activity £	Actual balance sheet for actual activity £
Sources of Funds			
Profit and Loss Account	NIL	NIL	2,500
Bank overdraft	18,000	22,500	20,000
Uses of Funds			
Stock on hand at standard	18,000	22,500	22,500

The Importance of the Standard Hour

In teasing out causes of divergence between the standard direct labour cost entitlement for production achieved, and actual direct labour cost which must be faced on the profit and loss account, anomalies between time allowed when standards were established and time actually taken are usually very significant. Such time comparisons underpin direct labour efficiency variances.

The basis for time allowances is a close study of the operating conditions during which the standards are to be in use, so that a fair estimate of the amount of production output which can be reasonably expected in one hour can be assessed. Calculating the productive capability of machinery and the potential achievement of operatives in a manual or mechanised environment is a highly skilled job.

'Normal operating conditions' are not easy to establish with a view to measuring potential output levels per hour. This problem is particularly pronounced when a new machine is being demonstrated on the premises of the supplier when conditions are likely to be ideal. The engineers of the company buying the machine must adjust a demonstrated output performance into line with the conditions which can be expected to accrue back at their base. Again, assessment of possible output per hour involves crystal-ball gazing when new products or production processes are involved of which management have no first-hand operational experience.

We shall be exploring possible causes of variances in due course; let it suffice at present that a 'standard hour' is a measure of output: in a bread factory, for example, a standard hour could be the number of loaves expected from one hour's production activity in a particular department. If production activity is mechanised, the expression 'standard hour' may be extended to 'standard machine hour' or even 'standard departmental operating hour', whereas in a manual department there could be 'standard direct labour hours' or 'standard labour hours'. In any event, a standard hour is the amount of output which is due from one hour's input effort into a production activity.

In many organisations, measurement of output as a number of standard hours is a vital step in agreeing direct labour payments. In such cases, when payment is by results at a rate per standard hour, there is usually a 'fall-back' clause whereby employees receive a basic hourly rate if standard hours of output fail to materialise. The workforce is protected from the full impact of machine breakdowns, lost time through lack of parts or materials etc, although understandably to maintain incentives the basic hourly rate is agreed at less than the rate per standard hour.

The expression 'piece rate' is sometimes used to describe payment by results schemes: the next examples in the series will illustrate how standard costing operates in such circumstances:

Example Four

In a factory the basis of payment is a basic rate plus a piece rate, as follows:

Standard basic wage £1.60 per hour worked.
Bonus rate, 80p per standard hour of production.

The following results are obtained:

Standard hours achieved	800
Actual hours worked	1,000
Actual wages paid	£2,600

Analysis of actual wages:

400 hours at £1.60	£640
300 hours at £2	£600
300 hours at £2.40	£720
	£1,960
Plus: bonus earned	
800 standard hours at 80p	£640
	£2,600

Required: calculate the direct labour variances. (Stock is valued at £2.40 per standard hour (80p + £1.60).)

Solution:

Measure and level of activity: *800 standard hours*

(a) Direct labour cost entitlement:

800 × £1.60 (basic pay) plus 800 × 80p (bonus)		= £1,920

(b) Actual wages paid:

	£	
800 × 80p	640	
400 hours at £1.60	640	
300 hours at £2	600	
300 hours at £2.40	720	2,600
Direct Labour Cost Variance (Unfavourable)		£680

Analysis

(1) Direct Labour Rate Variance

		£
(a) Actual hours worked at standard rate:		
1,000 × £1.60		1,600
(b) Actual hours at actual rates:	£	
400 at £1.60	640	
300 at £2	600	
300 at £2.40	720	1,960
Unfavourable Direct Labour Rate Variance		£360

(2) Direct Labour Efficiency Variance

Standard hours allowed for actual output	
× standard hourly rate: 800 × £1.60	1,280
Actual hours taken × standard hourly rate:	
1,000 × £1.60	1,600
Unfavourable Direct Labour Efficiency Variance	£320

Example Five

In a factory payment is by results. The budgeted output for an accounting period is 800 standard hours. However, actual output is 900 standard hours. The payment rate is £2 per standard hour achieved.

Required: calculate direct labour variances.

Solution:
Measure and level of activity: 900 standard hours.
Standard direct labour valuation of output achieved:
    900 × £2 =   £1,800
Actual payment made (by results):
    900 × £2 =   £1,800
Direct Labour Cost Variance   NIL

There can be no profit variance in this case: both the stock valuation and the cash payment stem from the same root source, a production schedule acknowledging the achievement of 900 standard hours of stock each worth £2, and authorising payment of 900 × £2 = £1,800 to the employees concerned.

Direct labour efficiency of 100% indicates that exactly one hour's worth of output has been achieved in one hour's worth of charged time. Clearly it is in a company's interest to seek an efficiency ratio in excess of 100%, frequently through the operation of a wage incentive scheme whereby, for example, the standard direct labour cost of the surplus of standard hours over actual hours worked might be split between the workforce and the company. Alternatively, a productivity agreement might be reached through which employees would receive higher wages per hour if they could produce more: a higher wage rate per hour would then be paid for a lower number of actual hours worked to achieve completion of a set job. The company would have an unfavourable direct labour rate variance which was exactly offset by a favourable direct labour efficiency variance.

Example Six
Job X is valued at 5 standard labour hours. A pay rise of 10% is agreed on top of the standard rate of £2 per hour. The company is unable to pass this 10% on to customers because of market pressures. What efficiency rate should be agreed by management and unions to prevent an unfavourable operating profit variance?

Solution:
At 100% efficiency, 5 hours are needed to produce 5 standard labour hours' worth of output. If each hour worked is now to be paid at a higher rate, there will need to be fewer hours worked.
    Let X = the revised actual hours which should be worked after a pay rise of 10%.
The approved unfavourable direct labour rate variance will be:
    X hours × £(2.2 − 2)
The required favourable direct labour efficiency variance will be
    (5 − X) hours × standard rate per hour (£2)
We know that the two variances must match:
    $X \times (2.2 - 2) = (5 - X) \times 2$
    $\therefore$ $2X = 10 - 2X$
    $\therefore$ $X = 50 - 10X$
    $\therefore$ $X = 4.55$ hours

The company require 5 hours' output to be produced in 4.55 hours. Therefore the required efficiency ratio is

$(\dfrac{5}{4.55} \times 100)\% = 110\%$ rounded.

This is a simple illustration of the close relationship between efficiency variances and efficiency ratios.

Example Seven

Job Y is worth 12 standard hours. If the direct labour force is working at 75% efficiency, how many actual hours will be taken? If direct labour is paid at £3 per hour (despite a standard rate of £3.50), what are the direct labour variances? Assuming Job Y to be the total of budgeted activity for the period, and that expense is paid from bank overdraft, prepare an appropriate balance sheet extract after transfer of variances to the Profit and Loss Account.

Solution:
After 12 hours of effort, the direct operatives concerned may wish to proceed to the inspection department for approval of their work. 'You're not finished', will be the inspector's response to their request to sign that the job is complete. If 12 hours = a $\frac{3}{4}$ complete stage, they will need to add another one third of 12 hours to see the job through: total, 16 hours.

	£
Stock valuation will be: 12 standard hours × £3.50	42
Actual wages paid will be: 16 hours × £3	48
Unfavourable Direct Labour Cost Variance	£6

An analysis is possible:

(1) Direct Labour Rate Variance	£
(a) Actual hours worked at standard rate per hour: 16 × £3.50	56
(b) Actual hours worked at actual rate per hour: 16 × £3	48
Favourable Direct Labour Rate Variance	£8

(2) Direct Labour Efficiency Variance:	£
(a) Standard hours allowed for work done × standard rate: 12 × £3.50	42
(b) Actual hours worked at standard rate: 16 × £3.50	56
Unfavourable Direct Labour Efficiency Variance	£14

Extract from Balance Sheets (direct labour content only)

	Budgeted balance sheet in view of actual activity	Actual balance sheet for actual activity
(Brackets = loss)	£	£
Sources of Funds		
Profit and Loss Account	NIL	(6)
Bank Overdraft	42	48
Uses of Funds		
Stock on hand at standard		
(12 standard hours at £3.50)	42	42

On occasion a rate variance may be wrongly exaggerated because the standard grade of labour specified for a particular product, job or process has not been used in practice. The wrong grade of labour can automatically lead to actual pay, even if standard for the grade, being the wrong standard for the work concerned. The calculation of a *Substitution Variance* to draw out that part of a Direct Labour Cost Variance, which is caused by using the wrong grade of labour, takes place on the assumption that the standard rate appropriate to this wrong grade is actually being paid; if it is not, a *rate* variance also applies.

Example Eight
The standard direct labour cost of a particular job is made up of 600 hours of Grade B operatives at a standard rate of £1 per hour. In due course, the actual cost of the job comprises 500 hours of Grade A operatives at £1.10 per hour. The standard cost of a Grade A operative is £1.20.
Required: calculate the direct labour variances.

Solution: calculation of Direct Labour Cost Variance
  (1) Actual hours charged × actual rate paid:

500 × £1.10 :	£550

  (2) Direct labour cost entitlement for actual activity achieved:

600 hours × £1 standard rate	£600
Favourable variance	£ 50

Analysis
  (a) *Efficiency Variance*
    (1) Standard hours allowed for job × standard rate per hour:

600 × £1	£600

    (2) Actual hours charged × standard rate per hour:

500 × £1	£500
Favourable variance	£100

  (b) *Substitution Variance*
    (1) Actual hours charged × standard rate for Grade B operative:

500 × £1	£500

(2) Actual hours charged × standard rate for actual
(Grade A) operative:

500 × £1.20	£600
Unfavourable variance	£100

(c) *Direct Labour Rate Variance*
  (1) Actual hours charged × standard rate for actual
    (Grade A) operative:

500 × £1.20	£600

  (2) Actual hours charged × actual rate for actual
    (Grade A) operative:

500 × £1.10	£550
Favourable variance	£ 50

Summary:			
	Efficiency	100	(F)
	Substitution	100	(U)
	Rate	50	(F)
	Cost	£ 50	(F)

Notice that the effects of a decision to allow the wrong labour grade were cancelled out between the efficiency and substitution variances: fewer hours were worked to complete the job, but each hour was paid at a higher rate. The net effect on profits was nil. *Another* decision, to pay a non-standard rate of £1.10 instead of the standard rate of £1.20, brought about a favourable profit variance of £50. The effects of this decision should not be merged into those of the first.

The final example in the direct labour series is taken from the Autumn 1978 Management Accounting Paper of The Institute of Chartered Accountants of Scotland. Many of the aspects dealt with individually in our previous examples are now treated within the framework of a single question.

Example Nine
Sea Pumps Ltd which operates a standard costing system sets its standard of performance and cost at the start of each financial year. A budgeted labour rate of £1.20 per hour was used to evaluate work in progress throughout the financial year ending 31st March 19X8, although the budgeted wage rate was revised to £1.32 per hour on 1st October 19X7.

The shop stewards within the machine shop have claimed that, contrary to management's view, the company is working efficiently and have suggested that a self financing productivity scheme should be introduced in order that they can share in the savings made.

The following information for the machine shop is available for the year ending 31st March 19X8:

	6 months to 30th September 19X7	6 months to 31st March 19X8
Production in standard hours	1,870	1,900
Extra allowances in standard hours	80	400
Allowed standard hours	1,950	2,300

Actual direct labour hours	1,900	1,925
Actual labour rate per hour	£1.25	£1.32
Actual wages paid	£2,375	£2,541

Required:
1. Prepare a statement setting out the labour variances for the year to 31st March 19X8.
2. Comment on the views of management and shop stewards about the efficiency of the machine shop.
3. Determine whether a self financing productivity scheme could be introduced and calculate the maximum percentage increase in wages that could be paid out based on the performance in the six months to 31st March 19X8.

Solution
Part (1): it is important to recognise the specific requirement that a statement be prepared. A set of working notes straggling down the page would only be well received if it formed a springboard to the formal statement requested. Where care and planning are brought to bear on statement preparation, the need for schedules of calculations can be minimised or even eliminated. However, practice is needed, and a cool head under examination conditions, before presentation of variances by simple comparison of statement columns can be achieved.
(See table on next page)

Comments on Solution to Part (1)
On this occasion the examiners have based the question on standard hours as the measure of activity. A total profit variance occurs as usual when the valuation of output for balance sheet stockholding purposes differs from the actual profit and loss charge for which the company is liable in creating that stockholding. The question in this case hinges on whether the company were prepared to charge their customers with 1,950 × £1.20 during the six months to 30th September 19X7 and with 2,300 × £1.20 for the second six months. Should this have been the case, the total profit variance caused by direct labour deviations, ie the direct labour cost variance, is clearly (1) £2,375 less 1,950 × £1.20 (£2,340) = £35 (Unfav) for the first six months and £2,541 less 2,300 × £1.20 (£2,760) = £219 (Fav) for the second six months. We are told that there was no revision of the budgeted labour rate of £1.20 during the year, and therefore in this case of the standard stock valuation rate of £1.20 per standard hour. There may, however, have been a re-think by management on the amount of chargeable output achieved (for ultimate sales invoicing purposes), in the actual time taken, so that they are satisfied with the prospect of balance sheet stock valuation of £5,100 (£2,340 + £2,760) for the year. Use of the word 'standard' implies that work output achieved can justify a charge of 1,950 + 2,300 = 4,250 times the standard rate. The solution has been prepared on that basis. The counter proposal that only 3,770 standard hours have formed the basis of stock valuation results in the following changes to the statement:
(See table on next page)

Solution to Example 9
Sea Pumps Ltd
Part 1

	(1) Basic output in st hours	(2) Extra allowances	(3) Allowed st. hours	(4) Act direct hours worked	(5) St hrs +/(-) act hours	(6) St rate per hr of output	(7) St value of output (3)×(6)	(8) Act rate per hour	(9) Act wages	(10) DL Rate Var (4) × |(8)-(6)|	(11) DL Effic'y Var (5)×(6)	(12) DL Cost Var (7)-(9)
6 mths to 30.7.X7	1,870	80	1,950	1,900	50	1.20	£2,340	1.25	£2,375	£95 (U)	£60 (F)	£35 (U)
6 mths to 31.3.X8	1,900	400	2,300	1,925	375	1.20	£2,760	1.32	£2,541	£231 (U)	£450 (F)	£219 (F)
Total	3,770	480	4,250	3,825	425	1.20	£5,100	—	£4,916	£326 (U)	£510 (F)	£184 (F)

Solution to Example 9
Sea Pumps Ltd
Part 1 (alternative)

	(1) Basic output in st hours	(2) Extra allowances	(3) Allowed st hours	(4) Act direct hours worked	(5) St hrs +/(-) act hours	(6) St rate per hr of output	(7) St value of basic output (1)×(6)	(8) Actual rate per hour	(9) Actual wages	(10) DL Rate Var (4) × |(8)-(6)|	(11) Extra allowances Var (2)×(6)	(12) DL Effic'y Var (5)×(6)	(13) DL Cost Var (7)-(9)
6 mths to 30.7.X7	1,870	80	1,950	1,900	50	1.20	£2,244	1.25	£2,375	£95 (U)	£96 (U)	£60 (F)	£131 (U)
6 mths to 31.3.X8	1,900	400	2,300	1,925	375	1.20	£2,280	1.32	£2,541	£231 (U)	£480 (U)	£450 (F)	£261 (U)
Total	3,770	480	4,250	3,825	425	1.20	£4,524	—	£4,916	£326 (U)	£576 (U)	£510 (F)	£392 (U)

The alternative statement, with the heavier unfavourable cost variances at column (13), uses the extra allowances as a device to ensure that genuine efficiency variances are only calculated after due weight has been given to changes in circumstances within the production area which render obsolete a straight comparison of the originally compiled 3,770 hours' entitlement and the 3,825 hours taken. What this approach means in effect is that the company are asserting that in view of an output of 3,770 standard hours, employees were entitled to charge 4,250 hours, and the fact that they actually charged 3,825 hours is very much a feather in their caps in terms of efficiency. The fact that the basis for invoicing customers may still only be 3,770 hours × £1.20 is, in the above argument, no fault of the workforce and another matter entirely.

Questions containing possible ambiguities can be countered by a brief note to the examiner. In the above case, those pursuing the line that balance sheet stockholdings would be based on 4,250 × £1.20 would be well advised to state: 'It is assumed that, while the rate of charging has been retained at £1.20 throughout the year, output of 4,250 (1,950 + 2,300) standard hours has been achieved for nominal ledger stock quantity assessment purposes.' Those adopting the alternative stance could write: 'It is assumed that the basis for evaluation of stock in the nominal ledger is only 3,770 (1,870 + 1,900) standard hours.'

Part 2

Whether or not balance sheet stock and customer charging are to be based on 4,250 hours, this is the total number of hours which the machine shop was expected to take for the output achieved over the year: the work was actually performed in 3,825 hours. There can be no doubt that on this basis the machine shop measures up very well in terms of efficiency, producing 111 hours' worth of output from every 100 hours of operation $(\frac{4,250}{3,825} \times 100)\% = 111\%$. When performance trend is analysed, the more recent six monthly period provides an efficiency ratio of $(\frac{2,300}{1,925} \times 100)\%$ = 119% which may lend weight to the shop stewards' view that *current* efficiency needs to be recognised in tangible terms.

The disparity between the extra allowances to 30th September and those to 31st March would need careful assessment. Clearly the substantial increase in the latter six months may have been agreed after long negotiation and delay, and may have been in recognition of conditions of working which applied during the earlier six months without any compensating adjustment. If the 80 hours during the first half of the financial year is parsimonious, the trend of improving efficiency referred to above may be unreliable.

It must be presumed that a major *raison d'être* of part (2) was to detect candidates who were content to measure efficiency by comparing 3,770 hours with 3,825 hours, the former having been recognised by management as unrealistic.

Part 3

The basis for a self-financing productivity scheme is the creation of additional output for additional wages, so that the company is not forced to make any increase in its unit valuation of stock, or ultimately to raise selling prices to recover pay increases.

In preparing a solution to this part of the question, the calculation again depends upon whether the output achieved has been taken as 1,900 or 2,300 for nominal ledger purposes.

Using 1,900, the question requires that this quantity of stock times the standard stock valuation rate of £1.20 should exactly equal the actual hours to be paid times the actual rate of pay per hour. If we let x = the rate of pay per hour:

$$1,900 \times £1.20 = 1,925x$$
$$\therefore x = £1.18 \text{ (rounded)}$$

The rate of £1.18 required to 'break-even' is well below the actual current wage rate in use, so that any increase in pay above £1.32 would clearly be totally uneconomic.

Changing the saleable output level to 2,300 standard hours certainly gives the shop stewards much more scope; let x = rate of pay per hour:

$$2,300 \times £1.20 = 1,925x$$
$$\therefore x = £1.43 \text{ rounded}$$

On this basis, a rate of pay of £1.43 per hour seems justified (an increase of approx $8\frac{1}{2}$%), provided that the workforce can maintain productivity at $119\% \left(\frac{2,300}{1,925} \times 100\right)\%$ in the future. With this in mind enquiries would be necessary as to whether operating conditions within the machine shop varied between summer and winter, and whether, for example, ventilation and poor buildings design could adversely affect performance in the six months to 30th September 19X8. In a UK environment, cynics might say that hot oppressive summer days rarely materialise to show up the effects of excessive roof glazing, poor air conditioning etc. Any evidence to support volatile working conditions across the year would prompt management to assess the viability of a self-financing productivity scheme on a full year's figures. The result emanating from study of the full year to 31st March 19X8 gives an acceptable wage rate of £1.33 rounded which argues caution in granting an 11p per hour increase. Part (3) of this question contains a narrative element, and the need to probe the above matters may well have been required by the examiners to capture full marks.

Unmeasured work

When work is incomplete, and/or there has been no opportunity to have it studied or measured, a company may well feel that the direct labour charged on such work should be split, perhaps on a 50–50 basis between good time and downtime, the latter being diverted away from direct labour and to the debit of an overhead control account. When such events are planned and these debits to overhead control accounts have been anticipated, they will be offset by factory overheads applied to work in progress and credited to overhead accounts.

CHAPTER 7

PRODUCTION AND ADMINISTRATION OVERHEAD VARIANCES

(1) Variable Works (or Production) Overheads

The remaining cost category which comes under the banner of variable works or production cost embraces all those items which vary in total cost with changes in output levels but which cannot be directly attributed to specific product units. (A product unit is taken to embrace jobs and processes.) Machine power costs provide a typical example. Typically electrical power, for example, may be coded to Variable Works Overhead Control Account in the nominal ledger when purchase invoices are analysed and, in the supporting subsidiary ledger, to a particular production cost centre which has provoked the expense. This arrangement is possible if electricity is purchased from an electricity board rather than generated within the company, and if meters operate to control the flow of electricity to specific departments. Neither the charge to the production cost centre nor the credit to the electricity board's personal account in the creditors' ledger form any part of the nominal ledger double entry book-keeping system:

Variable Works Overhead Control Account DR £X
Production Dept A Account DR £X (Subsidiary Ledger)
Creditors' Control Account CR £X
Electricity Board Personal Account CR £X (Subsidiary Ledger)

Within the Production Department A Account, a comparison will take place between incoming debits received as a result of invoice analysis, and what those debits *ought* to have been according to budget estimates. Each production department's account in the subsidiary ledger will show a list of expense classifications such as wages, payroll overheads such as superannuation fund payments, *machine power,* machine depreciation, and supervisors' salaries. The department's budget will have been prepared at this level of detail, so that the benefits of analysing actual costs and comparing them with budget can be optimised. As actual costs for items such as electricity enter a production department's account, the budgeted costs which have been prepared well in advance will already have been entered, so that variances between budget and actual costs, analysed by department and by expense class within department, can be teased out in a separate column as a natural consequence. The sum total of these variances, each controlled at departmental level by a specific individual, should agree with the balance on the Variable Works Overhead Variance Account in the nominal ledger. The reason is that whatever is debited to the Variable Works Overhead Control Account in the nominal ledger is also debited to subsidiary account 'actual cost' columns, and whatever is credited to Variable Works Overhead Control Account (and applied to Work in Progress) stems from exactly the same root source as all the 'budgeted cost' columns in the subsidiary accounts, namely the departmental budgets. So if there is a balance on the Variable Works Overhead Control Account, it means that the actual cost debits are out of step with the applied cost credits and by exactly the same amount in total and for the same reasons that the departmental actual and budgeted cost columns differ. Whatever is entered in the budgeted cost columns on departmental accounts forms the basis for the variable overhead recovery rate per unit of production achieved, which is used to credit Variable Works Overhead Control Account and debit Work in Progress Control Account.

The Use of Subsidiary Ledgers

If electricity or some other form of power is created within a company, the expenditure incurred directly in manufacturing the power concerned will be charged to Variable Works Overhead Control Account in the nominal ledger and directly to a Power Cost Centre Account in the subsidiary ledger supporting the control account. Within the Power Cost Centre Account there will be expense classifications through which to control actual costs against budget, drawn from the same expense classification list as referred to previously. The 'machine power' expense class line referred to earlier would be left blank as it would be the basis for an outgoing charge to other cost centres as customers of the power cost centre.

In neither of the above situations (purchased power and self-generated power) is any credit made to subsidiary account columns when *Work-in-Progress Control Account* is debited and the Variable Works Overhead Control Account credited. Debits to Work in Progress in respect of overheads are based on conglomerate totals of which, say, power cost might be only a small fraction. The charge rate to Work-in-Progress is:

$$\frac{\text{Budgeted variable works overhead cost at budgeted activity level}}{\text{Budgeted activity level}} \times \text{actual activity level}$$

To painstakingly support every use of the above pre-determined rate by going through the many overhead subsidiary ledger accounts winkling out and crediting small portions of cost would provide no benefits.

When one department such as the power cost centre charges part of its running cost to another department, production or otherwise, the nominal ledger is not involved. If power cost is an overhead when created and controlled, it is also an overhead when it reaches a production cost centre. Letting the cost lie in Variable Overhead Control Account permanently is correct. The incoming power cost to the latter department is recovered against production as a small or large constituent within that department's variable overhead recovery rate. So when a power cost centre's variable running costs of, say, £10,000 are recognised as having been incurred in bringing stock to its present condition and location (and therefore subject to inclusion in stock valuation), attempts will be made to find 'customers' within the company to receive this £10,000. If there are, say, two production departments A and B and a works canteen department using power in the proportions 50%, 40% and 10% respectively, the following entry would be typical:

Production Department A Account	DR	£5,000
Production Department B Account	DR	£4,000
Canteen Department Account	DR	£1,000
Power Department Account	CR	£10,000

When a system of standard costing is in operation, £10,000 will be the *flexed standard* cost to be passed on in the above way, ie the budgeted variable power cost flexed according to actual power output achieved for A, B and the canteen. If the actual cost was, say, £12,000, the variance of £2,000 would at least initially be left 'dead-weight', in the power department. Later, the £2,000 might be passed to 'customer' departments but only after considerable negotiations and eyebrow raising and under special revision of standard procedures.

If the canteen costs, including the £1,000 charged for power, totalled, say, £12,000 at standard cost and if the basis for apportionment of the canteen costs was 50–50 to A and B:

Production Department A Account	DR	£6,000
Production Department B Account	DR	£6,000
Canteen Account	CR	£12,000

Again, if the actual canteen costs incurred were, say, £13,500, the £1,500 would lie as a debit balance on the canteen account and would constitute part of any Variable Overhead Variance Account balance.

In due course, if production departments A and B could identify sufficient production activity, the following journal entry would be appropriate, assuming for the sake of simplicity that power and canteen were the only overheads incurred by each department:

Work-in-Progress Control Account – A	DR	£11,000
Work-in-Progress Control Account – B	DR	£10,000
Variable Works Overhead Control Account	CR	£21,000

The above details would be based on a pre-determined variable overhead rate per unit of production times the number of units produced.

The above background comments are to help the reader to understand something of the relationship between budgeted and actual variable works overheads costs which is imposed at departmental level by a sound standard costing system. Monitoring of results against plans becomes the responsibility of specific managers.

We move now to an examination of the basic variances likely to be faced in examinations. They have much in common with the direct material and direct labour variances which have gone before.

Example One

The following information is available for Theta Ltd for period 3:

	Budget	Actual
Production (units)	2,000	2,100

Variable production overheads   £4,000   £4,300
Required: calculate the variable production overhead cost variance.

Solution
Find the measure and level of activity: 2,100 units.
(a) Actual production achieved × standard variable works overhead
  cost entitlement per unit: $2,100 \times \dfrac{£4,000}{2,000}$ = £4,200
(b) Actual cost chargeable to the Profit and Loss Account   = £4,300
Unfavourable variable production overhead cost variance   £ 100

Until the point at which the 2,100 units are sold, the Balance Sheet will show a stock valuation at standard cost which includes £4,200 for variable works overhead, although cash will have been depleted by £4,300. Consequently, the Profit and Loss Account balance will be decreased by £100 to ensure that the balance sheet actually balances.

Extracts from Balance Sheets (situation on Variable Works Overhead only)

(Brackets = decline)	*Original budgeted balance sheet*	*Budgeted balance sheet in view of actual activity*	*Actual balance sheet for actual activity*
	£	£	£
Sources of Funds			
Profit & Loss Account	NIL	NIL	(100)
Bank overdraft (Note 1)	4,000	4,200	4,300
Uses of Funds			
Finished Goods Stock	4,000	4,200	4,200

Note 1 It is assumed that wages have been paid out of bank overdraft.

Example Two
The following information is available for Iota Ltd for period 4:

	Budget	Actual
Production (units)	200	180
Standard hours allowed per unit, 10		
Actual hours taken 1,700		
Variable overheads	£4,000	£3,000

Required:
  (1) calculate and analyse the variable production overhead variance.
  (2) Trace any balances on nominal ledger accounts to the company's trial balance. (Assume costs are paid from a bank account in overdraft.)
  (3) Prepare appropriate balance sheet extracts after closing out any variance balances to the profit and loss account in the nominal ledger.

Solution: (1)
Find the measure and level of activity: 180 units
  (a) Actual production achieved × standard variable production
     overhead cost entitlement per unit:

$$180 \times 10 \text{ hours} \times \frac{£4,000}{200 \times 10} \qquad\qquad £3,600$$

  (b) Actual variable production overhead cost
     chargeable to Profit and Loss Account   £3,000
     Favourable variable production overhead cost variance   £ 600

Analysis
(1) Calculation of Variable Production Overhead Rate Variance
  (a) Actual hours charged × standard rate per hour:

$$1,700 \times \frac{£4,000}{200 \times 10} \text{ (£2)} \qquad\qquad £3,400$$

  (b) Actual hours charged × actual rate per hour:
     (ie actual cost)   3,000
     Favourable rate variance   £ 400

(2) Calculation of Variable Production Overhead Efficiency Variance
  (a) Actual production achieved × standard variable
     production overhead entitlement:
     180 × 10hrs × £2   £3,600
  (b) Actual hours taken × standard hourly rate:
     1,700 × £2   £3,400
     Favourable efficiency variance   £ 200

Justifying the Split of Variable Overhead Cost Variances

Opinion is divided as to whether the above analysis of the cost variance is worth the candle. The split does show the effect which time savings in achieving a particular level of output can have on variable production cost incurrence. The suggestion is being made above that a saving of 100 hours against standard time (1,800 − 1,700 hours) may have caused £200 of the total favourable variance of £600. In some production environments machine running time may be the cause of variable production overhead costs, rather than production output achievement. In a laundry, for example, a twin-roller pressing machine used for pressing (or ironing) sheets will be operated using electrical power which is likely to be classed as a variable cost. There may well be quiet spells during which sheets are put through at slightly less frequent intervals. A day's machine power cost total may be assessed by multiplying units of output (sheets) by a unit cost rate, on the basis that the more sheets which are ironed, the greater the cost. In practice, however, the extent of machine running time has a definite bearing on the day's cost total. By converting costs to a rate per hour, and then preparing an efficiency variance by comparing standard hours achieved with actual hours taken, management can monitor the value of increasing throughput per hour and switching the twin-roller off to save cost. In cases where the machine is simply switched on at, say, 9am each morning and then off at 11am, regardless of the number of sheets to be ironed, the possibility of attributing fixed overhead status to machine power costs would need consideration.

Part 2
The constitution of a trial balance in this context will vary according to the operating stages reached or passed in operations and the consequent journal entries made. The following two stages can be regarded as typical rather than the rule:

Extract from Trial Balance – stage 1

	DR £	CR £
Work-in-progress at standard	3,600	
Bank overdraft		3,000
Variable production overhead efficiency variance		200
Variable production overhead rate variance		400
	£3,600	£3,600

Extract from Trial Balance – stage 2

	DR £	CR £
Finished goods stock account at standard	3,600	
Bank overdraft		3,000
Profit and loss account		600
	£3,600	£3,600

Journal entries would be used in the transition from stage 1 to stage 2.

Part 3
Balance Sheet Extract (variable production overhead element only)

	Original budgeted balance sheet £	Budgeted balance sheet in view of actual activity £	Actual balance sheet for actual activity £
Sources of Funds			
Profit & Loss Account	NIL	NIL	600
Bank Overdraft	4,000	3,600	3,000
Uses of Funds			
Finished Goods stock at standard	4,000	3,600	3,600

(2) Fixed Production Overheads

A company using absorption costing methods normally depends on the budgeted production activity level actually being realised. Fixed production overheads are absorbed (or recovered) in practice by charging (debiting) Cost of Production (or Work-in-Progress) Account with the actual number of units produced times: $\dfrac{\text{budgeted fixed production costs}}{\text{budgeted production activity}}$.

If the actual number of units produced falls short of the budgeted number, a part of the fixed production costs will fail to reach the work-in-progress target, ie will not be recovered in standard stock valuation. We will then have an unfavourable fixed production overhead volume variance. Of course a production level exceeding budget will cause more to be charged to work-in-progress at standard than was necessary to recover fixed costs, resulting in a favourable variance.

Again, if the actual fixed production costs differ from budget, the recovery rate calculated and used on the basis of a budgeted cost figure will fail to ensure a 'clean' debit to stock valuation of the appropriate actual amount spent, and so there will be an additional fixed cost variance known as the fixed production overhead expenditure variance. In cases where actual costs exceed budgeted costs, the variance will be the excess, which in all fairness, a pre-determined recovery rate per unit of production could never hope to recover in the process of debiting work in progress and crediting fixed production overhead control account.

Fixed production overhead volume variances can only arise when absorption costing is in use, because only then are fixed works costs absorbed into work-in-progress at a rate per unit, with the work-in-progress valuation including fixed costs. In other words, under marginal costing, you cannot have over- or under-absorption of fixed costs into work in progress, if, in the first place, you never take the necessary steps to absorb at all. Under marginal costing, fixed production costs are charged to a period's operating performance on period-end reports on a set-price, inflexible basis regardless of any variation between budgeted and actual production activity. A typical book-keeping method would be to debit Fixed Production Overhead Control Account and credit (say) Creditors' Control Account when the expense was first incurred. If this expense exceeded budget, the budgeted amount would be charged to the performance statement under the heading Cost of Production at Standard: thereafter the excess of actual over budget would also be charged, separately, as a fixed production overhead expenditure variance. In the event of production remaining unsold, only variable production cost of closing stock would be removed from the aggregate cost of production on the statement, thus forcing management to accept the full fixed costs for the period in determining period profits. The journal entries involved would be along the following lines (assume a budgeted fixed cost of £800):

(1) Fixed Production Overhead Control Account	DR (say)	£1,000
Creditors' Control Account	CR	£1,000
(upon purchase of fixed production services from outside suppliers: actual costs)		
(2) Cost of Production Account (at standard)	DR	£800
Fixed Production Overhead Control Account	CR	£800
(3) Fixed Production Overhead Expenditure Variance Account	DR	£200
Fixed Production Overhead Control Account	CR	£200
(to transfer balance on latter account to a new, variance account)		
(4) Cost of Sales Account (at standard)	DR	£800
Cost of Production Account	CR	£800

(5) Profit and Loss Account		DR	£800
Cost of Sales Account		CR	£800
(6) Profit and Loss Account		DR	£200
Fixed Production Overhead Expenditure			
Variance Account		CR	£200

The only fixed production cost variance possible when marginal costing applies (with stock valued at variable cost only, as described above) is the fixed production overhead expenditure variance.

This category of cost is again dealt with through examples:

Example One

The following information is available for Kappa Ltd for accounting period 4:

	Budget	Actual
Production (units)	100	110
Fixed production overheads	£2,000	£2,500

Required: (1) calculate fixed production overhead variances, assuming stock is valued at full standard cost.

(2) show the appropriate trial balance extract

(3) prepare appropriate balance sheet extracts

(4) show the situation in profit statement format.

Solution: Part 1

As with the preceding variable cost categories, it is advisable to shoot in-itially for a total variance, which in this case is the difference between the actual fixed cost to be charged to the Profit and Loss Account and the standard fixed cost valuation of production units achieved. Remember that standards attempt (usually in vain) to ensure that costs incurred (the debit to the Profit and Loss Account) and the stock which is on the balance sheet to show for this expense are identical; on a hope and a prayer the balance sheet then balances without any variances seeing the light of day. In such cases, 'cash minus' exactly equals 'stock plus' in nominal ledger, trial balance and balance sheet terms. The total variance referred to above, however, indicates the extent to which 'cash minus' has not been matched exactly by the 'stock plus'.

Calculation of Fixed Production Overhead Variance

(a) Standard fixed production cost evaluation of actual

activity achieved: $110 \times \dfrac{£2,000}{100}$ (£20)   £2,200

(b) Actual cost   £2,500

     Unfavourable variance   £300

Analysis

(1) *Expenditure Variance*

     Budgeted cost   £2,000

     Actual cost   £2,500

     Unfavourable variance   £500

(2) *Volume Variance*
   (a) Required activity (in this case budgeted activity)
       needed to absorb budgeted cost × standard rate
       per unit: 100 × £20   £2,000
   (b) Actual activity achieved × standard rate per
       unit: 110 × £20   £2,200
       Favourable variance   £200

Part 2   *Extracts from Trial Balance*

Stage 1	DR £	CR £
Fixed Production Overhead Control	2,500	
Bank Overdraft		2,500
	£2,500	£2,500

Stage 2	DR	CR
Bank Overdraft		2,500
Work in Progress at standard	2,200	
Fixed Production Overhead Control		NIL
Fixed Production Overhead Total Variance	300	
	£2,500	£2,500

Stage 3	DR £	CR £
Bank Overdraft		2,500
Work in Progress at standard	2,200	
Fixed Production Overhead Expenditure Variance	500	
Fixed Production Overhead Volume Variance		200
Fixed Production Overhead Total Variance		NIL
	£2,700	£2,700

Stage 4	DR £	CR £
Bank Overdraft		2,500
Work in Progress at standard	2,200	
Profit and Loss Account	300	
Fixed Production Overhead Expenditure Variance	NIL	
Fixed Production Overhead Volume Variance		NIL
	£2,500	£2,500

Part 3
Extracts from Balance Sheets (situation of Fixed Production Costs only)

(Brackets = decline)	Original budgeted balance sheet £	Budgeted balance sheet in view of actual activity £	Actual balance sheet for actual activity £
Sources of Funds			
Profit and Loss Account	NIL	200	(300)

Bank Overdraft	2,000	2,000	2,500
Uses of Funds			
Work in Progress at standard	2,000	2,000	2,200

Part 4

Profit Statement (extract showing the situation on fixed production costs)
((F) = favourable
(U) = unfavourable)

	(1)		(2)		(3)		(4)		(5)		
	Original Budget		*Adjustments into line with actual activity*		*Revised standard charge*		*Actual Profit & Loss Account*		*Variances affecting profits*		
									(a)	*(b)*	*(c)*
	Units	£	Units	£	Units	£	Units	£	*Vol*	*Exp*	*Total*
									£	£	£
Cost of Production											
Fixed costs	100	2,000	10	200	110	2,200	110	2,500	200 (F)	500 (U)	300 (U)

Example Two

A company values stock at full cost (including fixed works expenses). Its
fixed production costs are budgeted at £1,000 for period 3, in which it
plans to make and sell 1,000 units. Actual results show 1,100 units sold but
only 800 of these were made in the period. Actual fixed production expenses are £1,200. There is no closing stock.
Required: prepare fixed production cost variances.

Solution
Calculation of Fixed Production Overhead Variance
Find the measure and level of activity: 800 units
  (a) Standard fixed production cost evaluation of actual
     activity achieved (800) × standard recovery rate

     ($\dfrac{£1,000}{1,000 \text{ units}} = £1$) :   £800

  (b) Actual fixed cost incurred   £1,200
     Unfavourable variance   £400

Analysis
  (1) *Calculation of volume variance*
    (a) Standard fixed production cost evaluation of
      actual activity achieved (800) × standard

      recovery rate ($\dfrac{£1,000}{1,000 \text{ units}} = £1$)   £800

    (b) Production quantity required to absorb budgeted
      fixed overheads (ie budgeted production in this
      case) × standard recovery rate (£1)   £1,000
      Unfavourable variance   £200

(2) *Calculation of expenditure variance*

Budgeted cost	£1,000
Actual cost	1,200
Unfavourable variance	£200

300 units sold must have been made in a previous period. They would be held in the books of account at standard cost, and no fixed production cost variances would arise in respect of these units in the current period.

Example Three
Gamma Ltd had a production and sales budget of 1,000 units for period 2 with no opening stock on hand. The budgeted fixed expenses were £12,000. Analysis of actual results showed that only 900 units were made, and of these only 600 were actually sold. The actual fixed expense analysis showed expenditure of £12,150.
Required: (1) prepare fixed cost volume and expenditure variances.
　　　　　(2) indicate any features of the above situation which could cause you concern when you are preparing a statement of results for management.

Solution: (1)
In this case we *could* confine ourselves to calculating only the two variances requested. A total variance requirement is not implied in the wording of the question, nor is it helpful in double-checking fixed cost variances in a profit statement and balance sheet context as these, too, are not needed. However, the same start-point is maintained as in the previous question.

(1) *Calculation of Fixed Production Overhead Variance*

Actual stock achieved, at standard: $900 \times \dfrac{£12,000}{1,000}$	£10,800
Actual expenditure	£12,150
Unfavourable variance	£1,350

(2) *Calculation of Fixed Production Overhead Volume Variance*
900 units of production actually achieved

(a) Standard fixed production cost evaluation of actual activity achieved (900) × standard recovery rate $(\dfrac{£12,000}{1,000} = £12)$	£10,800
(b) Production quantity required to absorb budgeted fixed costs × standard recovery rate: 1,000 × £12	£12,000
Unfavourable variance	£1,200

(3) *Calculation of Fixed Production Overhead Expenditure Variance*

Budgeted cost	£12,000
Actual cost	£12,150
Unfavourable variance	£150

Part 2:
The fixed overhead recovery rate of £12 was based on the belief that 1,000

units would be produced and that this would be saleable sooner or later at a price which would include £12 for fixed expense. The cut-back in production to 90% of budget, and the retention of 33% of actual production as a closing stock figure ring alarm bells about the condition of the market for the company's product.

Secondly, and conversely, the fixed production overhead recovery rate is supposed to be based on a normal level of production activity. There must be doubt as to whether 1,000 units is such a level, or an optimistic estimate based on new growth which did not materialise. If the company's product is saleable and there is no anxiety about the level of selling prices, the fixed overhead cost per unit ought perhaps to have been based on the division of £12,000 by 900 units, giving a rate of £13.33 per unit. A figure below 900 units may in fact be a more normal level of activity, in which case the fixed overhead recovery rate should be even higher. Further investigation would clearly be needed before definite opinions could be held.

Further Analysis of Fixed Production Overhead Volume Variance
The variance which we have just been examining can be a hybrid, formed from a Fixed Production Overhead Capacity Variance and a Fixed Production Overhead Efficiency Variance: in other words it can stem from two separate causes, and the effect which each has in creating a deviation from budgeted profit can be given a monetary evaluation.

A Fixed Works Overhead Efficiency Variance comprises that part of a Fixed Works Overhead Volume Variance which results when actual direct hours worked during an accounting period are greater or less than the standard hours' worth of actual output in the period. The hours worked may be direct labour hours, departmental hours or machine hours: only chargeable hours are involved, not total clocked hours. When (a) actual direct hours worked exceed (b) the standard hours' output achieved, the resulting variance is unfavourable. It is calculated by multiplying the difference between (a) and (b) by the fixed works overhead recovery rate per standard hour.

A favourable variance leads automatically to an overall favourable *volume* variance provided that the direct hours worked equal or exceed the budgeted standard hours of output (ie provided the capacity variance is nil or favourable). In calculating the efficiency variance it is essential to convert budgeted output for the period concerned from units of product to standard hours.

A Fixed Works Overhead Capacity Variance comprises that part of a Fixed Works Overhead Volume Variance which results when actual direct hours worked during an accounting period differ from the budgeted standard hours of output for that period. The hours worked may be direct labour hours, departmental hours or machine hours. When actual direct hours exceed the budgeted standard hours, the variance is favourable; the hours difference is multiplied by the fixed overhead recovery rate per standard hour. In such cases, a complementary favourable fixed works overhead capacity *ratio* is also derived. A favourable variance (and ratio) lead automatically to a favourable overall volume variance (and ratio) provided efficiency in applying direct labour hours of charged time towards achieving standard hours of output can be maintained at 100% or more. It is essential in calculating the fixed works overhead capacity variance that budgeted output for the period be expressed in standard hours. Thus, if budgeted output for a period is 1,000 units of product A, the question would need to be searched to determine the standard hours' allowance per unit of product A. (If all that is being sought by examiners is a fixed works overhead volume variance, budgeted and actual output need not be converted to standard hours, although the correct answer will be achieved if the conversion takes place.)

Example Four
Part R goes through two departments, X and Y. The time allowed for one unit of Part R is 2 hours in department X and 4 hours in department Y. The company plans to make 1,000 of Part R in a given period: actual output is 900. The actual hours worked are 1,400 hours in department X and 3,100 in Y. The works overhead budgets for X and Y are £400 and £800 respectively. It is estimated that 50% and 60% of the works overheads of X and Y respectively are fixed.
Required: calculate and analyse the Fixed Production Overhead Volume Variance.

Solution:
(1) *Calculation of Volume Variance*
Each department is responsible for the control of its own fixed costs and their attribution to production achieved. Consequently there should be two volume variances, showing the extent to which the fixed expenses of X and Y have been separately absorbed into their respective levels of production.
(i) *Department X*
(a) Actual production achieved × standard recovery
rate per unit of production: $900 \times \dfrac{50\% \times £400}{1,000}$ (20p)   £180
(b) Production quantity required to absorb budgeted
fixed costs × standard recovery rate: 1,000 × 20p   200
Unfavourable variance   £20

(ii) *Department Y*
(a) As above $900 \times \dfrac{60\% \times £800}{1,000}$ (48p)   £432
(b) As above 1,000 × 48p   480
Unfavourable variance   £48

While some practitioners prefer to convert product units to standard hour equivalents immediately, as a preparatory toward analysis into efficiency and capacity constituents, the volume variance calculation does not require such a step.

(2) *Analysis of Volume Variance*
(i) *Department X*
Capacity Variance

(a) Budgeted output in standard hours × standard
fixed cost recovery rate *per hour:*

$1,000 \times 2\text{hrs} \times \dfrac{£200}{2,000\text{hrs}}$ (10p)   £200

(b) Actual direct hours worked × standard fixed
cost variance rate: 1,400 × 10p   £140

Unfavourable variance   £60

Efficiency (or Productivity Variance)
(a) Actual output achieved in standard hours ×
standard fixed cost recovery rate per hour:
900 × 2 × 10p   £180

(b) Actual direct hours worked to achieve actual
output × standard fixed cost recovery rate
1,400 × 10p   £140

Favourable variance   £40

(ii) *Department Y*
Capacity Variance
(a) As described above: $1,000 \times 4\text{hrs} \times \dfrac{£480}{4,000}$ (12p)   £480

(b) „   „   „ : 3,100 × 12p   £372

Unfavourable variance   £108

(ii) *Efficiency (or Productivity) Variance*
(a) As described above: 900 × 4 × 12p   £432
(b) „   „   „ : 3,100 × 12p   £372

Favourable variance   £60

Unfavourable capacity variances warn management that the number of
hours "booked" to achieve budgeted output, 2,000 and 4,000 for X and Y
respectively, were not charged in practice. Only 1,400 and 3,100 hours
were available to perform pre-determined workloads which, at 100% efficiency levels ought to have merited 2,000 and 4,000 hours. If, therefore, the
workforce have been unable for some reason to utilise budgeted time for
the work as planned, what hope is there that the company will have
achieved its budgeted output? The unfavourable capacity variances act as a
red warning light that, all else being equal, the company can expect trouble
at the volume variance level. If the workforce in such circumstances
adhered to a 100% efficiency plan (one standard hour of output for each
actual hour charged) the company could not escape from a volume
variance which was equal to the capacity variance. The volume variance
would then have been caused by failure to work sufficient chargeable hours.
   If less than one hour is taken to produce a standard hour of output, a
company can recover from the adversity of an unfavourable capacity
variance. In our example more output was achieved from each actual hour
available than the standards specified, so that some of the lost ground was
made up. In department X, only 1,400 hours appear to have been available
and by rights only 1,400 standard hours of output should have emanated,
operating at an efficiency rate of 100%. However, an extra 400 standard

hours were achieved which ate into the deficit of 600 standard hours of lost output which would otherwise have been the final volume variance result.

The challenge of working harder was again accepted by Department Y, who turned a threatened unfavourable variance of £108 around to the tune of £60; in this case 3,600 hours of output were achieved in 3,100 hours available. If only this highly satisfactory work-rate of $(\frac{3,600}{3,100} \times 100) =$ 116% had been $(\frac{4,000}{3,100} \times 100) = 129\%$, the company would have achieved its budgeted output against the odds.

At the back of any efficiency ratio above 100% there can be a productivity scheme, whereby employees are encouraged to produce extra output in each hour charged, for extra wages. Consequently, favourable efficiency variances may be more than offset by unfavourable direct labour rate variances: the whole broad canvas must be examined. Favourable efficiency variances are easy to initiate; I would be pleased to produce 20% more per hour if you paid me 40% more per hour for doing so. The company could then be a net loser. Everything would depend on the net effect on profits of producing (and selling) more output at enhanced cost.

Calendar Variances

Inconsistency in the constitution of accounting periods can cause distortions to the capacity variance discussed above. This is best illustrated in a practical example:

Example Five

The budgeted fixed production of ABC Ltd for year 5 was £72,000. During this year, the company's production target was 4,000 units, and the standard time allowance per unit was set at 1.5 hours. Output achieved in month 2 within year 5 was 400 units. Actual direct hours charged to production of these units totalled 450. Month 2 was not typical of an average operating month in that it had 2 extra days' holiday equivalent to 30 direct hours.

Required: calculate and analyse the fixed production volume variance for period 2.

Solution

The volume variance is based on a period 2 comparison of actual output achieved with budgeted output. To make this possible, all that can be done is to divide the annual budgeted output by 12 to derive a target or budget for a "typical month". We are already warned that month 2 is not a typical month. In fact in industry nowadays one rarely comes across a typical month.

As mentioned previously, the volume variance may be calculated without recourse to any conversion of output figures to standard hours. However, when the need for detailed analysis is known from the start, many proponents move into a state of readiness by converting immediately: the volume variance for month 2 is then:

(1) $\dfrac{\text{Budgeted output for year} \times \text{hours per unit}}{12} \times$ st. recovery rate per hour:

$$\dfrac{4{,}000 \times 1.5}{12} \times \dfrac{£72{,}000}{4{,}000 \times 1.5}(£12) \qquad = \qquad £6{,}000$$

(2) Actual output for month 2 converted to standard hours $\times$ standard recovery rate per hour:

$$400 \times 1.5 \ (600) \times £12 \qquad = \qquad \underline{£7{,}200}$$

Favourable volume variance $\qquad\qquad\qquad\qquad\qquad \underline{£1{,}200}$

The same result is obtained using units rather than standard hours:

(1) $\dfrac{\text{Budgeted output for year}}{12} \times$ standard recovery rate per unit:

$$\dfrac{4{,}000}{12} \times \dfrac{£72{,}000}{4{,}000} \ (£18) \qquad = \qquad £6{,}000$$

(2) Actual output for month 2 $\times$ standard recovery rate per unit:

$$400 \times £18 \qquad = \qquad \underline{£7{,}200}$$

Favourable volume variance $\qquad\qquad\qquad\qquad\qquad \underline{£1{,}200}$

Analysis of Volume Variance

A capacity variance can initially be calculated as in example four, but it will compare the 'booked' or budgeted hours needed in a typical month with the actual hours charged in a far from typical month, so that the variance will be distorted:

Total Capacity Variance

(1) $\dfrac{\text{Budgeted output for year in standard hours}}{12} \times$ st. recovery rate per hour:

$$\dfrac{6{,}000}{12} \times £12 \qquad = \qquad £6{,}000$$

(2) Actual hours charged $\times$ standard recovery rate per hour

$$450 \times £12 \qquad = \qquad \underline{£5{,}400}$$

Unfavourable variance $\qquad\qquad\qquad\qquad\qquad\qquad \underline{£600}$

This somewhat daunting variance is a coarse measure of events as it does not compare like with like at (1) and (2). Month 2 could never have been a typical month, so it is unfair to judge the actual hours charged (450) against 500 for an average month. If the management accountant of ABC Ltd were to ask the head of production: 'Why were the men only able to charge 450 hours this month?', an initial response might well be: 'This was a short month, didn't you know? Why are you accusing me of producing unfavourable variances when your targets are based on an impossible number of available hours?'. The management accountant needs to have a means of focusing more sharply on what really happened. The Calendar Variance is introduced for this purpose:

Analysis of Total Capacity Variance

(a) *Calendar Variance*

Hours lost in month 2 out of average month's hours $\times$ standard recovery rate per hour: $30 \times £12 = \underline{£360 \ (U)}$.

Of the total capacity variance of £600 caused by shortage of working hours, £360 can be excused because the available hours were 30 short of the 500 needed for month 2 to do the job demanded of a typical month. This leaves the threat of £240 of unabsorbed fixed overheads (all else being equal), because although 500 − 30 = 470 hours should have been worked in month 2, only 450 were actually worked:

(b) *Adjusted Capacity Variance*
  (1) Working hours actually available in period
    × standard recovery rate per hour: 470 × £12 = £5,640
  (2) Actual number of direct hours worked
    × standard recovery rate per hour: 450 × £12 = £5,400
    Unfavourable variance   £240

Now, in the above imaginary exchange between the head of production and the management accountant, the assertion by the former about a short month could be countered by the reminder: 'I've allowed for that: after deducting the effects of the short month, the operatives *still* failed to work to their adjusted target of 470 hours and it may have cost us £240 in unabsorbed fixed costs'.

The balance of the volume variance shows the extent to which operatives responded magnificently to the challenge of having fewer hours to work with than were needed to achieve a typical month's output. In the space of 450 hours, they produced 400 units, each entitling them to consume 1.5 hours:

Calculation of Efficiency Variance:
  (1) Actual output achieved in standard hours × standard
    recovery rate per hour: 400 × 1.5 × £12   £7,200
  (2) Actual hours charged × standard recovery rate per
    hour: 450 × £12   5,400
    Favourable variance   £1,800

An efficiency ratio of ($\frac{600}{450}$ × 100) = $133\frac{1}{3}\%$ has more than turned around the fixed costs absorption problem facing the company as a result of lack of capacity.

Calendar variances can work both ways, of course; there could be a holiday or some other capacity factor weighing in favour of a period which happened to have no holidays at all, while in our example the average month of $\frac{400 \times 1.5}{12}$ (500 hours) might be an average arrived at after due allowance for, say, a couple of days' holiday per month. In our example, month 2 having, say, 4 days' holidays rather than, say, a built-in average of 2 days could have caused the problem analysed above. If month 3 were then in practice to have, say, no days' holiday a favourable calendar variance would be needed to winkle out the distortion from a month 3 total capacity variance.

A capacity variance may be caused by an *unexpected* period of machine 'downtime', ie a spell during which machinery is *unexpectedly* idle, with production throughput totally absent. An hour of downtime is one in which there is nothing to show by way of saleable production, rather than an hour in which machinery is working below normal output levels. When the question of budgeting for output is being addressed, an allowance for normal downtime is made as a deduction from the gross hours of capacity available, so that the budgeted output becomes: total possible hours available for direct working on production, less an allowance in hours for downtime, multiplied by the number of units of production which can be expected in one direct hour's operation, working under normal operating conditions. Any monetary evaluation of a capacity variance which is caused by problems of downtime miscalculation must concentrate on the number of hours' difference between budgeted and actual downtime, and multiply this by the standard fixed cost recovery rate per hour.

We will deal with ratio counterparts to the above variances in the next chapter.

(3) ADMINISTRATION OVERHEADS

When a system of standard costing and flexible budgetary control is in operation, an examiner should give a clear indication as to whether the standard valuation of stock is to include administration overheads. He may assert that his imaginary organisation which is the basis for his examination question has administration costs which are incurred in bringing stock to its present condition and location (and such costs must be included in stock valuation), or he may deprive administration costs of any means of ingress into the valuation by stating that they do not have such a characteristic. More often than not a question will contain a simple instruction such as 'Value stock at full works and administration cost', or 'stock is valued to include variable and fixed works costs but excludes administration overhead'.

When a question contains administration costs, they are almost always regarded as fixed: if ever they are classed as variable, and are to be included in stock valuation, their treatment is identical to variable production overheads and similar variances arise. On any occasion in which variable administration overhead is to be excluded from stock valuation, they must be regarded as varying in sympathy with changes in selling activity, and can be treated in the same manner as variable selling overheads. When an examiner indicates that administration cost is fixed and included in stock valuation, it is treated exactly as fixed production overhead, with volume and expenditure variances being calculable. When such cost is to be kept away from stock valuation, the only variance to shoot for is the administration overhead expenditure variance.

Example
The stock of Eeta Ltd is valued at full standard cost, including administration overheads which are regarded as fixed costs. The following information is available for period 9.

	Budget	Actual
Production (units)	200	220
Administration overheads	£20,000	£19,000

Required: calculate administration overhead variances.

Solution:
Calculation of Administration Overhead Volume Variance
Find the measure and level of activity: 220 units
  (1) Actual production achieved × standard recovery rate per unit:

$$220 \times \frac{£20,000}{200} \ (£100) \qquad\qquad\qquad £22,000$$

  (2) Production quantity required (ie budgeted quantity)
     to recover budgeted administration costs × budgeted

recovery rate: 200 × £100	£20,000
Favourable variance	£2,000

Given a means of conversion of output to standard hours, and details of actual hours charged, it would of course be possible to analyse the above variance into capacity and efficiency constituents, but care would be needed to ensure that the benefits of such a supplement more than compensated for the extra effort involved. The cost of providing information should not exceed the monetary benefit derived from its use.

Calculation of Administration Overhead Expenditure Variance

(1) Budgeted cost	£20,000
(2) Actual cost	£19,000
Favourable variance	£1,000

The total profit variance resulting from administration overheads is therefore £3,000 (favourable).

Let us suppose that the examiner's instruction regarding administration cost had been to exclude it from standard stock valuation; the only profit variance would have been the £1,000 Expenditure Variance.

The comparative profit statement contents emanating from the above alternative solutions would be:

Profit Statement (extract showing the situation on fixed administration costs)
((F) = favourable)
((U) = unfavourable)

	(1) Original budget	(2) Adjustments into line with actual activity	(3) Revised standard charge	(4) Actual Profit & Loss A/c	(5) Variances affecting profits (a) Vol.	(b) Exp.	(c) Total
	Units £	Units £	Units £	Units £	£	£	£
1. Admin in stock valuation	200 20,000	20 2,000	220 22,000	220 19,000	2,000 (F)	1,000 (F)	3,000 (F)
2. Admin excluded	200 20,000	— —	220 20,000	220 19,000	—	1,000 (F)	1,000 (F)

Line 2 shows that for a standard charge to the Profit and Loss Account of £20,000 (see col (3)), the company paid only £19,000, so that the balance sheet is balanced in the usual way by attributing the difference of £1,000 to the credit of the Profit and Loss Account (see col (4)).

Until now we have been dealing with variances arising from *buying* activity (raw material price variances), and from *production* activity (the others). The remaining cost variances emanate from *selling* activity and are best left until a later chapter.

Some of the production cost variances which have been described and calculated have ratio counterparts, which are useful for providing non-accounting management with ready impressions of results and trends. We shall examine these in detail in the next chapter.

CHAPTER 8

PRODUCTION AND ADMINISTRATION COST RATIOS

The ratio counterpart to the Fixed Production Overhead Volume Variance is the Production Volume Ratio. Although 'The Terminology' booklet[1] advocates converting budget output and actual output achieved to their standard hours equivalents, it is not necessary to do this unless the intention is to go on and analyse the Production Volume Ratio into its two sub-sections: (a) the Efficiency (or Productivity) Ratio, and (b) the Capacity Ratio. To obtain any mileage from this analysis it is necessary to compare:

(a) actual direct hours worked with output achieved expressed in standard hours (efficiency ratio). If the latter exceeds the former, the ratio will be above 100%: a favourable ratio.

(b) actual direct hours worked with the standard hours of output needed to recover fixed costs (usually budgeted standard hours) (capacity ratio). If the latter exceeds the former, the ratio will be less than 100%: an unfavourable ratio.

The multiplication of (a) and (b) gives the 'senior' Production Volume Ratio. If this senior ratio is above 100%, the company will have over-recovered its fixed production costs (provided, of course, that it is valuing stock to include such costs).

Example One
The following information is available for XYZ Limited:

	Budget	Actual
Production (units)	5,000	6,000
Fixed costs for the period	£10,000	£11,000
Direct hours taken	15,000	19,000

3 hours are allowed per unit.

Required: (1) calculate and analyse the Production Volume Ratio
(2) what assumption has been made about the budgeted level of output?

---

[1] 'Terminology of Management and Financial Accountancy' (ICMA).

Solution:
(1) Calculation of Production Volume Ratio:

$$(\frac{\text{Output in standard hours}}{\text{Budgeted output in standard hours}} \times 100)\% =$$

$$(\frac{18,000}{15,000} \times 100)\% = 120\%$$

Analysis:
(a) Efficiency (or Productivity) Ratio:

$$(\frac{\text{Output in standard hours}}{\text{Actual direct hours charged}} \times 100)\% =$$

$$(\frac{18,000}{19,000} \times 100)\% = 94.7\%$$

(b) Capacity Ratio:

$$(\frac{\text{Actual direct hours charged}}{\text{Budgeted output in standard hours}} \times 100)\% =$$

$$(\frac{19,000}{15,000} \times 100)\% = 126.6\%$$

Notice that (a) × (b) = 120% (rounded)
(2) The assumption made is that the budgeted level of output is *normal*, and consequently that it has been used in determining the fixed cost recovery rate in line with the Statement of Standard Accounting Practice (SSAP 9). If 5,000 units cannot be so described, then the volume *variance* will be based on the following recovery rate:

$$\frac{\text{Budgeted fixed costs (BFC)}}{\textit{Normal} \text{ output level in st hours (NOL)}}$$

It will be calculated as follows:

(i) Normal output level × $\frac{\text{BFC}}{\text{NOL}}$

less:

(ii) Actual output level × $\frac{\text{BFC}}{\text{NOL}}$

If (ii) exceeds (i), the variance will be favourable.
   In the above circumstances it will still be possible to describe the volume ratio as showing the extent to which fixed costs have been over- or under-absorbed in percentage rather than monetary terms.

Example Two
Zeta Ltd intends having an efficiency ratio of 100% during period 5. The budget provides for the manufacture of 2,000 units, each taking one hour. In fact, 2,200 units are produced in 2,100 hours.
Required: calculate and analyse the production volume ratio.

Solution:
Production Volume Ratio
2,200 units of production achieved
   Convert to hours equivalent in anticipation of having to analyse the production volume ratio. At efficiency ratio of 100%, there must be a one for one relationship between an hour's effort and an hour's output. Therefore hours equivalent of 2,200 units = 2,200 hours.

Actual hours worth of output 2,200.
Expressed as % of budgeted output (in hours) (2,000) = 110%.
Analysed as follows:
  (a) Productivity (or efficiency) ratio:
    Actual hours of output expressed as % of actual hours worked:
    $(\frac{2,200}{2,100} \times 100)\% = 105\%$ (rounded upwards).
  (b) Capacity ratio:
    Actual hours worked expressed as a % of the hours planned
    to achieve 2,000 hours' worth of output (2,000):
    $(\frac{2,100}{2,000} \times 100)\% = 105\%$
    (a) × (b) = 110%.

Example Three
A company plans to produce 100 tonnes of castings in 20 hours during
accounting period 2. Instead it produces 60 tonnes, but operates for only
16 hours.
Required: (1) prepare and analyse the production volume ratio, showing
detailed workings.
(2) comment fully on uses to which the production volume ratio
and the analysis above might be put.

Solution
(1) Budgeted output 100 tonnes
  Budgeted output expressed in standard hours: 20 standard hours
  (ie 5 tonnes per hour).
  Actual output in standard hours $= \frac{60}{5} = 12$ standard hours.

  $$\text{Production volume ratio} = \frac{\text{Standard hours achieved}}{\text{Budgeted number of standard hours}}$$
  $$= \frac{12}{20} \times 100 = 60\%$$

  Analysis:
  (a) Productivity (or efficiency) ratio:
    $$\frac{\text{Standard hours achieved}}{\text{Actual number of hours worked}} \times 100 = \frac{12}{16} \times 100 = 75\%$$
  (b) Capacity ratio:
    $$\frac{\text{Actual hours worked}}{\text{Budgeted number of st. hours}} \times 100 = \frac{16}{20} \times 100 = 80\%$$
    (Proof: (1)×(2) = 75%×80% = 60% = production volume ratio.)
(2) When absorption costing is in use, fixed production costs are
  chargeable to work in progress. In such cases the production volume
  ratio shows the extent to which actual production will have absorbed
  fixed production overhead costs: eg if the ratio is 75% this means that,
  in the absence of fixed production overhead expenditure variances, £75
  of each £100 spent on fixed production overhead will have been
  successfully converted to saleable stock on hand.

The ratio can be used as a starting point when flexing budgeted cost allowances: if output is 75% of budget, the standard variable cost allowances for each variable production cost element should be flexed to 75% of original budgeted cost levels, and these flexed amounts compared with actual costs.

This ratio can also be used to put management on enquiry regarding potential threats or opportunities to other budgets such as sales or closing stock budgets. A production volume ratio of less than 100% could result, for example, in failure in due course to achieve the sales budget through not having sufficient finished goods on hand. Declining production, whether caused by inefficiency or a reduction in operating hours, could result in further decline through loss of customer confidence after failure to meet customer delivery deadlines.

The ratio expresses the monetary implications of the fixed production overhead volume variance in simple, non-monetary terms, and is therefore useful when conveying impressions to non-accounting management.

The productivity (or efficiency ratio) identifies whether one hour's worth of input effort achieved enough production output to saddle with one hour's worth of input costs: the ratio determines the degree of success in obtaining the output in an hour which was expected from that hour. This ratio recognises at the same time that in achieving more standard hours of output than were budgeted, undue strain may have been placed on the production facilities by using a disproportionately high number of operating hours (possibly) to the exclusion of other work.

An ostensibly good production volume ratio (in excess of 100%) can result in problems for a company if it relates only to one of several products competing for scarce working hour capacity: eg when analysis of a production volume ratio of more than 100% reveals an efficiency ratio of less than 100%, an actual contribution *per unit of key factor* (working hours) is being achieved which is below the budgeted contribution per unit of key factor.

Example: Budgeted number of standard hours' output: 10
Actual number of standard hours' output: 20
Actual hours worked: 30
Fixed costs to be recovered: £100
Variable costs: £2 per unit of product A
Selling price: £15 per unit of product A
1 Standard hour = 2 units of product A

	£
Sales 2 × 20 × 15 =	600
Variable costs 2 × 20 × 2	80
Contribution	£520

	Budget	Actual
Hours required	20	30
Contribution per hour	£26	£17.30

A decision to eliminate some other product in favour of product A may have been taken on the strength of an expected contribution from A of £26. Adverse efficiency ratios, when identified quickly, can be used to reconsider the apportionment of scare working hours over competing products.

The capacity ratio measures the extent to which a favourable production volume ratio was achieved at the expense of using too much unbudgeted working time. It measures the extent to which 'booked' working time (budgeted number of hours required) was actually taken up in practice, and the encroachment of one manager's manufacturing activity upon the booked operating time of another.

Elsewhere across the range of cost variances, ratio counterparts can be found without difficulty:

Example Four
£1,000 of direct materials and £2,000 of conversion cost is applied into a process, each at standard cost. 100 units are made in total, but good units which are saleable in due course are worth only £2,700 at standard cost. Normal scrap is 10% of total production units.
Required: calculate the Production Yield Variance, the Yield Ratio and the Scrap Ratio.

Solution
The start point would normally be a reconciliation of physical units to determine how many had been unexpectedly scrapped or alternatively had passed unscathed through inspection. These units would then be the basis for evaluation of the production yield variance. However, we are not given enough details to be able to approach a solution from the usual angle.

Standard unit output cost: $\dfrac{£(1,000 + 2,000)}{(100 - 10) \text{ units}} = £33.33$

$\therefore$ Good output $= (\dfrac{£2,700}{£33.33}$ $\qquad = 81$ units

$\therefore$ Yield ratio $= (\dfrac{81}{100} \times 100)\%$ $\qquad = 81\%$

$\therefore$ Scrap ratio $\qquad\qquad\qquad = \underline{19\%}$
$\qquad\qquad\qquad\qquad\qquad\qquad \underline{100\%}$

The production yield and production scrap ratios should equal 100%.

We can now proceed with the physical reconciliation:

Total units produced:		100
Whereof: Good units	81	
Normal scrap	10	
Abnormal scrap	9	
Total accounted for		100

Production yield variance $= 9$ units $\times \dfrac{£3,000}{90}$: $\qquad$ £300

Good output valuation: $81 \times \dfrac{£3,000}{90}$: $\qquad$ £2,700

Total cost accounted for $\qquad\qquad\qquad\qquad$ £3,000

Example Five

300 units of output are produced in aggregate: the normal loss to be expected is 10% of aggregate output. Each unit failing inspection has a standard sales value of 10p and this price is realised in practice. The standard and actual cost of manufacturing each unit is £1. Of the above 300 units, 295 were passed as good units.

Required: prepare (1) appropriate variances and ratios:

(2) an extract from a performance report incorporating variances.

Solution	Budget	Actual	
Yield ratio	90%	$(\frac{295}{300} \times 100)\% =$	98%
Scrap ratio	$\frac{10\%}{100\%}$	$(\frac{5}{300} \times 100)\% =$	$\frac{2\%}{100\%}$

Physical reconciliation

Total units produced		300
Whereof: good	295	
normal scrap	30	
abnormal scrap	(25)	
Total accounted for		300

The abnormal gain is the basis for the Production Yield Variance:

$$\text{Production Yield Variance} = 25 \times \text{Standard unit output cost}$$
$$= 25 \times \frac{£(300 - (30 \times 10p))}{(300 - 30) \text{ units}}$$
$$= 25 \times £1.10$$
$$= £27.50 \text{ (Fav)}$$

Scrap Yield Variance: £

(a) Standard scrap due from activity of 300 × standard
sales price: 30 × 10p   3.00

(b) actual scrap quantity × standard sales price: 5 × 10p   .50

Unfavourable variance   £2.50

A favourable production yield spins an unfavourable scrap yield variance: an unexpectedly high pass rate through inspection means an unexpectedly low volume of units for sale as scrap. The company can hardly 'have its cake and eat it'.

What standard costing tells us is that a good output level of 295 units entitled those concerned to spend 295 × £1.10 = £324.50. There is stock on the balance sheet to justify such expense. This stock is 25 units in excess of the expected level. The value of these 'bonus' units ought to have been 25 × 10p = £2.50; instead it is 25 × £1.10 = £27.50. The net effect is that £27.50 lies on the balance sheet by virtue of a success on production yield which was foreseen on the budgeted balance sheet, but £2.50 of income has failed to turn up on the actual balance sheet which was grafted on by rights to the budgeted balance sheet. The net effect is a profit variance of £(27.50 − 2.50) = £25 favourable.

We should realise that £324.50 is net after deducting 30 × 10p = £3 from the total cost for which good output is accountable. Therefore it is understated by 25 × 10p = £2.50 because this cash did not arrive. Therefore any profit figure derived after a charge of £324.50 would be overstated by £2.50. So the £2.50 is brought to bear on the faulty, under-stated standard cost to correct it to something in line with common justice:

Entries in Profit Statement Columns

	Standard charge to Production	Actual Profit & Loss Account	Variances affecting profits		
			(a) Prod'n Yield	(b) Scrap Yield	(c) Total
	Units £	Units £	£	£	£
Production					
Cost of gross production	300 300	300 300			
Less: normal scrap	30 3	30 3			
Standard good production	270 297	270 297			
Add back					
Favourable prod'n yield	25 27.50	25 2.50	27.50(F)	2.50(U)	25(F)
Good production	295 324.50	295 299.50	27.50(F)	2.50(U)	25(F)

Example Six

Gamma Ltd has a machine shop containing 20 similar lathes. The budgeted production for the quarter is as follows:

Products	A	B	C	D
Number of products per week	200	250	150	116
Standard hours per product	1.5	1.2	0.6	0.5

Further information relating to the budgets includes:
Budgeted operating efficiency is 110%
Budgeted downtime is 15%
All employees work a 40 hour week.
The actual achievement in week 5 was:

Products	A	B	C	D
Actual production	220	270	160	120

Labour details:
Machine operators-productive
hours clocked: 760
Required: prepare appropriate ratios to help to explain the above situation.

Solution

Total practical capacity should be expressed in hours: as the department is fully mechanised, lathe operating hours are the essence of ratio analysis, rather than man-hours. It is important to sense what is happening in the machine shop. For example, it is anticipated that a unit of product A will require 1.5 hours on a lathe, rather than a certain period of attention from a group of employees.

Gross capacity within which the budgeted output may be achieved is:
20 lathes × 40 hours: 800
To determine the budgeted net (practical)
capacity, deduct 15% 120
Budgeted productive hours 680

Within 680 hours, the budget expects 748 standard hours of output to be achieved:

		Standard hours
Product A	200 × 1.5	300
„ B	250 × 1.2	300
„ C	150 × .6	90
„ D	116 × .5	58
		748

This result is compatible with a budgeted efficiency ratio of 110%.
(680 × 110% = 748).

A table can therefore be prepared, comparing actual and budgeted results in ratio format:

	A Original Budgeted results	B Revised results (actual downtime)	C Actual results	Line Ref:
Gross capacity (hours)	800	800	800	1
Downtime	(15%) 120	(5%) 40	(5%) 40	2
Gross capacity utilisation	(85%) 680	(95%) 760	(95%) 760	3
Output at 100% efficiency (standard hours)	680	760	760	4
Output at budgeted efficiency of 110% (standard hours)	748	836	—	5
Output at actual efficiency of 106% (standard hours)	—	—	810*	6
Production volume ratio (% of 748)	100%	112%	108%†	7
Capacity ratio	91%	102%	102%	8
Efficiency ratio	110%	110%	106%	9

* = Note 1 † = Note 2

Note 1	Product A	220 × 1.5	330
	„ B	270 × 1.2	324
	„ C	160 × .6	96
	„ D	120 × .5	60
			810

Note 2 All ratio calculations have been rounded. Had operatives maintained the agreed 110% efficiency rate, the company could have expected 836 standard hours of output instead of the 810 hours which materialised. The 40 hours of actual downtime is a 'forced' figure, after deriving 800 hours of gross capacity and being given actual productive hours of 760.

There is an important distinction between the gross capacity utilisation at line 3 and the capacity ratio at line 8. In the first case the gross possible capacity of 800 hours at line 1, with no incidence of breakdown, is being planed down to the hours which ought to have been available for direct charging (column A), or those which were available (columns B and C). On the strength of B and C, the maintenance engineers can ostensibly bask in the plaudits of the production function: downtime has fallen well short of expectations. At line 8 we see the direct relationship between the budgeted output in standard hours (748) and the actual hours available to perform this task (line 3).

A small diagram shows the relationships for column C.

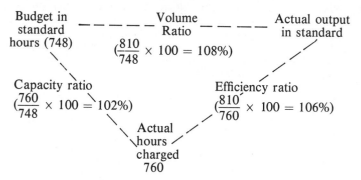

For column A, the relationships are:

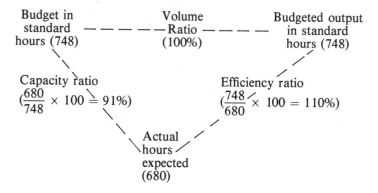

The downtime and gross capacity utilisation ratios must total to 100% in all three columns.

Management's overall performance in the machine shop is attested by a final ratio which relates total gross hours available (800) to the output achieved (810 standard hours). The calculation of a *machine shop effectiveness* ratio of $\frac{810}{800} \times 100 = 101.25\%$ cuts across all deceptions and excuses, and asks: 'When all is said and done how did management deploy the aggregate time at their command?' Top management are likely to pay only perfunctory tribute to any impressive ratios within the detailed range if, at the culmination the effectiveness ratio is showing a deteriorating trend. Whether 101.25% was impressive would depend on comparison with preceding periods.

Conclusion
Among the more intractable classes of management, variances and other representatives of the unfamiliar are generally disliked. However, ratios, by removing the emphasis from monetary evaluation of events, and transferring it to comparisons between actual and budgeted physical activities, often convey information which becomes clearer to non-accounting personnel.

'Ratios are also useful as pointers to areas which require further investigation. They put the reader on enquiry. They are particularly effective when prepared in sets to reveal trends. As with standard costing variances, each ratio should be regarded as reflecting only part of the total broad canvas of a company's affairs.'[1]

[1] 'Understanding Management Accounting', by the author (Gee & Co (Publishers) Ltd).

CHAPTER 9

SALES AND SELLING COST VARIANCES

Each sales variance which we calculate in this publication again has the prefix 'Profit variance caused by...'. Therefore, we do not calculate and utilise what I would refer to as 'turnover variances'. For example, if a company sells 500 units at £1 each instead of a budgeted 400 units at £1 each, its sales invoice total will be £100 above budget, and its turnover will be £100 above budget. However, the company's actual profit will not exceed budgeted profit by £100, because the cost of the extra 100 units needs to be charged against the extra turnover; the profit variance will be only the extra *profit* gained in the books of account from selling an extra 100 units. We would not offer a standard costing variance of:

$$500 \times £1 = £500$$
less $400 \times £1$ 400

Favourable result   £100 ...

... on any schedule of variances.

Sales Volume Variance

When stock is valued at full absorption cost, the sales volume variance is: (unit standard sales price − unit standard cost of sales) × number of un-budgeted units sold; or × number of units by which actual sales fall short of budget. Cost of sales includes fixed expense.

When stock is valued at marginal cost, the sales volume variance is: (unit standard sales price − unit standard variable cost of sales) × number of unbudgeted units sold; or × number of units by which actual sales fall short of budget.

A sales volume variance is calculated at standard selling prices and also assumes that standard costs have actually applied in practice. A favourable variance may be achieved at the expense of an adverse sales price variance which may more than compensate in monetary terms, creating a net adverse profit variance as an overall result of selling/marketing action.

A sales volume variance may show the aggregate result of two basic deviations from plan when more than one product is involved. The first involves changes between total actual bulk and planned bulk, the second deviations within actual bulk so that standard product mix is not achieved. Analysis of the sales volume variance is then needed.

Whether or not a sales price variance is involved, a favourable sales volume variance may indicate that products are underpriced, or too high in quality for prices charged.

Favourable sales volume variances can also arise at the expense of unfavourable cost variances elsewhere on the profit (or operating) statement, not least of which may be selling cost variances. As has been implied earlier, there may be a significant difference between standard and actual cost of sales, the former being used in calculating sales volume variances. There may also be a shortfall between budgeted and actual closing stock quantities, the latter being the lower, and this could prejudice ensuing periods' marketing plans or cause failures in customer service.

In general, a sales volume variance can be a pointer towards mis-reading of market potential or demand; as its presence in sizeable form can be caused by miscalculation at the time of budget preparation, it should put management on enquiry regarding other possible faulty budgeting which may have featured in respect of the current period.

Sales Price Variance

Underlying the sales price variance is the need to identify actual sales quantities achieved, ie actual sales activity levels, in the same way that raw material price variances prepared at time of purchase depend on ferreting out actual current purchasing activity in the given period, and direct labour rate variances are based on actual direct hours worked. The formula is (1) actual quantity at standard selling prices, less (2) actual quantity at actual selling prices; if the latter is greater, the price variance is favourable. Alternatively the variance may be expressed as: actual quantity sold × (actual − standard) selling prices; a positive answer means a favourable variance.

A sales price and a sales volume variance can frequently emanate from the same root source, a decision to deviate from standard selling prices: if the price is pushed up, quantities may decline and vice versa. Management consequently tend to look for the net effect on profits of combined price and volume variances. This approach is also reflected in most examination questions, which focus on situations in which the need to calculate and report upon both types of variance is clearly apparent. From time to time examiners ask for the calculation and presentation of the effect which the sales function has had on budgeted profits.

Examples showing Sales Volume and Price Variances
Example One
The nominal ledger of ABC Ltd shows the following situation:

	Budget	Actual
Sales (units)	1,000	850
Selling price per unit	£8	£9
Cost of sales per unit	£6	£8

Required: calculate the sales price variance and the sales volume variance.

Solution
Calculation of sales price variance:
Actual quantity sold × (actual − standard) selling price:
850 × £(9 − 8) = £850 (favourable)
Calculation of sales volume variance:
(actual − budgeted) units sold × (standard selling price − standard
cost of sales):
150 × £2 = £300 (unfavourable)
The net effect is therefore £(850 − 300) = £550 (favourable). Notice
how deviations between standard and actual cost of sales are ignored at
this stage. Elsewhere within reporting procedures, explanations of cost
variances will normally be forthcoming, hopefully at a more detailed level
than a mere 'Cost of Sales Variance' of 850 × £(8 − 6) = £1,700 (unfavourable).

Example Two

ABC Ltd have the following results for period 4:
Budgeted sales
300 of product A at £8 each (standard cost of sales £5 per unit)
200 of product B at £4 each („   „ „ „ £3 „ „)
Actual sales
320 of A at £8.50 each and 150 of B at £5 each.
Required: calculate the sales variances.
The absence of any actual cost details reinforces my earlier remark that
only standard cost figures are required to answer such a question.

Sales Variances

(1) *Sales Price Variance*
Actual quantity sold at standard selling prices

	£	£
A: 320 at £8.00p	2,560	
B: 150 at £4.00p	600	3,160
Actual quantity sold at actual selling prices		
A: 320 at £8.50p	2,720	
B: 150 at £5	750	3,470
Sales price variance (favourable)		£310

(2) *Sales Volume Variance*
Budgeted sales at standard profit per unit

A: 300 at £3	900	
B: 200 at £1	200	1,100
Actual sales at standard profit per unit		
A: 320 at £3	960	
B: 150 at £1	150	1,110
Sales volume variance (favourable)		£10

Analysis of Sales Volume Variance
(a) *Mix*
    Actual sales according to standard mix

A: $\frac{3}{5}$ × 470 at £3 standard profit	846	
B: $\frac{2}{5}$ × 470 at £1 standard profit	188	1,034

    Actual sales : actual mix

A: 320 at £3	960	
B: 150 at £1	150	1,110
Mix variance (favourable)		£76

(b) Budgeted Bulk Quantity

A: 300 at £3	900	
B: 200 at £1	200	1,100

    Actual quantities : standard mix

A: $\frac{3}{5}$ × 470 (282) at £3	846	
B: $\frac{2}{5}$ × 470 (188) at £1	188	1,034
Bulk quantity variance (unfavourable)		£66

When the mix variance at (a) is being calculated, the actual quantity sold is used throughout. The problem which requires monetary evaluation is that this actual sales quantity, fully admitted by management, did not contain the standard proportions or blend within the 470 units which management expected. Clearly A offers a much higher profit per unit than B, and if it is sold in the proportion $\frac{320}{470}$ of total sales, instead of $\frac{3}{5}$ths of total sales, the sales functions are generating higher profits from 470 units than management had a right to expect from 470 units when budgets were prepared. By 'enriching' the mix of A and B, an excess of £76 of actual profit over budget has been created: the full title of this variance might be: 'That part of the profit variance caused by the proportions of individual products sold being different from the budgeted proportions.'

While establishing the effect of selling a different aggregate quantity from plan at (b), the company assumes that 'all else is equal', eg that the proportions of A and B are as budgeted. The monetary evaluation is of the missing aggregate bulk, assuming it is constituted as $\frac{3}{5}$ths of A and $\frac{2}{5}$ths of B.The missing profit is therefore caused by not selling 30 units of which, for the purposes of this variance, 18 would have earned £3 each and 12 £1 each: total £66 (unfavourable variance).

Example Three
(Institute of Chartered Accountants of Scotland, Management Accounting Examination, Spring 1976)

Luscious Fruits Ltd, produce merchants, prepares budgets for 13 four-weekly periods annually.

Budget details for period 3 (4 weeks to 25th March 19X6) are as follows:

	R	S	T	
	Products			
Sales – units	3,000	4,000	8,000	
Selling price per unit	50p	60p	40p	
Variable or direct cost per unit	40p	45p	15p	
Fixed overhead budgeted for period 3				£1,500

Actual results of the period are as follows:

	R	S	T	
	Products			
Sales – units	2,500	5,000	9,000	
Selling price per unit	55p	50p	45p	
Fixed overhead				£1,650

Other information:
Actual variable or direct costs per unit for period were as budgeted.

Required:
1. Prepare a comparative statement of budgeted and actual profit for period 3, 19X6.

2. Analyse the variance between budgeted and actual contribution due to:
   (a) sales price
   (b) sales volume.

Solution
No attempt is being made by the company to value its production stock of individual products to include fixed costs. Two factors emanate from this arrangement: (a) A 'contribution per product' line is necessary on whatever reporting format is chosen (showing sales less variable (or direct) costs per unit): (b) the only fixed overhead variance which is possible is a fixed overhead expenditure variance. Volume variances stem from over- or under-absorption into production on a per unit basis, and this is impossible if no attempt at absorption is being made in the first place.

Two presentation styles are offered in answer to this question. The first is only appropriate in this case because of the dearth of narrative lines down the left-hand side. Notice how each of these must be repeated for each product, and there is also a total line for each. Had the situation been more complicated, with opening and closing stock figures, and with the variable costs analysed into categories, this presentation format would have involved spilling over onto a second and probably a third page which would have made it too unwieldy. The second format takes the strain of having multi-product sales *across* the page.

Part 1

Luscious Fruits Ltd
Comparative statement of budgeted and actual profit

Presentation style No 1   Period 3

	(1) Original Budget		(2) Adjustments into line with actual activity		(3) Revised standard charge		(4) Actual Profit & Loss A/c		(5) Variances affecting profits			
									(a) Sales price	(b) Sales vol. Col (2)	(c) Fixed O/Hd expend.	(d) Total
	Units	£	Units	£	Units	£	Units	£	£	£	£	£
Sales R	3,000	1,500	(500)	(250)	2,500	1,250	2,500	1,375	125 (F)	—	—	125 (F)
S	4,000	2,400	1,000	600	5,000	3,000	5,000	2,500	500 (U)	—	—	500 (U)
T	8,000	3,200	1,000	400	9,000	3,600	9,000	4,050	450 (F)	—	—	450 (F)
	15,000	7,100	1,500	750	16,500	7,850	16,500	7,925	75 (F)	—	—	75 (F)
Variable Costs R		1,200		(200)		1,000		1,000	—	—	—	—
S		1,800		450		2,250		2,250	—	—	—	—
T		1,200		150		1,350		1,350	—	—	—	—
		4,200		400		4,600		4,600				
Contribution R		300		(50)		250		375	—	50 (U)	—	50 (U)
S		600		150		750		250	—	150 (F)	—	150 (F)
T		2,000		250		2,250		2,700	—	250 (F)	—	250 (F)
		2,900		350		3,250		3,325	—	350 (F)	—	350 (F)
Fixed Overhead		1,500				1,500		1,650			150 (U)	150 (U)
Profit		1,400		350		1,750		1,675	75 (F)	350 (F)	150 (U)	275 (F)

The actual profit of £1,675 (col (4)) represents an increase of £275 (col 5(d)) over original budgeted profit of £1,400 (col (1)). £1,675 is £75 less than could have been expected at the revised activity levels (col (4) − col (3)).

Part 2
(a) Analysis of sales price variance is shown at col 5(a) of Part 1
(b) Analysis of sales volume variance

Due to quantity		R		S		T	Total
Budget units		3,000		4,000		8,000	15,000
Contribution per unit		10p		15p		25p	
Budgeted contribution (£)		300		600		2,000	2,900
Actual units – standard mix	(3)/(15)	3,300	(4)/(15)	4,400	(8)/(15)	8,800	16,500
Revised contribution $\frac{16,500}{15,000} \times 2,900$		330		660		2,200	3,190
Variance due to quantities		30 (F)		60 (F)		200 (F)	£290 (F)

Due to mix		R		S		T	Total
Budget units	(3)/(15)	3,000	(4)/(15)	4,000	(8)/(15)	8,000	15,000
Actual – actual mix		2,500		5,000		9,000	16,500
Actual – budgeted mix	(3)/(15)	3,300	(4)/(15)	4,400	(8)/(15)	8,800	16,500
Difference		800		(600)		(200)	—
Contribution per unit		10p		15p		25p	
Variance due to mix		£80 (U)		£90 (F)		£50 (F)	£60 (F)
Total Sales Volume variance							£350 (F)

Luscious Fruits Ltd
Comparative statement of Budgeted and Actual Profits

Presentation style No 2   Period 3

Line refce		Budget Units R	S	T	Total	Budget £ R	S	T	Total	Actual Units R	S	T	Total	Actual £ R	S	T	Total
1	Sales at standard	3,000	4,000	8,000	15,000	1,500	2,400	3,200	7,100	2,500	5,000	9,000	16,500	1,250	3,000	3,600	7,850
2	Less: Variable cost of sales at standard					1,200	1,800	1,200	4,200					1,000	2,250	1,350	4,600
3	Budgeted Contribution					300	600	2,000	2,900								
4	Standard Contribution on actual sales quantities													250	750	2,250	3,250
5	Sales price variances (Note 1)																
6	– Favourable/(adverse)					125	(500)	450	75					125	(500)	450	75
7	Sales volume variances																
8	– Favourable/(adverse)																
9	– quantity (Note 1)					30	60	200	290								
10	– mix (Note 1)					(80)	90	50	60								
11						375	250	2,700	3,325					375	250	2,700	3,325
12	Fixed overhead at standard								1,500								1,500
13	Fixed overhead expenditure variance (adverse)								—								(150)
14	Profit (line 3 – line 12)								1,400								
15	(line 11 – lines 12 and 13)																1,675

Note 1
Details would be presented to the examiners as shown at presentation No 1.

Presentation style No 2 gives standards their chance until proved wrong. Budgeted and actual sales quantities are presented *at standard prices* on line 1. The fact that the actual prices were different is faced and evaluated at line 6. Costs are assumed to be in line with standard costs at line 2. Had actual variable costs been different in practice, there would have been variance accounts in the nominal ledger, with balances requiring posting to the Profit and Loss Account in the nominal ledger (the actual column *is* the Profit and Loss Account). These variances would have been shown in the 'actual' column just prior to the fixed overhead expenditure variance, and the actual profit at line 15 would accordingly have required changing. The principle of showing standard costs initially in the 'Actual' column is sustained for fixed costs, at lines 12 and 13.

Example Four
Alpha Ltd have the following budgeted sales pattern for accounting period 4:

Product	Selling Price per unit	Production & Administration Cost of Sales per unit	Sales quantity
A	£10	£8	1,000
B	£11	£6	1,000
C	£12	£6	1,000

Variable costs are considered to represent 50% of the above selling prices. In practice, however, the following sales pattern emerges:

Product	Selling Price per unit	Production & Administration Cost of Sales	Sales quantity
A	£9	£8	1,100
B	£12	£7	850
C	£13	£8	1,050

Required
Calculate and analyse the change between budgeted and actual profits which the sales function have effected, assuming that altered selling prices and changes in quantities sold were their responsibility. (Ignore selling expenses.)

Solution

PROFIT AND LOSS ACCOUNTS

	Budget								Actual							
	Units				£				Units				£			
	A	B	C	Total	A	B	C	Total	A	B	C	Total	A	B	C	Total
Sales at standard	1,000	1,000	1,000	3,000	10,000	11,000	12,000	33,000	1,100	850	1,050	3,000	11,000	9,350	12,600	32,950
Production and admin. cost of sales at st.					8,000	6,000	6,000	20,000					8,800	5,100	6,300	20,200
Budgeted Profit					2,000	5,000	6,000	13,000								
Standard Profit on actual quantity													2,200	4,250	6,300	12,750
Add/(deduct) fav/(unfav) price variance (note 1)					(1,100)	850	1,050	800					(1,100)	850	1,050	800
Add/(deduct) fav/(unfav) sales vol. var. (a) Quantity (note 2)					—	—	—	NIL								—
(b) Mix (note 3)					200	(750)	300	(250)								
Profit on actual quantity, at actual selling prices					1,100	5,100	7,350	13,550					1,100	5,100	7,350	13,550
Less: any unfavourable cost variances													(X)	(X)	(X)	(X)
Add: any favourable cost variances													X	X	X	X
Actual Profit (Note 4)													X	X	X	X

Note 1
Sales Price Variance

Product	Act Qty	Actual +/(−) budget (£) (1)	Variance Fav/(unfav) (£)
A	1,100	(1)	(1,100)
B	850	1	850
C	1,050	1	1,050
			£ 800 (fav)

Note 2
Sales Volume Variance: Quantity

Product	Act Qty st mix	St Qty st mix	Qty diff	Standard profit per unit	Variance fav/ (unfav)
A	1,000	1,000	—	2	—
B	1,000	1,000	—	5	—
C	1,000	1,000	—	6	—
	3,000	3,000	—		—

Note 3
Sales Volume Variance: Mix

Product	Act Qty st mix	Act Qty Act mix	Qty diff	Standard profit per unit	Variance fav/ (unfav)
A	1,000	1,100	100	2	200
B	1,000	850	(150)	5	(750)
C	1,000	1,050	50	6	300
					(250)

Summary re Notes 2 and 3
The effect on profits caused by changes made by the selling function is £550 (fav), made up of £800 (fav) for Sales Price Variance, and £250 (U) for sales volume variance. This variance is the difference between the budgeted profit of £13,000 and the final line total of £13,550.

Note 4
This layout would be completed by showing *cost* variances in the actual column only, in questions which asked for the comparison of budgeted and actual profits on a performance report, profit and loss account or operating statement. The final figure in the actual column would be ACTUAL PROFIT. The standardised layout with columns (1) to (5) across the page would be difficult where three products and a total column were required, compounded by the need for units and pounds (£).

Selling Cost Variances
Such costs are taken to include 'marketing' costs. A variable selling costs variance shows the difference between the actual cost incurred at the actual *selling* activity level, and the cost which ought to have been incurred (the standard, allowed, cost) at that actual level. To achieve the latter revised

budget, one has to take the variable selling cost given in a question for the original budgeted sales activity, and flex it into line with the actual activity level. When budgeted and actual fixed selling costs are compared, management may confine themselves to the calculation of a fixed selling cost expenditure variance, although if it is considered beneficial to show the over- or under-absorption of fixed selling costs caused by an unexpected sales activity level, a volume variance may also be prepared.

Example

The following information is available for Lamda Ltd for period 3:

	Budget	Actual
Sales (units)	800	900
Variable selling costs	£10,000	£10,500
Fixed selling costs	£20,000	£19,000

Absorption costing is in use.
Required: calculate selling cost variances.

Solution
Calculation of variable selling cost variance
Find the measure and level of *selling* activity: 900 units
(a) Standard variable cost entitlement for actual activity
achieved: $900 \times \dfrac{£10,000}{800} = $ £11,250
(b) Actual variable cost incurred: £10,500
Favourable variance   £750

Other variable cost variances can be split into rate (or price) and efficiency (or usage) segments, but such analysis of what must be regarded as the Variable Selling Cost Variance is normally impossible.

Fixed Costs
(1) *Expenditure*

Budgeted cost	£20,000
Actual cost	19,000
Favourable variance	£1,000

(2) *Volume*
  (a) Budgeted sales needed to absorb fixed costs
      × standard recovery (or absorption) rate:
      $800 \times \dfrac{£20,000}{800}$ (£25)   £20,000
  (b) Actual sales × standard recovery
      rate: 900 × £25   £22,500
      Favourable variance   £2,500

Total favourable variance: £3,500

The *raison d'être* behind the volume variance is that, through increasing the standard cost of sales charge from a budgeted figure of £20,000 to £22,500, the favourable Sales Volume Variance resulting from increased sales is being reduced by £2,500, somewhat artificially: but the profit gain from extra sales is doubtless very real and, all else being equal, ought not to have been cut back by £2,500. Let us suppose in this case that the standard and actual selling price per unit of product is £40. Ignoring other costs of sales (eg production) for the sake of simplicity, a profit statement would show the following:

((F) = favourable
(U) = unfavourable)

	(1) Original Budget		(2) Adjustments into line with actual activity		(3) Revised standard charge		(4) Actual Profit & Loss Account		(5) Variances affecting profits £				
									(a) Sales Volume col(2)	(b) Var Selling Cost	(c) Fixed Expense Volume	(d) Fixed Exp Expend.	(e) Total
	Units	£	Units	£	Units	£	Units	£					
Sales	800	32,000	100	4,000	900	36,000	900	36,000					
Variable selling cost		10,000		1,250		11,250		10,500		750(F)			750(F)
Fixed selling cost		20,000		2,500		22,500		19,000			2,500(F)	1,000(F)	3,500(F)
Total		30,000		3,750		33,750		29,500					
Profit	800	2,000	100	250	900	2,250	900	6,500	250(F)				250(F)
Profit variances									250(F)	750(F)	2,500(F)	1,000(F)	4,500(F)

Notice how the sales volume variance at column (2) has been greatly reduced by the imposition of the fixed selling cost variance of £2,500 in the same column. An alternative presentation would exclude any reference to fixed selling cost volume variance, showing nothing at column 5(c) and nothing on the same line at column (2). The result would be to increase the sales volume variance by £2,500 so that the end result (a total profit variance of £4,500) would be the same. Management can exercise their discretion as to whether to split what is in fact a gross sales volume variance of £(2,500 + 250) = £2,750 into sales volume and fixed selling cost volume.

In the nominal ledger the fixed cost situation would develop along the following lines:

(1) Fixed Selling Cost Control Account   DR   £19,000
     Creditors, etc   CR   £19,000
     (upon receipt of services, etc classed as fixed selling costs)

(2) Cost of Sales at Standard   DR   £22,500
     Fixed Selling Cost Control Account   CR   £22,500
     (900 units sold × £25)

(3) Profit and Loss Account   DR   £22,500
     Cost of Sales at Standard   CR   £22,500
     (transfer of cost of sales at standard to the P & L A/c)

(4) Fixed Selling Cost Control Account   DR   £3,500
     Fixed Selling Cost Variance Account   CR   £3,500
     (creation of variance account through the transfer of the
         Control Account balance)

(5) Fixed Selling Cost Variance Account   DR   £3,500
     Profit and Loss Account   CR   £3,500
     (transfer of variance account balance to P & L A/c)

CHAPTER 10

PROFIT STATEMENTS

The culmination of variance accounting is reached when actual and budgeted results for an accounting period are presented and compared on a statement of performance. Many examination candidates who are adept at variance calculation falter when faced with this task. Yet there is scarcely a question which involves merely hacking out a report after a fashion; most demand a good presentation style. Report formats can be easily memorised and will serve virtually without fail. Candidates should suppress any notions that they are obliged to create original art-works when designing performance reports.

We have already used the two formats which should suffice in an examination environment. The layout which sets out columns (1) to (5) across the page is particularly useful when only one, or perhaps two products are involved. On occasions when multi-product situations arise the framework illustrated on page XX, which is recommended in 'Standard Costing: an Introduction to the Accounting Processes' (ICAEW) can be a preferable option, with the columns (1) to (5) layout threatening to break down through lack of space. In a question involving three products, column (1), for example, would have three units columns for each of the three products, plus a total units column.

The purpose of this chapter is to illustrate how large-scale examination questions which call for statements of actual and budgeted results and detailed explanations (by way of variances) of differences between the two, can best be handled using the pre-conceived, standardised reporting formats referred to above.

Example One
(The Institute of Chartered Accountants of Scotland (ICAS), Management Accounting Examination, Autumn 1977)
Bacon Ltd produces meat slicers. An integrated system of standard costing and budgetary control is operated. The undernoted data is available for four weeks ending 30th July 19X6.

Production in units – budget	260
– actual	240
Sales in units – budget	275
– actual	250

	£
Budget sales value per unit	200
Standard cost per unit –	
Material	80
Labour	20
Production overhead – fixed	10
– variable	10
	£120

	£
Budget selling expenses – fixed	2,750
– variable	5,500
Actual sales	52,000
Materials issued at standard price	19,040
Materials purchased at standard price	22,320
Materials purchased at invoiced price	22,030
Actual labour costs	4,950
Actual production overhead – fixed	2,500
– variable	2,300
Actual selling expenses – fixed	2,800
– variable	5,400
Finished stock at standard cost, 2nd July 19X6	84,720
Raw materials at standard price, 2nd July 19X6	21,200

Required:
1. Prepare a statement for the period showing the appropriate budget, actual and variance figures.
2. State the stock values at 30th July 19X6 of raw materials and finished stock.

Bacon Limited: Performance Statement for period ending 30th July 19X6

	(1) Original Budget		(2) Adjustments into line with actual activity		(3) Revised standard charge		(4) Actual Profit & Loss A/c		(5) Variances Affecting Profits (£)							
									(a) Sales Price	(b) RM Usage	(c) RM Price	(d) Cost	(e) FO Vol	(f) FO Exp	(g) Sales Vol	(h) Total
	Units £		Units £		Units £		Units £									
Sales	275	55,000	25	5,000	250	50,000	250	52,000	2,000 (F)							2,000 (F)
Current Production Costs	260		20		240		240									
Material (st. price £80 per unit)		20,800		1,600		19,200		18,750		160 (F)	290 (F)					450 (F)
Labour		5,200		400		4,800		4,950				150 (U)				150 (U)
Prod'n o/head – fixed		2,600		200		2,400		2,500					200 (U)	100 (F)		100 (U)
– variable		2,600		200		2,400		2,300				100 (F)				100 (F)
Total	260	31,200	20	2,400	240	28,800	240	28,500								
Add: opening finished stock	706	84,720	—	—	706	84,720	706	84,720								
Total prod'n costs of units available for sale	966	115,920	20	2,400	946	113,520	946	113,220								
Less: closing stock	691	82,920	5	600	696	83,520	696	83,520								
Prod'n cost of Sales	275	33,000	25	3,000	250	30,000	250	29,700								
Add: selling expenses Fixed		2,750		—		2,750		2,800				50 (U)				50 (U)
Variable		5,500		500		5,000		5,400				400 (U)				400 (U)
Total Cost of Sales	275	41,250	25	3,500	250	37,750	250	37,900								
Profit	275	13,750	25	1,500	250	12,250	250	14,100	2,000 (F)	160 (F)	290 (F)	500 (U)	200 (U)	100 (F)	1,500 (U)	350 (F)

(g) 1,500 (U) = (col (2) total)

(F) = favourable variance; (U) = unfavourable variance

Opening and closing stock quantities are valued at standard cost of £120 per unit in all columns.
The total at column 5(h) shows the total profit variance, ie the difference between the totals at cols (1) and (4).
To derive the difference between actual profit of £14,100 [col (4)] and the profit which should have been derived at those production and activity levels [col (3)], deduct the sales volume variance of £1,500 (U) at 5(g) from the £350 (F) at 5(h): answer £1,850 (F).

Calculation of Raw Material Price Variance

Creditors for July purchases	22,030
Standard price	22,320
Favourable variance	£290

This variance which emanates from the activities of the buying department, has been credited to the actual performance at col (4) on the performance statement. The £18,750 comprises materials issued at standard price £19,040 less the £290 above.

Part 2   Raw Material Stores Control Account

Opening Stock at st.	21,200	Requisitions at st. during July	19,040
Purchases at st.	22,320	Closing stock at st.	24,480
	£43,520		£43,520

31st July Balance b/down £24,480

Finished Goods Stores Control A/C

Opening Stock at st.	84,720	Transfers to Cost of Sales at st.	30,000
From W in P	28,800	Closing Stock at st.	83,520
	£113,520		£113,520

31st July Balance b/down £83,520

The adjustment figures which you see in column (2) of the operating statement relating to production costs are to revise the company's standard stock valuation into line with actual levels of production [column (3) units column]. The column (1) evaluation shows standard cost of the stock which the company budgeted to produce, and column (3) the stock valuation of the actual stock which it *did* produce. Stock valuation includes a portion of fixed cost for each unit produced as stock is being valued at *full* works cost. Therefore, the more stock produced, the higher the stock valuation level. We use the same fixed cost recovery (or absorption rate) for each unit produced throughout the period. As stock quantities rise, the balance sheet standard value rises, and this can be *expected* to be achieved *at no extra fixed cost* as the budget for fixed cost remains static. Therefore any over-absorption represents a stock increase for no equivalent cash decrease, and the profit and loss account receives a favourable uplift for the amount of the over-absorption. Under-absorptions, which may also be illustrated at column (2), show expected/budgeted cash declines for fixed costs which will not be countered by equivalent stock increases, and diminish the profit and loss account balance in the balance sheet. When *actual* fixed overhead expense differs from budget, the company will of course over- or under-absorb a faulty budgeted fixed cost. The ultimate balance sheet position has also to reflect this deviation between budgeted and actual fixed costs and this difference is shown by comparing column (1) with column (4).

The variances which are likely to appear in column (2) when there are production and selling activities in the question, are: (a) Sales Volume Variance [total of column (2)]; (b) Fixed Production Overhead Volume Variance; (c) Fixed Administration Overhead Volume Variance and, if useful, (d) Fixed

Selling Overhead Volume Variance: (a) and (d) disappear if there is no selling activity.

Example Two
(Based on ICAS Management Accounting Examination, Autumn 1977)
In this example, sales variances are not specifically asked for, but no profit statement (which *is* specified as a requirement) would be complete without them:

A C Wilcox Ltd use a standard costing and flexible budgetary control system to control the manufacture of its single product, a tape recorder. The standard costs of this tape recorder are:

	£
Raw materials	
A – 8 units at £0.50	4
B – 20 units at £1.60	32
Direct Labour	
6 hours at £2.00	12
Overhead	
Variable	6
Fixed	18
Total standard cost	72

The following information is available for August 19X7:

	A	B
Raw material stocks at 31st July 19X7	6,000 units	7,000 units
Raw material stocks at 31st August 19X7	24,000 units	43,200 units

Finished goods stock at 31st July 19X7	£21,600
Finished goods stock at 31st August 19X7	£7,200

	Budget	Actual
Tape recorders manufactured	1,500	1,200
Hours worked	9,000	7,500
Payroll costs	£18,000	£15,750
Variable overhead	£9,000	£7,400
Fixed overhead	£27,000	£26,300
Raw material purchases of A	28,000 units – £13,720	
Raw material purchases of B	60,000 units – £97,200	
Sales of tape recorders : actual	1,400 units at £80 each	
Sales of tape recorders : budget	1,500 units at £80 each	

Required
Prepare a profit statement for August 19X7 to show the effect on standard profit of the following variances:
1. Labour rate;
2. labour efficiency;
3. material price;
4. material usage;
5. variable overhead;
6. fixed overhead volume;
7. fixed overhead expenditure.

A C WILCOX LTD PROFIT STATEMENT FOR AUGUST 19X7

Column (5) = Variances Affecting Profits (£); (F) = favourable (U) = unfavourable

	(1) Original Budget — Units	£	(2) Adjustments into line with actual activity — Units	£	(3) Revised standard charge — Units	£	(4) Actual Profit & Loss A/c — Units	£	(5a) Price/Rate	(5b) Volume	(5c) Usage/efficiency	(5d) Cost	(5e) Expenditure	(5f) Total
Sales	1,500	120,000	100	8,000	1,400	112,000	1,400	112,000	NIL					NIL
Costs (a) Current	1,500		300		1,200		1,200							
Raw materials		54,000		10,800		43,200		44,000 *	920 (U) (Price)		120 (F) (Usage)			800 (U)
Direct Labour		18,000		3,600		14,400		15,750 †	750 (U) (Rate)		600 (U) (Efficiency)			1,350 (U)
Variable Overhead		9,000		1,800		7,200		7,400				200 (U)		200 (U)
Fixed Overhead		27,000		5,400		21,600		26,300 ‡		5,400 (U)			700 (F)	4,700 (U)
Total current cost	1,500	108,000	300	21,600	1,200	86,400	1,200	93,450	1,670 (U)	5,400 (U)	480 (U)	200 (U)	700 (F)	7,050 (U)
(b) Opening stock at standard cost	300	21,600			300	21,600	300	21,600						
(c) Available for sale	1,800	129,600	300	21,600	1,500	108,000	1,500	115,050	as above					7,050 (U)
Less: (d) Closing stock at standard	300	21,600	200	14,400	100	7,200	100	7,200						
Cost of sales	1,500	108,000	100	7,200	1,400	100,800	1,400	107,850	as above					7,050 (U)
Profit	1,500	12,000	100	800	1,400	11,200	1,400	4,150	as above					7,050 (U)
Sales volume variance (col 2)										800 (U)				800 (U)
Profit variances									1,670 (U)	6,200 (U)	480 (U)	200 (U)	700 (F)	7,850 (U)

* Note 1   † Note 2   ‡ Note 3

Column (3) again shows what the profit ought to have been from producing 1,200 units and selling 1,400, had all transactions been exactly in line with standards. Column (4) shows the profit actually earned. Column 5(f) shows the total difference between col (1) and col (4): if the £800 (U) is deducted from 5(f) to give £7,050, we have the difference between (3) and (4). An alternative layout to that at Example One is shown at the foot of Column (5) to draw attention to the sales volume variance of £800 (unfavourable).

Note 1   Calculation of actual raw material cost for entry into col 4

	Raw Material A		Raw Material B	
		£		£
Opening stock at standard	6,000	3,000	7,000 at 1.60	11,200
Purchases during August at standard	28,000	14,000	60,000	96,000
	34,000	17,000	67,000	107,200
Less: closing stock at standard	24,000	12,000	43,200	69,120
Usage at standard	10,000	5,000	23,800	38,080

Add unfav/(deduct) favourable RM price variances

on full purchases	28,000 at 50p	14,000	60,000 at 1.60	96,000	
less: actual cost price		13,720	actual cost price	97,200	1,200
charge to column (4) (ensuring full price variance charged)		(280)			39,280
					4,720
		£4,720			£44,000

Total at column (4)

Usage variances

	A	B
Actual usage standard prices	£5,000	£38,080
less:		
Standard entitlement at standard prices 1,200 × £4	4,800	
1,200 × £32		38,400
Favourable/(unfavourable)	(200)	320
Total usage variances (Favourable)		£120

Note 2   Calculation of Direct labour variances

			£
Standard hours allowed for current production	1,200 × 6 = 7,200		
at standard rate per hour (£2)			14,400
Actual hours worked		7,500	
at standard rate per hour (£2)			15,000
(1) Efficiency variance (unfavourable)			£600
Actual hours at standard rate			15,000
Actual hours at actual rate			15,750
(2) Rate variance (unfavourable)			£750
Total Direct wage cost variance col (3) – col (4) (U)			£1,350

Note 3   Expenditure variance =
col (1) – col (4)
= £700 Favourable
Volume variance =
col (3) – col (1)
= £5,400 Unfavourable

As in this next case, some questions contain two sections, the first requiring the preparation of an operating or profit statement, the second some interpretative comment on the results obtained. To answer the second part with any enthusiasm, you should stand in the place of an imaginary owner of the business upon which you are reporting, and try to answer your own questions. The centre point of your comments should be *actual profit,* and why it differed from expectations. To give your answer credibility you need to practise ferreting out possible causes of each class of variance. Marks do not appear to come easily in this type of question. When a question asks candidates to 'comment briefly' on results which have been obtained at an earlier part of the question, there are two possible categories of response: (1) *interpretative* comment, indicating in a nutshell what the actual profit was, and mentioning among other things the total profit variance (total of column (5)): (2) *investigative* comment, indicating areas of concern, and possible causes of variances. It would appear that a heavy proportion of marks is awarded for the latter category. In addition the allocation of adequate time to the narrative aspects of such a question is a prerequisite of high marks.

Example Three
(ICAS Management Accounting Examination, Spring 1978)
The Handyman Company has organised its activities into product divisions and each product has an internal transfer price which assumes a profit of 10% on the budgeted costs at the beginning of each year. The company operates a system of flexible budgetary control and standard costing to measure the performance of each division.

In the hacksaw blade division steel sheet is sheared into squares which in turn are punched into hacksaw blades. The blades are transferred to the finished goods store from which they are sold to other divisions within the company. The weight of each finished blade is 2lbs and a standard allowance of 10% of the weight of the finished blade is included in the standard materials cost of the blades to provide for the weight loss in punching and shearing.

In the budget standards have been set at 75p per lb for the purchase of raw materials and 25p per lb for the sale of scrap.

The following information is available for Period 1 19X8:

	Budget	Actual
Raw material:		
Purchases	3,000 lbs	2,800 lbs
Cost of purchases	£2,250	£1,960
Issues	2,200 lbs	2,240 lbs
Shearing and punching costs:		
Labour	£500	£560
Overhead: Variable	£200	£186
Fixed	£200	£224
Blades finished and sold	1,000	950
Sales value of scrap	£50	£68
Sales value of blades	£2,750	£2,613

Raw materials stocks are valued at standard materials cost and finished goods stock is valued at full standard cost.

Required
1. Prepare a profit statement for period 1 incorporating variances and comparing actual results with budgeted results.
2. Comment briefly on the results shown in the statement.

The Handyman Company: Hacksaw Blade Division – Profit statement for period 1

	(1) Original Budget		(2) Adjustments into line with actual activity		(3) Revised standard charge		(4) Actual Profit & Loss A/c		(5) Variances affecting Profits (£)					
									(a) Sales Price	(b) Sales Volume	(c) Fixed O/head Exp.	(d) Fixed O/head Vol.	(e) Cost	(f) Total
	Units	£	Units	£	Units	£	Units	£						
Sales	1,000	2,750	50	137.5	950	2,612.5	950	2,613	0.5 (F)					0.5 (F)
Cost of Sales	1,000		50		950		950							
Direct materials (Notes 1 and 2)		1,600		80		1,520		1,472				Note (2)	48 (F)	48 (F)
Direct Labour		500		25		475		560					85 (U)	85 (U)
Variable Overheads		200		10		190		186					4 (F)	4 (F)
Fixed Overheads		200		10		190		224			24 (U)	10 (U)		34 (U)
Total cost of sales	1,000	2,500	50	125	950	2,375	950	2,442						
Profit	1,000	250	50	12.5	950	237.5	950	171	0.5 (F)	12.5 (U)*	24 (U)	10 (U)	33 (U)	79 (U)

* transferred across from foot of column (2)

Notes on Profit Statement

		£
1.	Direct material costs	
	Column (1) 100 × 2.2lbs × 75p	1,650
	less: sale of punching & shearing loss	
	200lbs @ 25p per lb	50
	Net material cost	1,600
	Column (2) 50 × 2.2lbs × 75p	82.5
	less: sale of scrap 10lbs @ 25p	2.5
		80
	Column (3) 950 × 2.2lbs × 75p	1,567.5
	less: sale of scrap 190lbs @ 25p	47.5
		1,520
	Column (4)	
	Total actual cost given for 2,800lbs	1,960
	less: unused quantity (560lbs) valued	
	at standard cost 75p	420
		1,540
	less: actual income from scrap	68
		£1,472

2. Analysis of raw material cost variance (£48 (F))

	£
(a) Standard weight allowance for good blades	
produced (950) = 950 × 2.2lbs	2,090lbs
Actual weight used (given)	2,240lbs
Excess usage	150lbs
Raw material usage variance = 150 × 75p	£112.50 (U)
(b) Scrap selling price variance	
Actual scrap qty 2,240 − (950 × 2)lbs	340
Standard value 340 × 25p	£85
Actual income	68
Variance	£17 (U)
(c) Standard cost of total purchases 2,800 × 75p	2,100
Actual cost of total purchases	1,960
Raw material price variance	£140 (F)
(d) Extra scrap yield variance	
Expected scrap qty 950 × .2lbs	190lbs
Actual scrap	340lbs
Extra scrap sold above budget	150lbs
At standard selling price (25p)	£37.5 (F)

Summary

(a) Raw material usage variance	£112.5 (U)
(b) Scrap selling price variance	17 (U)
(c) Raw material price variance	140 (F)
(d) Scrap yield variance	37.5 (F)
Total raw material cost variance	£48 (F)

Part 2
From an actual sales turnover of £2,613 (col (4)) from the sale of 950 blades, the division made a profit of £171. This compares with an originally budgeted profit of £250 (col (1)) from the sale of 1,000 blades. At actual production and selling levels, the division would have made a profit of £237.50 (col (3)) rather than £171, if standard selling prices, standard costs and standard levels of efficiency had been achieved throughout the division. The actual profit of 7% on actual costs compares unfavourably with 10% originally envisaged (column 1).

The division has based its cost recovery and profit uplift on production and sale of 1,000 units; failure to achieve this target has reduced profits by £10 and £12.5 respectively (total £22.5).(See col (2) fixed overheads and profit lines.)

Disturbingly high labour costs resulted in an unfavourable direct labour cost variance of £85. It may be that the cheaper materials purchased (favourable price variance of £140) proved very difficult to work, and that longer times were taken in production than planned. Production problems with cheap materials can be evidenced also by an unfavourable usage variance of £112.50 which is alleviated by sale of excess scrap to derive a net unfavourable yield variance of £112.50 − 37.50 = £75.

In summary, much of the division's poor profitability probably stems from cheaper sheet steel purchases.

Example Four
(ICAS Management Accounting Examination, Spring 1974)
In this next example, three different departments are involved, each responsible for its own fixed cost recovery rate and absorption against its own production. The many performance riddles which management as a whole must face require segmentation into line with the company's distinctive organisation structure.

A brick-making company operates a flexible budgetary control and standard costing system. Bricks made and dried are passed through an inspection department before being fired in the kilns; on withdrawal from the kilns, a further inspection takes place before transfer to the finished goods yard. Scrap at each inspection stage is written off as having no value. The standard unit product costs incorporate the standard scrap allowances. The undernoted information is available from the budget and control accounts for period 1. All figures are thousands of units or thousands of pounds as appropriate:

	Budget	Actual
Bricks made and dried	100.00	120.00
Bricks sold	81.00	80.00
Making and drying costs		
Labour	5.00	6.10
Overhead – Variable	2.00	2.20
– Fixed	2.00	2.50
Kiln costs		
Labour	1.80	2.10
Overhead – Variable	1.80	2.20
– Fixed	3.60	4.50

Yard costs		
Labour	3.24	4.00
Overhead – Fixed	0.81	1.20
Sales value	24.30	24.80

Other information is –

The budget allows a scrap level of 10% at each inspection point. Actual numbers of bricks scrapped in period 1 are –

At 1st inspection point	15,000
At 2nd inspection point	6,300

Finished goods stock is valued at full standard cost.

There is no change in work-in-progress level at the end of the period.

The effective cost of materials is a royalty included in variable overhead.

Required:

1. For period 1, produce in summary form a statement incorporating variances, comparing actual results with budgeted results.

2. Comment briefly on the results shown in the statement.

Solution

This presentation shows a single column of monetary variances at column (5), with titles at a new column (6). At part 2 of the question, an amplification is shown initially on the pretext that the examination question might have called for a full-scale narrative commentary. Thereafter, the solution text reverts to answering the specific 'comment briefly' requirement. The double-bracketed sections cannot be completed in this particular question through lack of both information and examiner's instruction, but the framework wordings are included in this text as a guide to where comments would be placed if needed.

(1) STATEMENT OF OPERATING RESULTS

(All figures are thousands of £'s or units as appropriate)	(1) Original budget Units	(1) £	(2) Activity Change/Flexing of Standard Charge to Production Units	(2) £	(3) Flexed Budget/Standard Charge to Production Units	(3) £	(4) Actual Results Units	(4) £	(5) Variances affecting profits	(6) Description of variances
SALES	81	24.30	1	.3	80	24	80	24.8	.8 (F)	Sales Price Variance
COSTS OF PRODUCTION										
Making and Drying	100									
Labour		5.00	20	1.00	120	6.00	120	6.10	.10 (U)	D Labour cost var.
Overhead										
Variable		2.00		.40		2.40		2.20	.20 (F)	V Prod'n o/h cost var.
Fixed		2.00		.40		2.40		2.50	.10 (U)	Fixed prod'n o/h cost var.
		9.00		1.80		10.80		10.80		
Less: scrap – normal	(10)	—	(2)	(.30)	(12)	(.30)	(12)	—	—	
– abnormal			(3)		(3)		(3)		.30 (U)	Production Yield Variance
	90	9.00	15	1.50	105	10.50	105	10.80	.30 (U)	
Kiln										
Labour (Note 1)		1.80		.30		2.10		2.10	—	
Overhead										
Variable (Note 1)		1.80		.30		2.10		2.20	.10 (U)	Var prod'n o/h cost var.
Fixed (Note 1)		3.60		.60		4.20		4.50	.30 (U)	Fixed prod'n o/h cost var.
		16.20		2.70		18.90		19.60		
Less: scrap – normal	(9)	—	(1.5)	.84	(10.5)	.84	(10.5)	—	.84 (F)	Production Yield Variance
– abnormal			4.2		4.2		4.2			
	81	16.20	17.7	3.54	98.7	19.74	98.7	19.60	.14 (F)	
Yard Costs										
Labour (Note 2)		3.24		.708		3.948		4.00	.052 (U)	D Labour cost var.
Overhead										
Variable (Note 2)		—		—		—		—	—	
Fixed (Note 2)		0.81		.177		.987		1.20	.213 (U)	Fixed o/h cost var
TOTAL CURRENT COSTS	81	20.25	17.7	4.425	98.7	24.675	98.7	24.80	.125 (U)	
Less: Closing stock (Note 3)		—	(18.7)	4.675	(18.7)	4.675	(18.7)	4.675	—	
COST OF SALES	81	20.25	(1)	(.25)	80.0	20.0	80.0	20.125	.125 (U)	
PROFIT	81	4.05		(.05)		4.0		4.675	.675 (F)	

(Amplification of part 2 of examination question into full-scale report)

ALPHA LIMITED
Results for period 1

1. *Results and Comparisons*

   From a turnover of £24.8, the company made a profit of
   £4.675 for the period (18.8% on sales), [[the net profit
   represents____% on capital employed of £____]].
   The actual turnover for the period is up £0.5 (2%) on budget,
   and the profit is up by £0.625 to 18.8% on sales. [[The actual
   capital employed of £____is only____% of budgeted capital
   employed, so that a return of____% on capital employed
   compares very favourably/badly with budget (____%).]]
   At our actual sales and production activity levels we could have
   achieved a profit of £4.0, if actual selling prices, costs,
   general efficiency and scrap levels had been in line with budget.
   That we actually achieved £4.675 illustrates the overall
   effects of selling price increases, cost increases and decreases
   and general improvements or disappointments in the use of our
   resources.

2. *Significant Variances*

   (a) *General review*

   Four departments have contributed to the overall results.
   - (1) Making and Drying
   - (2) Kiln
   - (3) Yard
   - (4) Sales and marketing

   (1) On a throughput of 120 units (budget 100) the *Making and
   Drying Department* incurred costs of £10.80, although for the
   good output achieved of 105 the allowed cost level was £10.50
   The only significant variance was caused by the scrap level of
   12.5%, the cost of the excess scrap over budget 10% being
   £0.30.
   (2) Again, the *Kiln* had to cope with an activity level of 105
   units against a budget of 90 units. Increased costs of
   operating the Kiln caused cost variances of £.40 on overheads,
   but the situation was relieved by a significant reduction in
   the level of scrap to 6% against budgeted scrap of 10%.
   (3) The *yard* handled 98.7 units against a budget of 81 units.
   Operating expenses have risen particularly for fixed overheads,
   and this is a cause for concern.
   (4) There was a decline in units sold of ONE against budgeted
   sales of 81 units. This had the effect of reducing the standard
   profit expectation by £0.05 from £4.05 to £4.00.
   However a price rise of £0.01 per unit resulted in an increase

in profits of £0.8 against the profits which would have accrued on actual sales of 80 had prices been pegged.

2. (b) *The cost of abnormal scrap levels*
The anomaly between the two production departments is a cause for concern as it reflects possible weaknesses in inspection policy. However the net effect between the two departments is favourable.

2. (c) *Stock levels*
The closing stock level of 18.7 units when related to a budgeted closing stock of NIL gives cause for great concern, in particular because
(1) It co-incides with a decline in sales turnover against budget.
(2) fixed expenses of £1.43 are included in the closing stock valuation and will need to be faced and recovered in ensuing periods. $(18.7 \times (\frac{2}{90} + \frac{3.6}{81} + \frac{0.81}{81})$
(3) it may reflect an acute unwillingness on the part of customers to pay higher prices.

3. *Possible causes of variances*
The following possible causes are put forward for consideration.
(1) Insufficient time spent on budgeted cost details (all departments).
(2) Failure to distinguish clearly between fixed and variable expenses (especially in the Yard).
(3) Too stringent quality control of Making and Drying Department output, causing a sharp decline in scrap levels in the Kiln.

4. *Profit Margins*
(a) *General*
The profit margin of 18.8% on sales depends on carrying forward unbudgeted closing stock of 18.7 units at full cost.
In itself the unbudgeted price rise to customers does not seem excessive, but without it the profit margin would have dropped to 16.1%. $((\frac{4.675 - .8}{24}) \times 100\%)$.

The valuation of unsold bricks at full cost including costs incurred in maintaining and depreciating production facilities could cause severe problems in later periods.
(b) *Significance of level of capacity/activity and stock valuation*
In valuing stock a budgeted level of production activity of 100 units in the Making and Drying department has been used for the recovery of fixed expenses, 90 for the kiln and 81 for the Yard. This has had the effect of *increasing* the overhead recovery rate per unit used in closing stock valuation. This is a dangerous practice if the actual level of 120 units is the normal level for the M & D department, 108 for the Kiln and 97.2 for the Yard.

5. *Availability of Capacity*
   [[At the actual production level of_____units,_____% of practical
   capacity was utilised, leaving plenty of/some/no room for
   expansion.
   Market capacity is presently fully utilised/under utilised]].
6. *Conclusion*
   Period 1 results must be read with caution. The key objective
   must be to increase sales turnover. Although the product sold
   is non-perishable, there are limits to the company's capacity
   to stockpile in the yard. It is possible that the production
   activity level during ensuing periods may need to be reduced until
   stocks are reduced.
   'Comment Briefly' (Specific examination requirement)
   1. From a turnover of £24.8, the company made a profit of
      £4.675 for the period (18.8% on sales).
   2. The actual turnover for the period is up £0.5 (2%) on
      budget, and the profit is up by £0.625 to 18.8% on sales.
   3. The profit margin of 18.8% on sales depended on carrying forward
      unbudgeted closing stock of 18.7 units at full cost.
   4. In itself the unbudgeted price rise to customers does not seem
      excessive, but without it the profit margin would have dropped
      to 16.1%.
   5. The valuation of unsold bricks at full cost including costs incurred
      in maintaining and depreciating production facilities could cause
      problems in later periods.
   6. The very high unbudgeted closing stock could illustrate acute
      unwillingness of customers to accept higher prices.
   7. Certain fixed costs may in fact be variable, in particular as regards
      yard overhead expenses.
   8. The inspection of bricks leaving the Making and Drying department
      may be too stringent, and this may be resulting in bricks of
      unusually high quality reaching the Kiln where scrap levels are
      well below budget.

Example Five
Frederick Bloggs between attempts at the CA exams – Part II – becomes a
part-time baker: he makes and sells currant buns, fern cakes and almond
fingers. He expected to sell a total of 3,000 items in January 19X9, com-
prising equal numbers of all three products. His standard variable costs and
selling prices per unit for each item is as follows:

	Currant Buns	Fern Cakes	Almond Fingers
	pence	pence	pence
Material	1	2	2.5
Labour	0.5	1.5	1.5
Variable overhead	0.5	0.5	1
Total	2	4	5

Standard selling prices	6	7	8
Contribution per unit	4	3	3

Mr Bloggs expected his fixed expenses for January 19X9 to be:

	£
Bakery	30
Selling	15
Administration	15
Total	60

He generally apportions fixed expenses across products on the basis of budgeted activity levels: there are no opening and closing stocks of products: in any case fixed expenses must be written off in the period in which incurred. An analysis of actual results for the month shows:

(1) *Production and sales*
    quantities and prices

		£
Currant buns	800 @ 7p	56
Fern cakes	1,100 @ 7p	77
Almond fingers	1,300 @ 8.5p	110.50
	Total	£243.50

(2) *Costs*

	£
Materials	60
Labour	30
Variable overhead	28
Bakery fixed costs	41
Selling	9
Administration	16
	184

Required: prepare a statement which compares actual and budgeted results.

Frederick Bloggs: Statement of Performance for January 19X9

Line refs		Budget				Actual			
		C/ Buns	F/ Cakes	A/ Fingers	Total	C/ Buns	F/ Cakes	A/ Fingers	Total
	Sales quantities (units)	1,000	1,000	1,000	3,000	800	1,100	1,300	3,200
1.	*Sales at standard (£)*	60	70	80	210	48	77	104	229
2.	*Variable cost of sales (at standard) (£)*								
3.	Material	10	20	25	55	8	22	32.5	62.5
4.	Labour	5	15	15	35	4	16.5	19.5	40
5.	Variable overhead	5	5	10	20	4	5.5	13	22.5
6.	Total variable costs	20	40	50	110	16	44	65	125
7.	Budgeted contribution	40	30	30	100				
8.	Standard contribution on actual sales, standard selling prices (£)					32	33	39	104
9.	Add/(deduct) favourable/(unfavourable) price variance (See note 1)	8	—	6.5	14.5	8	—	6.5	14.5
10.	Add/deduct favourable/(unfavourable) sales volume variance – quantities (See note 2)	2.68	2.01	1.98	6.67				
11.	Add/deduct favourable/(unfavourable) sales volume variance – mix (See note 3)	(10.68)	.99	7.02	(2.67)				
12.	Standard contribution on actual sales, actual selling prices (£)	40	33	45.5	118.5	40	33	45.5	118.5

Line refs		C/ Buns	F/ Cakes	A/ Fingers	Total	C/ Buns	F/ Cakes	A/ Fingers	Total
12.	Standard contribution b/fwd (£)	40	33	45.5	118.5	40	33	45.5	118.5
13.	Fixed costs (at standard) (£)								
14.	Bakery	10	10	10	30	10	10	10	30
15.	Selling	5	5	5	15	5	5	5	15
16.	Administration	5	5	5	15	5	5	5	15
17.		20	20	20	60	20	20	20	60
18.	Standard profit on actual sales, actual selling prices (£)	20	13	25.5	58.5	20	13	25.5	58.5
19.	Add/(deduct) favourable/ (unfavourable) cost variances (£)								
20.	Material					—	—	—	2.5
21.	Labour					—	—	—	10
22.	Variable overhead					—	—	—	(5.5)
23.	Bakery fixed overhead					—	—	—	(11)
24.	Selling fixed overhead					—	—	—	6
25.	Administration fixed overhead					—	—	—	(1)
26.	Net profit (£)	20	10	10	40	—	—	—	59.5

Note 1 Calculation of sales price variances (F) = favourable

Line refs		C/ Buns	F/ Cakes	A/ Fingers	Total
1.	Actual quantities	800	1,100	1,300	
2.	Standard selling price	6p	7p	8p	
3.	Actual selling price	7p	7p	8.5p	
4.	Difference: line 4 − line 3	1p (F)	—	.5p (F)	
5.	Line 4 × line 1	£8 (F)	—	£6.5 (F)	£14.50

Note 2 Calculation of sales volume variance − quantities

Line refs		C/ Buns pence	F/ Cakes pence	A/ Fingers pence	Total
1.	Standard unit selling price	6	7	8	
2.	Standard variable cost of sales	2	4	5	
3.	Standard unit contribution	4	3	3	
		Units	Units	Units	
4.	Budgeted quantity	1,000	1,000	1,000	3,000
5.	Actual quantity (properly mixed) say	1,067	1,067	1,066	3,200
6.	Difference (line 5 − line 4)	67	67	66	200
7.	Line 6 × line 3	£2.68	£2.01	£1.98	£6.67

Note 3 Calculation of sales volume variance − mix

Line refs		C/ Buns	F/ Cakes	A/ Fingers	Total
1.	Actual quantity (see line 5 above)	1,067	1,067	1,066	3,200
2.	Actual quantity (actual mix)	800	1,100	1,300	3,200
3.	Difference actual + /(−) standard	(267)	33	234	—
4.	Contribution per unit	4p	3p	3p	—
5.	Line 3 × line 4 Variance (Brackets = Unfav)	(£10.68)	£.99	7.02	(£2.67)

Frederick Bloggs
'Comment briefly on the results shown on your statement ... '
Results and Comparisons
1. From a turnover of £243.50 during January 19X9, Frederick Bloggs made a profit of £59.50; this compares with a budgeted profit of £40 on a budgeted turnover of £210. In terms of bulk, 3,200 items were sold, 6.6% up on budgeted bulk of 3,000 items.
2. An unbudgeted increase in selling prices effected an improvement in the profit position of £14.50 against budget; the market for Mr Bloggs' produce was undamaged in that there was also an increase in volume, achieving a further gain in profits against budget of £4. However, the sales performance for currant buns, the highest contributor to profits on a per unit basis, is disappointing and a profit shortfall of £8 against budget on this line is alleviated by gains on fern cakes and almond fingers.

3. At actual selling activity levels, the profit of £59.50 would have been £44 if selling prices, cost prices and rates and efficiency levels had been exactly in line with budgets and standards. The difference of £15.50 is the accumulated effect of selling price increases, efficiencies in the use of resources and economies in costs and buying prices. (£15.5 = 14.5 + 2.5 + 10 + 6 − (5.5 + 11 + 1)).
4. Regarding costs, bakery fixed overheads are far in excess of budget, but there was a sharp decline of 25% on variable direct labour costs.

Matters for concern
5. Budgeting of costs appears somewhat haphazard, with significant variances against many elements of cost.
6. The practice of apportioning fixed expenses across the three products sold has little merit; the contribution derived from each product to help to recover fixed expenses is of paramount importance, especially as an aid to sensible pricing and as a guide as to where to place emphasis in stocking and marketing policies. The budgeted net profit figures per item, of £20, £10, and £10 for C/Buns, Fern Cakes and A/Fingers respectively and the itemised standard profit figures at line 18, have an appearance of accuracy which is unjustified.
7. The fundamental and vital issue of comparative budgeted and actual time spent by Mr Bloggs in achieving the results shown cannot be ascertained by examination of the report. Ostensibly an actual net profit figure 48.75% in excess of original budget is very impressive, but this result could be disappointing if Mr Bloggs' additional time spent against budget is out of proportion.

Example Six
A company operates a flexible budgetary control and standard costing system. A summary of key figures from the standard product cost files for four products is shown below:

	A £	B £	C £	D £
Per unit −				
Material cost	10	12	8	15
Variable labour cost	3	6	3	9
Variable works overhead	1	2	1	3
Fixed works overhead	4	7	4	11
Standard margin	12	13	14	27
Variable distribution cost	2	3	1	4
Fixed selling overhead	5	5	5	5
Fixed administration overhead	4	7	4	11
Standard net profit (loss)	1	(2)	4	7

	Units	Units	Units	Units
Per annum −				
Budgeted production	15,000	5,000	20,000	17,500
Budgeted sales	16,000	6,000	20,000	15,000

A summary of trading figures for the year relative to the four products and the department in which they are produced is shown below:

Solution in SWE package

	A Units	B Units	C Units	D Units	Total Units
Opening stock	1,300	1,500	1,600	1,400	5,800
Produced	15,200	4,800	22,000	18,100	60,100
Sold	15,700	6,200	19,600	15,500	57,000
Closing stock	600	100	3,500	3,700	7,900

	£
Material issues	651,200
Variable labour costs	325,600
Variable works overhead	112,400
Fixed works overhead	366,100
Variable distribution costs	130,400
Fixed selling overhead	290,200
Fixed administration overhead	349,600
Sales	2,314,500

Required:
1. Present the total column of a summary trading statement for the year, incorporating variances.
2. Show a check reconciliation of the net profit without incorporating variances.
Note: Work in thousands to one decimal place. Value stock at standard cost of material, labour and works overhead.

SUMMARY TRADING STATEMENT

PART 1
(All amounts are thousands or units as appropriate)

Line Ref'ce		Budget Total Units	Total £	Actual Total Units	Total £	Notes
1	Sales at standard	57	2,295	57	2,314.5	1 & 2
2	Standard cost of production	57.5		60.1		
3	Material		632.5		657.1	3

4	Variable labour		292.5	303.3	4
5	Variable works overhead		97.5	101.1	5
6	Fixed works overhead		367.5	381.5	6
7			1,390	1,443.0	7 & 8
8	Standard incr/(decr) in stock	.5	50	90.4 / 3.1	
9	Standard production cost of sales	57	1,340	1,352.6 / 57	
10	Standard gross profit		955	961.9	
11	Standard gross profit-actual sales				
12	Standard selling/admin costs				
13	Variable distribution		130	131.6	10 & 11
14	Fixed selling		285	285	12 & 13
15	Fixed administration		351	355.1	14 & 15
			766	771.7	
17	Budgeted net profit (10 – 16)		189	190.2	
18	Standard net profit on actual sales (11 – 16)			190.2	16
19	Sales volume variance – mix		1.2		
20	Sales volume variance – qty		—		
			190.2		
	Cost variances				9
21	Stock loss			(23)	
22	Material cost (actual – 3)			5.9	
23	Variable labour (actual – 4)			(22.3)	
24	Variable works overhead (actual – 5)			(11.3)	
25	Fixed works overhead volume (6)			14	
26	Fixed works overhead expenditure (actual – 6)			1.4	
27	Variable distribution costs (actual – 13)			1.2	
28	Fixed selling volume (14)			—	
29	Fixed selling budget (actual – 14)			(5.2)	
30	Fixed admin volume (15)			4.1	
31	Fixed admin budget (actual – 15)			1.4	
32	Actual net profit			156.4	

Note 1

Product	Units SP (£)	Budget Qty (000)	Sales Value (£000)
A	30	16	480
B	40	6	240
C	30	20	600
D	65	15	975
		57	2,295

Note 2

Product	Units SP (£)	Actual Qty (000)	Sales Value (£000)
A	30	15.7	471
B	40	6.2	248
C	30	19.6	588
D	65	15.5	1,007.5
		57.5	2,314.5

Note 3

Product	Unit Mat'l Cost (£)	Budget Qty (000)	Budgeted Total Cost (£000)	Actual Qty (000)	Budgeted Total Cost (£000)
A	10	15	150	15.2	152
B	12	5	60	4.8	57.6
C	8	20	160	22	176
D	15	17.5	262.5	18.1	271.5
		57.5	632.5	60.1	657.1

Note 4

Product	Unit Variable Labour cost	Qty (000)	Budgeted Total Cost (£000)	Actual Qty (000)	Budgeted Total Cost (£000)
A	3	15	45	15.2	45.6
B	6	5	30	4.8	28.8
C	3	20	60	22	66
D	9	17.5	157.5	18.1	162.9
		57.5	292.5	60.1	303.3

Note 5

	Budget Unit Variable Works o/head cost	Qty (000)	Total Cost (£000)	Actual Qty (000)	Budgeted Total Cost (£000)
A	1	15	15	15.2	15.2
B	2	5	10	4.8	9.6
C	1	20	20	22	22
D	3	17.5	52.5	18.1	54.3
		57.5	97.5	60.1	101.1

Note 6

	Budget Unit Fixed Works overhead cost	Qty (000)	Total Cost (£000)	Actual Qty (000)	Applied Total Cost (£000)
A	4	15	60	15.2	60.8
B	7	5	35	4.8	33.6
C	4	20	80	22	88
D	11	17.5	192.5	18.1	199.1
		57.5	367.5	60.1	381.5

Note 7

Valuation of budgeted change in stock levels (( ) = decrease)

Product	Qty (000)	Unit Cost (£)	Valuation (£000)
A	(1)	18	(18)
B	(1)	27	(27)
C	2.5		95
D	.5		50
		38	

Note 8 Standard valuation of standard change in stock level (( ) = decrease) + (in view of actual sales)

Product	Qty (000)	Unit Cost (£)	Valuation (£000)
A	(.5)	18	(9)
B	(1.4)	27	(37.8)
C	2.4	16	38.4
D	2.6	38	98.8
	3.1		90.4

Note 9 Valuation of stock losses

Product	Qty (000)	Unit Cost (£)	Valuation (£000)
A	.2	18	3.6
B	—	—	—
C	.5	16	8.0
D	.3	38	11.4
	1		23

Note 10 Variable distribution costs – budgeted sales at standard

Product	Qty (000)	Cost	Total cost (£000)
A	16	2	32
B	6	3	18
C	20	1	20
D	15	4	60
	57		130

Note 11 Variable distribution costs – actual sales at standard

Product	Qty (000)	Cost	Total cost (£000)
A	15.7	2	31.4
B	6.2	3	18.6
C	19.6	1	19.6
D	15.5	4	62
	57		131.6

Note 12 Fixed selling costs – budgeted sales at standard

A	5	16	80
B	5	6	30
C	5	20	100
D	5	15	75
		57	285

Note 13 Fixed selling costs – Actual sales at standard

A	5	15.7	78.5
B	5	6.2	31
C	5	19.6	98
D	5	15.5	77.5
		57	285

Note 14 Fixed Administration overhead – budgeted sales at standard

Product	Cost	Qty (000)	Total Cost (£000)
A	4	16	64
B	7	6	42
C	4	20	80
D	11	15	165
		57	351

Note 15 Fixed Administration overhead – actual sales at standard

A	4	15.7	62.8
B	7	6.2	43.4
C	4	19.6	78.4
D	11	15.5	170.5
		57	355.1

Note 16   Calculation of Sales Volume Variance (Mix)

	A	B	C	D	Total
Budget (000's)	16	6	20	15	57
Actual (000's)	15.7	6.2	19.6	15.5	57
Actual +/(−) Budget	(.3)	.2	(.4)	.5	
Unit Profit	1	(2)	4	7	
Variance	(.3)	(.4)	(1.6)	3.5	1.2

Part 2   CHECK RECONCILIATION (£000)

Actual sales			2,314.5
Production costs			
Materials		651.2	
Variable labour		325.6	
Variable works overhead		112.4	
Fixed works overhead		366.1	
		1,455.3	
Increase in stocks:			
Difference between production & sales	90.4		
Stock losses	23		
		67.4	
Production cost of sales			1,387.9
Gross profit			926.6
Less:			
Distribution		130.4	
Selling		290.2	
Administration		349.6	
			770.2
Actual Net Profit			156.4

Example Seven

The profit budget for XYZ Ltd for 19X7 is shown below:

(000's)

Sales		3,000
Standard cost of sales		2,580
Gross profit		420
Selling expense	200	
Research and development expense	100	
Administrative expense	200	500
Net profit/(loss) before tax		(80)

An analysis by product of the above information appears below.

	Products			
	1	*2*	*3*	*4*
Sales quantities (000's)	200	400	1,000	1,000
Sales prices per unit	£1	£2	£1.50	50p
Standard costs per unit				
Material	20p	£1.00	60p	10p
Direct labour	30p	40p	40p	10p
Variable over head	10p	20p	20p	10p
Total variable cost	60p	£1.60	£1.20	30p
Budgeted fixed overheads	40,000	80,000	100,000	100,000
Total standard costs per unit	80p	£1.80	£1.30	40p

Actual sales turnover and costs for 19X7 were as follows:

(000's)

		£
Sales		3,100
Standard cost of sales (Note 1)	2,680	
Net standard cost variances	40	
Actual manufg cost of sales		2,720
Gross profit		380
Selling expense		220
Research and development expense		120
Administrative expense		210
		550
Net loss		(£170)

Operating statistics for 19X7 (000's) are as follows:

	Products			
	1	2	3	4
Unit sales	300	600	800	800
Price per unit	80p	£2.10	£1.60	40p
Production (000's)	300	600	600	600

There is no closing stock of any product at the end of 19X7.

Actual manufacturing costs:

	(000's)
Material	1,000
Labour	680
Overhead	700

Required: Prepare an analysis of variance between actual profits and budgeted profits for 19X7. Assume actual fixed expenses are the same as budget.

SUGGESTED SOLUTION: (See next page)

XYZ Limited: Operating Statement 19X7

Line Ref	Product	Budgeted					Actual				
		1	2	3	4	Total	1	2	3	4	Total
1	Sales (000 units)	200	400	1,000	1,000	2,600	300	600	800	800	2,500
2	Sales (at standard) (£000)	200	800	1,500	500	3,000	300	1,200	1,200	400	3,100
3	Production (000 units)	200	400	1,000	1,000	2,600	300	600	600	600	2,100
4	Standard costs of production										
5	Materials	40	400	600	100	1,140	60	600	360	60	1,080
6	Direct labour	60	160	400	100	720	90	240	240	60	630
7	Variable overhead	20	80	200	100	400	30	120	120	60	330
8	Fixed production overhead	40	80	100	100	320	60	120	120	60	300
9	Total (£000)	160	720	1,300	400	2,580	240	1,080	780	240	2,340

No.	Item						
	Add:						
10	Opening Stock (at standard)				260	80	340
	Line 1 – Line 3				1,040	320	2,680
11	Standard cost of sales		240	1,080			
12	Budgeted gross profit (2 – 9) 40	80	60	120	160	200	420
13	Standard profit on actual sales (2 – 11)	60	100	80	80	80	420
14	Sales price variance (actual at line 1 × (st – act) S Price per unit) (60) ( ) = unfavourable	(60)	(60)	60	80	(80)	—
15	Sales volume variance						
16	– Quantity						
17	See Note 1	(1.4)	(3)	(7.8)	(3.9)	(16.1)	
18	Sales volume variance						
19	– Mix						
20	See Note 2	21.4	43	(32.2)	(16.1)	16.1	
			180	240	180	240	420
						—	420

21	Fixed expenses at standard		
22	Selling	200	200
23	Research/development	100	100
24	Administrative	200	200
25	Standard profit (loss) on actual sales, actual prices		(80)
26	*Cost variances*		
27	Materials		80
28	Labour		(50)
29	Variable overheads		(50)
30	Selling		(20)
31	Research/development		(20)
32	Administrative		(10)
33	Fixed overhead volume		(20)
34	Profit/(Loss) (£000)	(80)	(170)

Note 1 (from Line 17)
Calculation of sales volume variance – quantity

Product	Actual @ Standard mix	Standard	Variance	Standard Gross Profit	Total (Line 17)
1	193	200	(7)	20p	(1.4)
2	385	400	(15)	20p	(3)
3	961	1,000	(39)	20p	(7.8)
4	961	1,000	(39)	10p	(3.9)
	2,500	2,600	(100)		(16.1)

Note 2 (from Line 20)
Calculation of sales volume variance – mix

	Mix Standard	Mix Actual	Variance	Standard Gross Profit	Total
1 2/26 × 2,500	193	300	107	20p	21.4
2 4/26 × 2,500	385	600	215	20p	43
3 10/26 × 2,500	961	800	(161)	20p	(32.2)
4 10/26 × 2,500	961	800	(161)	10p	(16.1)
	2,500	2,500			16.1

Example Eight
The final example reverts to the columns (1) to (5) layout and, like
Example Six, the solution to which was presented in the other format, in-
cludes the treatment of stock losses.

Given for ABC Ltd

Opening stock at standard cost	50 units @ £10 × £500
Production budget	200 units
Actual production	230 units
Actual closing stock	40 units
Actual sales	210 units
Budgeted sales	220 units
Budgeted selling price per unit	£14
Actual selling price per unit	£13
Variable (or direct costs) per unit at standard	£7
Fixed costs for the period	£1,000 (budget)
Fixed costs for the period	£1,100 (actual)
Actual variable costs	£1,380

Required: Prepare a statement showing actual and budgeted results, with
detailed variances. Value closing stock at full standard cost.
Ignore selling expenses. FIFO is in operation.

Treatment of Stock Losses

Line ref		(1) Original budget Units	(1) £	(2) Adjustments into line with actual activity Units	(2) £	(3) Revised standard charge Units	(3) £	(4) Actual Profit & Loss A/c Units	(4) £	(5)(a) Sales price Var. £	(b) Abn. stock losses £	(c) Cost £	(d) Fixed O/head vol. £	(e) Fixed O/head exp. £	(f) Sales vol. £	(g) Total £
1	Sales	220	3,080	10	140	210	2,940	210	2,730	210 (U)						210 (U)
2	Current Production	200		30		230		230								
3	Variable costs		1,400		210		1,610		1,380			230 (F)				230 (F)
4	Fixed costs		1,000		150		1,150		1,100				150 (F)	100 (U)		50 (F)
5	Total	200	2,400	30	360	230	2,760	230	2,480							
6	Add: opening stock	50	500	—	—	50	500	50	500							
7	Book stock available for sale	250	2,900	30	360	280	3,260	280	2,980							
8	Less: abnormal stock losses	—	—	30	360	30	360	30	—							
9	Net available for sale	250	2,900	—	—	250	2,900	250	2,980		360 (U)					360 (U)
10	Less: closing stock	30	360	10	120	40	480	40	480							
11	Cost of sales	220	2,540	10	120	210	2,420	210	2,500							
12	Profit	220	540	10	20	210	520	210	230	210 (U)	360 (U)	230 (F)	150 (F)	100 (U)	20 (U)	20 (U) / 310 (U)

(from col (2))

Unless specific guidelines are offered, an assumption must be made in such questions on the *timing* of any stock loss. In this case it is assumed that the missing units had full doses of cost attached to them prior to their 'disappearance', and also that they were a part of the total *current* production activity of 230 units. They have therefore been valued at the full current standard cost of £12 each, which comprises: (1) variable (or direct) costs per unit, £7 plus (2) fixed costs: $\dfrac{\text{£1,000 (Budgeted cost)}}{\text{200 (Budgeted production)}}$: (£5).

Clearly, if FIFO is in operation as indicated in the question, any stock produced in preceding periods and valued at £10 per unit (top line of question) will have been sold and its cost must remain in Cost of Sales rather than in any closing stock valuation.

The abnormal stock loss variance of 30 × £12 = £360 is a 'cousin' to the Production Yield Variance. The units involved are only those which were *unexpectedly* lost, in the same way that the units used in a production yield variance are those unexpectedly scrapped.

Closing stock is valued at standard cost in all columns, including column (4), this latter valuation being on the basis that the actual balance sheet will be showing the standard stock valuation. Column (4) deals strictly with 'actuals' and it is an actual fact that closing stock is to be valued at standard. An effect of this is to force the current period cost of sales at column (4), line 11, to bear the brunt of all variances. Line 10, columns (3) and (4), are taken to show a physically proven quantity: never use faulty book stock quantities on such a line.

Commenting on operating results

To revert finally to the narrative aspects of such questions, the basic contents may be committed to memory. Actual profit is the *essence* of any figure-work report, and any supporting comments must echo and reinforce actual profit and why it is not as expected.

Framework of typical answer to question:
'Comment briefly on the results shown in your statement'.

1. Actual results in a nutshell	Turnover
	Actual profit
	Gross profit % of sales
	Profit % of capital employed
	Profitability
2. Comparisons	Actual profit with original profit
	Actual profit with revised profit
	Actual profitability with budgeted profitability
	Actual turnover with original turnover
3. Significant variances	Highlight and quantify: offset with other variances
4. The cost of abnormal scrap levels	Quantify: offset with other variances
5. Possible causes of variances	See Chapter Eleven for potential causes

6. Significance of product mix changes

Quantify sales volume variance, analysed if possible between quantity and mix

7. Profit margins

Contribution level
Gross profit level
Net profit level
(Gross profit % shows extent to which manufacturing and admin costs may be allowed to rise without increase in selling price)
Significance of financing charges

8. Availability of capacity

For expansion

9. Usage of capacity

Whether additional hours worked have resulted in additional saleable output

10. Waste of capacity which must still be paid for

Fixed expense costs are based on maintaining facilities to produce in a state of readiness

11. Significance of level of capacity chosen for overhead recovery

Overhead rate should be based on normal practical capacity

12. Significance of stock valuation and of stockholding versus budget

Stockholding represents delayed charging of costs because ensuing period will benefit

13. Provisos/assumptions

Eg 1. 'It has been assumed that stock should be valued to include all works cost and admin costs'
2. 'It has been assumed that scrap was discovered at point of completion'
3. 'It has been assumed that 'in line with budget' means that unit cost rates, eg for raw materials, were as expected. Consequently flexing of budgeted costs has taken place according to activity levels'
4. 'Raw material price variances have been calculated at the time of material purchase rather than at the time of requisitioning from stores'

Guidance on Interpretation of Results

In commenting on operating results it is vital not to jump to conclusions on the strength of a single variance. All variances must be digested and a consensus formed. For example, in a typical question there could be a massive favourable sales price variance, but if you took the time and trouble to look

around your operating statement you could find a massive unfavourable
sales volume variance, and perhaps some unfavourable production cost
variances, indicating an unbudgeted change in product quality (extra costs)
which involved an unbudgeted sales price uplift, but which was not at all
popular among potential customers: overall result, negative.

Two or more variances can emanate from the same root source; for
example a decision to buy cheaper materials than budgeted can cause a
favourable raw material price variance, but there can be extra difficulties in
trying to work with such materials, causing extra raw material scrap, and
perhaps declines in labour efficiency. Look at the entire canvas of operating
results before drawing your conclusions.

CHAPTER 11

CAUSES OF VARIANCES

Over the task of ensuring the credibility of standard costing hang the threats of attributing wrong causes to variances, and of succumbing to the parallel lure of forcing managers concerned to produce plausible causes of variances for the sake of appearances when these can be no more than guesswork. While management should be seen to be in command of the nuances of the evidence, possible causes of deviations from plan may best come out in malleable flows of conversation rather than in stereotyped reports. However, as regards the more familiar variances which we have already considered, there is a catalogue of accepted wisdoms which is worth presenting. Some of the causes shown are received in practice with gallows humour because they are difficult, and in some atmospheres of minimum co-operation, virtually impossible to eliminate. In short, variances may have the appearance of credibility and be a stark deception, or they may be incisive in exposing deviations from plan while, as non-controllable, they provoke little more response than a helpless shrugging of management shoulders. The most likely causes of key variances are listed below: each factor has to be *unexpected,* or present to a greater or lesser degree than expected, before a variance can be caused, as anticipated factors will be built into standards.

1. *Raw Material price:*
    (a) a general increase in market prices, agreed by all or most suppliers: or a change in prices peculiar to a company's own supplier(s).
    (b) a change in quality caused by the usual (or standard) quality not being available. This could be caused by world or national shortage, but also by expansion within the company resulting in having to look to other suppliers for the additional material requirements.
    (c) buying in small quantities, causing loss of discounts and/or additional freight costs added to price: alternatively, bulk buying to reduce costs. Buying in small quantities can be the result of a positive stock reduction programme, but such purchases can result in loss of discounts, and in additional freight charges and supplier's setting up costs being charged.
    (d) inadequate information about sources of supply resulting in vulnerability to price increases.

2. *Raw Material usage:*
   (a) deviations from planned quality. This cause could possibly be evidenced by a compensating favourable price variance.
   (b) deviations from expected wastage levels caused by changes in handling or loading arrangements, or changes in levels of skill or care exercised by operatives.
   (c) deviations in the quality of work performed by earlier departments.
   (d) higher or lower standard of machine capability, perhaps caused by changes to maintenance timing and frequency.
   (e) production tooling modifications.
   (f) inability to measure actual usage accurately, through lack of precision equipment or through non-availability or by-passing of equipment.
   (g) unusual operating conditions, eg a second shift, or night shift.

3. *Direct Labour rate*
   (a) a wage agreement (details of which were not anticipated).
   (b) wrong grade of labour.
   (c) a change in operating conditions, eg involving working with 'difficult' material.
   (d) an unscheduled productivity scheme, whereby operatives receive higher wages per hour for producing more output units per hour.

4. *Direct Labour efficiency*
   (a) operations not being performed in accordance with standard procedures.
   (b) the amount of output which can be achieved in one hour may have been misjudged when standard of performance (output level per hour) was assessed.
   (c) idle time charged to direct labour. Idle time may arise when waiting for instructions, or during 'bottlenecks' in departments handling earlier processing stages, or when machines have broken down or are under preventive maintenance. Conversely, productive time may be charged to idle time, so that the direct hours charged are reduced on work records and output achieved appears unexpectedly high.
   (d) deviations from planned material qualities causing a change in speed of handling and throughput.
   (e) an unscheduled productivity scheme (see 3(d) above).

5. *Fixed production overhead volume*
   (a) misjudgment of *total capacity* available for possible use when budgeted output in standard hours was calculated.
   (b) misjudgment of *practical capacity* level (ie total capacity less deductions for stoppages etc) likely to be available when budgeted output in standard hours was calculated. (Re (a) and (b), it is assumed that the fixed production overhead recovery rate is based on recovery of budgeted fixed costs against budgeted output (ie that budgeted output is normal)).
   (c) an increase or decrease in actual hours directly charged, without any

alteration to efficiency levels (ie a capacity variance without any compensating efficiency variance: capacity + efficiency = volume).

(d) an increase or decrease in efficiency levels without any deviation from plan in the number of hours directly charged: this may be caused by an unscheduled productivity scheme.

(e) miscalculation of the level of output which can be expected in one hour's operation (ie the efficiency level).

(f) a change in the level of customer demand.

(g) the emergence of a limiting factor which restricts production levels (eg oil scarcity), or conversely an unexpected increase in supplies of what was expected to be a limiting factor.

(h) failure to communicate to management that the consistent achievement of a given level of production is essential to recover the fixed overheads.

6. *Fixed production overhead expenditure*

(a) faulty cost estimation during budget preparation: this can be aggravated by uncertainty about impending inflation levels.

(b) increases or decreases in activity when there have been inaccuracies in distinguishing clearly between fixed and variable costs.

(c) introduction of unexpected new fixed costs because the company has inadvertently moved out of a relevant range of activity whereby fixed costs are no longer completely static in total.

7. *Production yield*

(a) misjudgment of normal operating conditions, and consequently of the output which can reasonably be expected within the operating period concerned.

(b) actual operating conditions may be more or less favourable than (correctly assessed) normal operating conditions.

(c) an unplanned wage incentive scheme.

(d) changes in labour grades used.

(e) capitalisation: replacing operatives and/or manual processes by machinery; or changes to the level of capitalisation.

(f) technological break-through, so that operatives 'tease out' more from the same machinery in the same time through better handling or timing, or through the exploitation of skills.

(g) operatives may be made responsible for handling greater quantities of raw materials, to improve productivity.

(h) changes in quality of raw materials.

(i) extra (reduced) manning so that more (less) is produced in one departmental hour, but there is a higher (lower) wage bill per hour.

(j) a change in supervision levels.

(k) changes in inspection standards resulting in a higher or lower failure rate of finished goods than expected.

(l) faulty measurement of output, caused by lack of, or by-passing of precision measuring equipment.

(m) non-standard quality of input, eg size or density of coal entering a coke production plant.

(n) departmental management may lose sight of key objective, eg to manufacture coke from coal, if they are given significant credits for unusually high yields of by-products (eg, following naturally from unusually low coke yields).

8. *Sales volume*
   (a) miscalculation of market demand when budgeted sales were agreed.
   (b) unexpected market developments such as new competition from other suppliers, or elimination of a competitor.
   (c) production problems filtering through to affect sales levels.
   (d) deviations in product mix, whereby the proportions of either higher or lower profit contributors are increased in relation to budgets.
   (e) whether or not a sales price variance is involved, a favourable sales volume variance may indicate that products are underpriced, or too high in quality for prices charged: the converse may also be true.
   (f) overspending against budget on selling costs, eg advertising. In general, while there may be a favourable volume variance, the company may have succumbed in the process to compensating unfavourable cost of sales variances.

Criteria for Investigating Causes of Variances

A variance is a symptom of a problem which has a cause. Whether investigation of causes is worth the candle is largely a matter of managerial experience and intuition. In many instances one can draw a parallel with a headache, which again is a symptom of a malaise which has a cause. If a headache is very severe, or persists, or recurs frequently, the sufferer is likely to probe causes and look for remedial treatment of causes, rather than resort to aspirins to alleviate the headache symptom. Thus if a variance is very large, or takes place over, say, three consecutive periods, or is likely to strike at several monthly performance reports within a year, the company concerned is likely to deploy accounting and other functional management manpower in finding out reasons.

Relative and absolute size of a variance are two important characteristics which are weighed before time and money are committed to investigations. Relative size usually involves measuring a variance as a percentage of budgeted or actual cost, and the absolute size criterion would recognise the importance of probing any variance over a certain monetary size regardless of its size relative to budgeted or actual cost. Again size of variances may combine relative and absolute measures, eg a direct labour rate variance of a particular department might be probed if it was more than 2% of budgeted direct labour cost, provided the absolute amount was in excess of £1,000.

Degree of persistence of a variance is also important. Again, whether variances can actually be corrected after causes are found is a factor which has a bearing, along with the possible cost of attacking causes and eliminating the variances concerned, and the possible cost savings which would result from investigation and corrective action. The nature of a variance will also influence management as to whether a variance should be investigated. For example, many companies are concerning themselves with probing physical variances such as production yield, direct labour efficiency and raw material usage variances which respond to internal management action, while spending less time on variances which arise through misjudging inflation. Again, some favourable variances may trigger bonuses to employees: unfavourable variances could then become an emotive issue, which could provoke determined efforts by employee representatives to discover reasons for disappointing results.

CHAPTER 12

ENSURING CREDIBILITY

There is a clear dividing line between the problems of *setting up* and those of *operating* a standard costing system.

Setting up difficulties

(1) *Cost justification and company-wide management support*
Standard costing systems can be very expensive both to set up and to operate, so that cost justification becomes a prime difficulty. In some companies the proponents of standard costing are required to 'spell out' net cost savings which would be expected to emanate from the system. With this in mind, sets of typical variances in simulated format can be prepared, and direct questions can provide ingress to management's real needs: (a) Could it have saved you any money to have known about these?; (b) How much money?; (c) How soon would you have needed them?; (d) Would you ever have switched any of the business resources at your disposal on the strength of such information and could this have saved you money?; (e) Conversely, is lack of information in the right format and at the right time losing you money? Obviously these heavy questions have somehow to be handled in a lighter vein, lest the management accountant be regarded as lurking outside managers' doors like a bad fairy to signify their carelessness in the past. Normally a standard costing system is very broad based and involves most if not all of the business functions, and most if not all levels of management. It becomes important to canvass support from as wide a range of managers as possible, to spread the setting-up cost over a variety of functions, departments and locations likely to benefit from increased productivity, improved efficiency and cost control emanating after initiation (or start-up).

Setting-up costs require to be approved at budget time and grafted onto the overall costs to be borne by individual managers; this is a sensitive area. On the other hand, managers at the receiving end of attempts to charge actual costs to their departments or other responsibility areas when no costs have been budgeted are likely to go off like righteous roman candles.

The fact that standard costing tends to be all-embracing is both a help and a hindrance: a help because an aware manager does not like to go around wearing blinkers, but wants to see the ramifications of his actions elsewhere in the business: a hindrance in that *everyone* needs to be convinced of the worth of such an expensive system, rather than isolated management pockets.

(2) *Controllable and Non-Controllable Variances*
A second setting-up difficulty is in distinguishing between controllable and non-controllable variances. Their separation should be attempted while the system is still at the design stage. Distinctions are not easy to make unless related firstly to *costs*. Managers are more inclined to discuss control of costs than responsibility for creating and then 'taking blame' for variances. Many variances are initially listed as non-controllable and considerable persuasion has to be brought to bear on individual managers before agreement is reached that they are in fact controllable.

In practice it is often difficult to fix responsibility for a given cost because two or more persons may have a direct influence on the cost, or some person(s) may indirectly influence costs that appear to be under the direct control of another.

Turning then to controllable *variances,* the English Institute's book on standard costing has this to say: 'It is essential in standard costing statements to distinguish controllable variances from those which are uncontrollable. The distinction will depend upon the person for whom the accounting statement is prepared, because a particular item may be controllable within the business as a whole although not by the manager of a department which is affected by a particular item. A typical variance analysis will show efficiency variances for which responsibility must rest on the departmental managers concerned; whereas it must be the general manager and not departmental managers who is responsible for the capacity variances. Similarly, the materials usage variances are the responsibility of the departmental managers, whereas the material prices variances (if controllable at all) will be the responsibility of the buyer. This question of distinguishing between controllable and uncontrollable variances is therefore largely one of presentation and should be given careful attention in the construction of costing statements with the aim of ensuring:
  (1) That statements presented to any particular individual will distinguish clearly the variances for which that individual can properly be held responsible.
  (2) That statements presented to the general manager will indicate the individuals who can properly be held responsible for the variances shown.
  (3) That statements presented to the directors distinguish clearly those variances which are controllable within the business from those over which the business has no control.'

(3) *Level of Detail Required*
The optimum degree of detailed variance analysis is difficult to establish, and many mistakes can be made unless simulation tests are carried out at the systems design stage, or even earlier, at the feasibility stage, to test the

value of proposed variances to users. Each sub-variance has to be justified before becoming part of the routine reporting system. Variances which do not lead to any corrective action or to better resource deployment may do more harm than good, because they may weaken the impact of the whole report upon the reader, diffusing the focus of his attention. Conversely, if the level of detail finally selected is insufficient, with aggregate variances being produced which fail to answer management queries, ad hoc requests can pour in for manual back-up analysis to expose required levels of detail, and this can be very costly and time consuming. If, on the other hand, a demanding, precise level of detail is called for, in due course various unjustified assumptions may need to be made on an ongoing basis for force transaction data into over-detailed categories.

(4) *Lack of Experience Among Staff*
A fourth difficulty of setting up standard costing relates to the problems of lack of experience of systems investigation, planning, design and implementation among staff. This interesting area cannot be covered here, but it should be made clear that many problems stem from lack of clear definition of management's *future* as well as current information requirements, and failure to see the possibilities of improvement in information across a broad enough canvas: total systems which help everyone are the best but they are difficult and costly to produce. So often the lead is taken by a newcomer to the business who cannot know whether the conditions under which he is testing capacity usage, levels of activity, efficiency, material usages, and scrap levels are typical, or *normal*. Standard costing depends on so many estimates, and the greatest of these is the pre-vision of what normal operating conditions are going to be *like;* consequently there must be (a) detailed early enquiries across all functions, (b) flexibility in revision procedures when mistakes are found, and (c) sound knowledge of cost behaviour at varying activity levels.

(5) *Insufficient Details of the Past*
Most people know the old computer system adage 'Garbage in, garbage out,' the 'GIGO' theory, and a standard costing system of information output reporting can only be as good as the data fed into the system will allow. Often there is insufficient detail regarding past performance and costs available from the system preceding the standard costing system to enable trust to be placed in the first year's reports. There will usually be a serious lack of detail at product/process/job level on which to base standard product specification sheet information. There will be the temptation to make guesses, particularly if the introduction of the system is running to a tight deadline. To obviate the sharpest effects of insufficient data, there should be minimum arbitrary guesswork in the initial year(s), eg by relating reports solely to product groups, instead of individual products, or to high value products only, and/or to *routine* products which have consistent resource ingredients of materials, labour and overheads.

(6) *Initial Administrative Burden*
There is an accounting burden in preparing standard cost specification

sheets (SCS sheets) prior to start-up, for no immediate benefit. This can be a daunting task in periods of rapid technological change and when there is a wide range of products. This work-load has to be placed at a sensible point on the calendar, and manpower found to achieve it within deadlines. Nevertheless, a parallel can frequently be drawn with painting the Forth Bridge: no sooner are standards prepared than they require revision. A part-remedy is to avoid excessive detail on SCS sheets: for example, overhead charges may be categorised as 'variable works', 'fixed works', etc, without analysis into details such as machine power, works rates, maintenance, supervision, etc. Within an overhead charge there may be a 'buffer' to allow for changes without the laborious task of amending hundreds of product specification sheets, a task which would befall if each element was shown on SCS sheets concerned.

(7) *Timing of Output Reports*

Every adherent wants timeous reports from the system, but their timing depends on how early the raw data to generate the reports can be batched and fed into the system. In total reporting systems, providing information to everyone in the business, reports may all be delayed until the very last batch of inputs from the 'slowest' manager has been rushed in. The computer may have 98% of its input ahead of schedule, but this is hardly the point if the balance of 2% proves to be a few days late. Most systems nowadays have some form of cut-off procedure whereby late batches miss the computer run, or are the subject of some late routine which affords them ingress by a 'side-door'. In short, the speed of output reports to manager X may depend on the speed of data input to the system from manager Y. Friction can emanate from differing output reporting data requirements from potential management users.

(8) *'Forced' Standardisation*

In some companies conditions change rapidly and in addition no two products or jobs may be exactly alike. There is the danger of attempting to standardise dissimilar output for the sake of the system.

(9) *Training Needs*

At training sessions, so many participants insist on nodding their heads to signify understanding of points made when, in fact, they would be shaking their heads in bewilderment were it not for the fact that the clock indicated an alarming lateness of the hour. The key features of good training in this environment are (a) ample *discussions,* (b) training sessions involving simulation of planned operations with well prepared practical examples, (c) written procedures to support spoken presentations/lectures, (d) clear definition of individual responsibilities which will accrue from any new procedures.

Operating Difficulties

Many of the problems which arise on a day-to-day basis can be prevented through care and attention to details before the routine system commences. Assuming, however, that a conscientiously prepared system has been introduced, what form are operating difficulties likely to take?

(1) *Rapid Technological Change*
When operations are constantly marked by such changes, review of standard cost specification sheets is essential, more or less on a continuous basis, to prevent variances from becoming more and more unwieldy. The changes to specifications in this case are physical rather than merely to cost rates. They involve adding complete new entries or deleting whole lines, or completely re-working an entire sheet. One has to consider whether to create new standard cost specification sheets or alter existing ones. One of the defensive measures which may be taken is to streamline the system to cut out certain levels of variance, or to give an altered product a complete new entity in its own right with a new specification sheet: this latter course ultimately leads to sales volume variances caused by mix deviations, but overall, if management decisions have been well founded, any profit variances should be favourable and should reflect to some extent the merits of the improved technology.

(2) *Assessing Standards of Performance*
Most companies attempt at the initiation stage of a standard costing system to measure and introduce standards of performance which are attainable with some extra effort as compared with preceding periods. However, in a continually changing environment, adherence to this principle becomes quite a challenge. For example, there has to be a continuing fertile association between increased productivity and increased wages. The relationship between additional output and additional remuneration requires constant fine tuning. The threat of paying higher wages for meeting easily attainable standards of output lies over standard costing like a blanket. The corollary is an over-reaction whereby management become hardened in their conviction that the standards of performance can be substantially improved and new output targets become impossible to attain under normal operating conditions.

A choice has to be made when deciding on the level of output to be achieved from a given mix of resources. This output must be identifiable and capable of definition, eg given a descriptive measure such as tonnes or direct labour hours, and capable of measurement. Easily attainable standards of performance result in actual levels of output being frequently in excess of budgeted levels, as operatives are not required to extend themselves in reasonably determined efforts to improve 'throughput'. As a consequence, individual products may well be over-valued when valued at standard rates which call for costs to be spread over fewer units of output than actually materialise. In due course they may be over-priced on the market. A series of favourable variances in the nominal ledger will warn in such an eventuality, but these variances may be difficult and costly to relate via analysis to individual products/jobs. Fixed expense recovery rates are too high and over-absorption of fixed expenses takes place with resulting favourable fixed overhead volume variances.

A natural consequence of easy standards is complacency, with failure to achieve increased productivity and general growth. The converse is true when standards of performance set demand from employees more output than they are capable of achieving in the normal course of operations under normal conditions. Actual costs regularly exceed the standard cost entitlements in view of outputs achieved. Adverse variances appear throughout the nominal ledger, and stocks valued at standard, and ultimately standard cost of sales, are undervalued to the extent of the variance monetary balances. In extreme cases, staff may become demoralised and cease to care about adverse variances.

Most companies try to set standards of performance which are not easy to attain but which can be reached with some extra effort (in relation to previous demands made) under normal operating conditions. Such a policy attempts to secure continuing expansion of productivity which benefits both the organisation and its employees.

Whichever policy is adopted with regard to performance standards, output to be achieved from a given mix of resources can be adjusted by using negotiated efficiency ratios, which effectively increase or decrease the target levels of output to be sought in a given period. For example, if budgeted output at 100% efficiency was 100 units, a revised budgeted output would be 110 units if operatives agreed to work for the same number of hours (say 100) at a 110% efficiency rate. The benefits of this arrangement can be kept within the organisation: the customer pays standard rate for 110 units when costs incurred are for 100 hours. Alternatively, prices may be cut by one-eleventh in this case, so that prices are more in line with actual costs.

Standards which are ideal (difficult to achieve), easily attainable, or attainable with some effort under normal operating conditions each produce their own pressures. The amendment of standards of performance on a routine basis calls constantly for decisions as to which *type* of standard is preferable.

(3) *Departmental Inter-dependence*
One operating department can materially influence the performance of another: because there is so much inter-dependence, there is difficulty in establishing the controllability of variances. Is an efficiency variance attributed to a specific department really brought about by the actions of persons outside the department? Management believe wholeheartedly in the need for efficiency and its measurement, but if efficiency variances are laid at the wrong doors, the management accountant's periodic reports can be greeted with fits of the snarls and the snaps. Thorough research into operating conditions and a spirit of team-work can prevent awkward confrontations.

(4) *Variances at Wrong Levels*
Many so-called detailed variances are found in practice, and despite initial research, to be issued at an insufficiently detailed level, making discovery of causes difficult. An exercise can be undertaken to simulate various levels of variance to assess whether they are worthwhile and whether their causes *can* be resolved and at what cost in time and money.

(5) *Timing of Revisions*
If trends of favourable or unfavourable variances are developing, manage-

ment must decide when they are signalling the need to revise standards, or whether to introduce revision variances as a stop-gap. Decisions as to when variances have established themselves permanently must be taken in the light of future trading and operating conditions; then standards may be revised outright, *or* unwieldy variances may be slimmed down by teasing out those parts of total variances which are distorting overall comparisons of actual and budgeted results because they are caused by some *uncontrollable* factors which render the standards unrealistic. Revised standards should be carried through to a revised stock valuation, with credit being taken in the profit and loss account through, for example, a credit to a price variance account. This practice assumes that the revised standard cost of stock carried forward will be fully recoverable in ensuing periods.

(6) *Over-reaction by Management*
Management training towards interpretation of operating statements and variances included therein can obviate some of the threat of over-reaction to variances which may not require action, eg because cumulatively a situation will improve after initial production training is complete. Many standards are intended to apply for some time, and unfavourable variances during initial periods of new products or new techniques may well be planned, and later offset by compensating favourable variances which produce a net profit variance which is close to nil. In such cases, the optimum reaction may be no reaction.

(7) *Constant Need to Estimate*
Standards are based on informed guess-work about the potential behaviour of each resource of the business under future operating conditions. This feature leads to the need to segregate variances caused by misjudgment of costs or operating conditions from efficiency deviations which are manageable and which can be accentuated if worthwhile and eliminated if not. The standard cost of output, for example, requires estimates of normal scrap levels, which in turn depend on operating conditions being normal. Many companies operating standard costing have single, 'one-off' customer orders for which it is inconvenient for reasons of cost or administrative effort to prepare formal standard cost specification sheets. It is vital for estimating departments in such cases to use exactly the same criteria as are used in the preparation of standards: otherwise, estimated costs and quite possibly sales prices can be badly adrift.

Revision of Standards and Revision Variances
Standards will normally be revised at least once per annum, as they operate in conjunction with budgets which are prepared annually. During inflationary periods, however, quarterly budget periods are common; as each quarter's trading is completed, a fresh quarter's projection is added and an earlier quarter deleted so that a moving situation of one past quarter and three future quarters is maintained. In such circumstances it is clearly preferable to update standards so that at the detailed product level they remain comparable with totals at budget level.

Alternatively, annual budgets may be amended at some point in the year, but in such cases the original budget figures are retained on the reporting format. Standards are revised to support the accomplishment of the *revised* annual budget, but the difference between the revised budget and the original budget becomes a form of revision variance. In this way the company maintains a strong reporting tie-back to the original annual budget which has been the basis for so many plans. Total variances between actual costs and original standard costs are reported as well as variances between revised standard costs and actual costs.

Standards are intended to be a close approximation of actual costs. They are also intended as targets for management's future performance. However, as soon as these two criteria become unworkable, and quite apart from the annual reviews suggested above, the possibility of revising standards must be considered. Delay during inflation leads to faulty stock valuation with the possibility of inappropriate quotes and selling prices.

The following factors need to be considered:

(1) Whether the obsolescence of standards will continue for the foreseeable future, or whether the situation could be retrieved through management effort.

(2) Whether the future is certain enough to enable durable new standards to be agreed.

(3) Whether there is time and manpower available to undertake the tasks of revising standards.

(4) Whether, in the case of alterations to standards through technological and other physical processing changes, enough care has been taken in defining normal operating conditions and in establishing machine and operator capabilities, to establish new standards with confidence.

(5) Whether opportunities should be taken to compound levels of variance detail or conversely to introduce simplifications. In other words, it might be appropriate not only to revise standards, but also the standard costing *system*.

The frequency with which a revision is undertaken must, however, always be a matter for decision in the light of the circumstances of a particular business. A complete revision of standards will normally involve a considerable amount of work which ought not to be undertaken unless it is necessary; on the other hand, the work involved should not be allowed to act as a deterrent if the existing standards are sufficiently out of date as to make them no longer useful as standards against which to measure experience.

The introduction of new wage rates could lead management into a revision of standards rather than an analysis of the variance from the previous standard. Massive rate variances are all very well but frequently they will constitute a red alert to revise standards: variances may become less and less meaningful the further a company operates from the original base line of when the standards were set.

The alternative to revising standards is to continue to operate with standards which are known to be irretrievably out of date but to draw out from a total variance for a particular category of cost, that part of it which is caused by the standards being obsolete, and to classify this as a revision variance. A revision variance is therefore a profit variance brought about when the standard cost entitlement for a particular product, process or job is out of date, and part of the ensuing total profit variance is caused by failure to revise the standards concerned. In monetary terms, the revision variance quantifies the extent to which an out-of-date standard cost entitlement, usually debited to Work in Progress Control Account (or Cost of Production at standard) ought to be adjusted (normally upwards as far as obsolete standard cost rates or prices are concerned). On the other hand, improved technology or production methods frequently mean that the un-revised *times* allowed per standards are excessive and revision variances can counter the distortions to efficiency variances which are being caused by obsolete time entitlements. Revision variances are those segments of total variances which are caused not by poor budgeting or cost estimating on the one hand, nor by efficiency or inefficiency of operations on the other, but rather by failure to maintain up-to-date standards. Revision variances preparation and reporting procedures should continue while new standards cannot be set with any degree of accuracy and/or durability, eg when current cost patterns are unsettled, and unlikely to stabilise in the foreseeable future. Revision variances for a particular cost category, generally regarded as belonging to the 'non-controllable' class of such afflictions, are extracted to enable management to concentrate on resolving the balance of the total profit variance for that cost category, which thankfully has often considerable 'controllable' segments.

Example
Job X is evaluated as having a direct labour content of 5 hours, according to standards of performance currently in use in ABC Ltd. The standard direct labour cost is £2 per hour, but this rate now lags well behind the negotiated rates within the industry to which the company belongs, and is also unrealistic in the light of other local wage rates for compatible work. It is now felt that £2.60 would be a more realistic labour rate per hour. When time sheets and wages sheets are analysed in due course, however, Job X is found to have taken 6 hours to complete and the actual wage rate paid is £3.

Required: calculate direct labour variances.

Solution
Calculation of Direct Labour Cost Variance
   (1) Standard direct labour cost of Job X:
         5 hours × £2   £10
   (2) Actual wages paid: 6 hours × £3   £18
       Unfavourable variance   £8

(On the balance sheet, cash of £18 will have been replaced by sufficient work in progress stock to justify a standard evaluation of £10.)
Analysis
   (a) *Revision Variance:*
      (1) Standard direct labour cost of Job X:
         5 hours × £2   £10
      (2) Standard hours allowed (5) × £2.60   £13
         Unfavourable variance   £3

(b) *Rate Variance*

(1) Actual hours taken (6) × £2.60		£15.60
(2) Actual hours taken (6) × £3		£18
Unfavourable variance		£2.40

(c) *Efficiency Variance*

(1) Actual hours taken (6) × £2.60		£15.60
(2) Standard hours allowed (5) × £2.60		£13.00
Unfavourable variance		£2.60

Notice how the Revision Variance maintains the original number of hours allowed intact: the time to be taken (5 hours) is not considered suspect and in need of revision. As usual the Rate Variance is based on actual hours charged: despite an uplift of 60p to the more realistic sum of £2.60, someone has *still* approved an actual rate which is 40p above the 'going rate', so that the cause for concern, a rate variance of 6 hours at 40p (£2.40) can be considered *manageable*.

An alternative calculation of the Revision Variance as: 6 hours × £2 less 6 hours × £2.60 = £3.60 (U), with a compensating diminution of the Efficiency Variance to 6 × £2 less 5 × £2 = £2 (U) would switch the focus of attention from the extra hour spent, laying more blame on 'general inflation' and less on an internally created problem of allowing too leisurely a pace. In fact, the full efficiency variance of £2.60 as previously calculated has been directly condoned by management action and this approach of self-criticism ought to be taken by management in containing any future cost variance problems within reasonable bounds. Allowing an extra hour to be worked and paid for has directly cost the company £2.60: paying £3 for that extra hour has cost another 40p and this amount is laid at the door of personnel management (or whoever is answerable for such deviations) as part of the 6 hours × 40p (£2.40) rate variance. To 'pass the buck' for 60p of the £2.60 above into the unmanageable (or uncontrollable) Revision Variance would be contrary to sound principles. Moreover, such a policy could work against those concerned if, in due course, *fewer* hours were charged to similar jobs in the future than were specified in standards.

CONCLUSIONS

If variance analysis is to be used successfully, variances must be categorised in ways which will optimise management decision making and action. Towards this end, standards must be prepared with great care and, as far as is practicable and economic, kept up to date.

In addition, variances which are controllable by persons within the organisation should be segregated from those which are not controllable. The greatest care must be taken with the use of the word 'controllable'; what is controllable to the Board may not be to a works foreman.

Regarding the level of detail of variance analysis, those variances which are caused by deviations in rates of pay and prices of materials and overhead services must be segregated from those which are the result of operating efficiencies/inefficiencies. Basically these separate categories of variances are the responsibilities of separate sections of management.

Controllable variances in the 'efficiency' class should only be reported as such if the recipient (or his subordinate) is in control of the production variables such as the supply and quality of tooling, the quality of material to be worked, etc.

Continual emphasis of variances as being *profit* variances can encourage manipulation of input and output figures on, say, raw materials, especially if precision measuring equipment can be by-passed in favour of guesswork/estimating of quantities. Again, yields on by-products may be favourable whenever yields on main-products are not, and this credit or 'gain' on by-products can diffuse the attention of management away from the fact that the yield of the vitally important main product is not enough to meet later processes' needs.

Standard costing should lead to prolific discussions and enquiries, rather than their demise: questions are provoked by such a system more than answers are provided. The solving of riddles can be assisted by narrative comments supporting figure-work reports. As in an examination environment, the practitioner must take sufficient time and trouble with explanatory and investigative comments to encourage sound reactions to the figures from busy colleagues. Two or three lines, scrawled in a cornered-rat vein when the report issue deadline has already passed, discredit standard costing in the eyes of non-accounting management.

As standard costing has the name of being very technical, and hardly the province of non-accounting personnel, the management accountant must endeavour at all costs to have his company's system regarded and referred to by his colleagues as 'our system' rather than 'his system'. Nowhere else in the field of industrial accounting is team-work more important.

GLOSSARY OF TERMS AND EXPRESSIONS USED

Activity: the degree to which the capacity of an organisation has been exploited, usually expressed as a number of units of output (for production activity) or sales (for selling activity). It is essential when answering examination questions involving production or selling activity (or both) to define the *measure* of that activity (eg, steel blades, jars of jam, castings, passenger-miles), and then to identify the actual level of that activity which has been achieved (eg, 950 steel blades produced).

Budgetary Control: 'The establishment of budgets relating the responsibilities of executives to the requirements of a policy, and the continuous comparison of actual with budgeted results, either to secure by individual action the objective of that policy or to provide a basis for its revision.'[1]

Budgets: 'Financial and/or quantitative statements, prepared and approved prior to a defined period of time, of the policy to be pursued during that period for the purpose of attaining a given objective. They may include income, expenditure and the employment of capital.'[1]

Calendar variance: that part of a fixed works (or production) overhead capacity variance which is caused by a difference between the budgeted output in standard hours for a particular accounting period and the actual direct hours which were *practicable* and *available* within that period (but not necessarily worked). The budgeted output for a particular month may be based for example on one-twelfth of an annual budget, but that month may have less than one twelfth of the total practical capacity because of the incidence of holidays. The calendar variance is calculated by multiplying the difference between the hours of a *typical* or average period (month, etc) and the hours *available* in a particular period (month, etc) by the fixed works overhead recovery rate per standard hour.

Capacity: hours available for possible application to production effort. Capacity may be a theoretical maximum (eg, 7 days × 24 hours per day = 168 hours) or a practical capacity (eg, 5 days × 8 hours per day = 40 hours). Capacity can also be expressed in production unit terms, eg,'1,000 tonnes per week'.

Capacity Ratio: 'The actual number of direct working hours charged (in an accounting period) divided by or expressed as a percentage of the budgeted number of standard hours.'[1] A ratio higher than 100% indicates that more hours were utilised in practice that were earmarked (booked in advance), so that when direct operatives exploit these actual hours used at an efficiency of at least 100% (one hour's worth of output from one hour's effort), the production area concerned will produce an output level in excess of budget.

Contribution: the difference between the selling price of a product, process or job and its marginal cost.

Contribution Margin Ratio: that part of each pound of sales which can be set aside, after variable costs have been paid, to help to recover fixed costs and to boost profits.

Control accounts: are nominal (or general) ledger accounts which are maintained for stock accounts and debtors' and creditors' accounts, and which reflect the total situations to be found in detailed accounts within subsidiary ledgers. The use of the word 'control' implies that a subsidiary ledger is maintained, detailing separate subsidiary ledger accounts for each job, process, product, raw material or finished goods part, etc. The balance of a control account should always equal the total of the balances on the individual accounts in the subsidiary ledger.

Controllable variances: variances, the size and persistence of which can be influenced by persons within the organisation concerned. In reporting formats, variances which are controllable by persons within the organisation should be segregated from those which are not. In the presentation of a report to a particular individual the greatest care must be taken with the use of the word 'controllable'; what is controllable to the Board may not be to a works foreman.

Controllable costs: 'Costs which may be directly regulated at a given level of managerial authority, either in the short run or in the long run.'[3]

Cost rationing: This occurs when a firm sets an absolute limit on the size of one or more expenditure budgets, although benefits could arguably accrue if additional expense were to be incurred. The principal reason for such action is that some firms are reluctant to engage in external financing (borrowing or issuing shares): there may also be a fundamental worry about exceeding overdraft limits.

Cost Centre: the full title is 'cost collection centre'. It is an area of responsibility for which costs may be collected to promote business objectives, eg, the spreading of manufacturing costs over units of production passing through a particular centre. Cost centres are used as points of cost control, where actual and expected costs are compared by specific managers.

Cost Control: procedures whereby actual costs incurred at actual production and selling activities are compared on an ongoing basis against the costs which, according to pre-determined calculations, ought to have been incurred at such (actual) levels. Clearly original, budgeted cost levels have to be flexed or adjusted to bring expense entitlement levels into line with actual activities.

Cost of Sales: this may be 'the total cost of production, marketing, general administration and research and development, attributable to the products or services and during a specified accounting period'[1] or it may relate only to the production cost of sales, or to the production and administration cost of sales, depending on the level of profit assessment ('gross', 'net', etc) required. In any event, 'COST OF SALES' should have an appropriate prefix, eg, 'Total Cost of Sales' or 'Production Cost of Sales'.

Direct Labour: all labour which is directly chargeable by means of time sheets, etc, to specific products, processes or jobs without arbitrary splitting or apportionment.

Direct Labour Cost Variance: the total financial impact on the budgeted profit due at the actual production level, which is brought about by having to pay a different amount for direct wages than was expected (according to standards) at that level. This variance can often be analysed into rate and efficiency variances.

Direct Labour Efficiency Variance: that part of a total variance (between actual profit and the budgeted profit at actual output levels), which is brought about when the difference between actual direct hours charged and the number of hours which *ought* to have been charged (according to standards) at the actual production level is evaluated at the standard rate per direct labour hour.

Direct Labour Rate Variance: that part of the total variance above which is brought about by using actual hourly wage rates which differ from standard rates. The difference is evaluated using the actual direct labour hours worked.

Direct Material: raw material which, via invoices or stores requisition slips or other basic documentation, can be charged to specific products, jobs or processes without the need for some arbitrary re-apportionment, or guess-work as to how a total charge for that material can best be split over more than one product. Consumables such as paint and lubricating oil for manufacturing machinery are not regarded as direct materials when they can only be directly charged to departments or cost centres and then spread on some arbitrary basis over a number of products through inclusion in overhead recovery procedures.

Direct Material Cost Variance: the total financial impact on the budgeted profit due at the actual production level, which is brought about by having to use a different quantity of raw materials at different prices from standard. This variance can often be analysed into the usage and price variances.

Direct (or Raw) Materials Mix Variance: this variance comprises the difference between the actual quantity of mixed ingredients used, in *actual* proportions, valued at standard raw material unit prices, and the actual quantity used, in *standard* proportions, valued at standard raw material unit prices. Such a variance is only calculable when more than one raw material is being fed into the production process.

Direct Material Price Variance: better practice involves evaluating the difference between actual quantity purchased at standard buying prices and actual quantity purchased at actual prices. This variance is again a part of the total profit variance referred to previously: alternatively, actual quantities used may be substituted.

Direct (or Raw) Material Scrap Price Variance: the actual saleable scrap weight derived in practice times the standard selling price per measure of scrap: *less* the actual saleable scrap weight derived in practice times the actual scrap selling price per measure of scrap. A negative result in the above comparison indicates a favourable variance.

Direct (or Raw) Material Scrap Yield Variance: the number of units produced times the standard weight measure of scrap expected per unit times the standard selling price per measure of scrap: *less* the actual saleable scrap weight derived in practice times the standard scrap selling price per measure of scrap. A negative result in the above comparison indicates a favourable variance.

Direct (or Raw) Material Yield Variance: this variance may be that part of a *direct (or raw) material usage variance* which is caused by using excess or short measure of input bulk of ingredients mixed in standard proportions in a manufacturing process (as compared with standard total bulk allowed for the given production activity level). However when there is *only one* raw material ingredient, the direct material yield variance is the same as the direct material usage variance, in which case the latter expression is preferred. When more than one raw material ingredient is in use, R. M. Usage Variance = R. M. Mix Variance + R. M. Yield Variance.

Direct Material Usage Variance: that part of a total variance which is brought about by a difference between the quantity of direct materials actually used at the actual production level and the quantity which ought to have been used (according to standards) at that level. The difference is evaluated at the standard unit price of the materials concerned.

Downtime: time which is a part of the capacity of a manufacturing unit but during which production has ceased, either on a planned or unexpected basis. Budgeted downtime may be expressed as a percentage either of total capacity or of practical capacity. It may sometimes represent the difference between practical capacity (in hours) and activity (in hours).

Elements of Cost: (see Expense classifications)

Exception Reporting: Reporting operating performance or overall results in such a way that deviations between actual and planned results are highlighted to promote speedy remedial action on the part of recipients.

Expense Classifications: categories of cost which are used to facilitate the analysis of total expenditure into manageable and meaningful elements, so that deviations between actual and budgeted costs become more significant and can bring about management action. Examples: salaries; training costs; recruitment costs; travelling expenses.

Fixed Costs: those costs the total of which does not fluctuate with movements in activity levels: fixed production costs, for example, do not change with production level changes, and fixed selling costs are likewise insensitive to changes in sales activity. It must be remembered that fixed costs may remain fixed only within certain ranges of activity. For example, after a certain level of production has been reached, new machinery may be involved which necessitates additional fixed costs such as preventive maintenance and insurance.

Fixed Production Overhead Expenditure Variance: the difference between the budgeted fixed production overhead cost and the actual cost for an accounting period. This variance forms part of the total profit variance already mentioned.

Fixed Production Overhead Variance: the sum total of the fixed production overhead expenditure variance and the fixed production overhead volume variance.

Fixed Production Overhead Volume Variance: the extent to which budgeted fixed expenditure has been over- or under-absorbed (recovered) by units of production. The standard fixed cost recovery rate is multiplied by the excess of actual units over budgeted units or by the shortfall if actual production is less. This variance provides part of the explanation as to why actual profit is greater/less than the originally budgeted profit. This variance is only possible when absorption costing is in use.

Fixed Works (or Production) Overhead Capacity Variance: that part of a fixed works overhead volume variance which results when actual direct hours worked during an accounting period differ from the budgeted standard hours of output for that period. The hours worked may be direct labour hours, departmental direct hours or direct machine hours. When actual direct hours exceed the budgeted standard hours, the variance is favourable. The hours difference is multiplied by the fixed overhead recovery rate per standard hour.

Fixed Works (or Production) Overhead Capacity Ratio: that part of a fixed (or production) overhead volume ratio which shows direct hours worked in a period as a percentage of budgeted standard hours for the period. If direct hours worked exceed budgeted standard hours, the percentage is above 100% and the ratio is favourable. The basic data used are the same as for a simple capacity ratio (see separate definition).

Fixed Works (or Production) Overhead Efficiency Variance: that part of a fixed works (or production) overhead volume variance which results when actual direct hours worked during an accounting period are greater or less than the standard hours' worth of actual output in the period. The hours worked may be direct labour hours, departmental direct hours or direct machine hours: only chargeable hours are involved, not total clocked hours. When (a) actual direct hours worked exceed (b) the standard hours' output achieved, the resulting variance is unfavourable.

Fixed Works (or Production) Overhead Efficiency Ratio: that part of a fixed (or production) overhead volume ratio which shows standard hours of output achieved as a percentage of direct hours worked (expressed as a percentage). If standard hours achieved exceed direct hours worked, the percentage is above 100% and the ratio is favourable. The basic data used are the same as for a simple productivity or efficiency ratio (see separate definition).

Fixed Works (or Production) Overhead Volume Ratio: actual standard hours of output achieved expressed as a percentage of budgeted standard hours for the period concerned. If actual standard hours exceed the budget, the ratio is favourable.

Fixed Works (or Production) Cost (or overhead): a cost which accrues in relation to the passage of time and which, within a certain production output range of activity, tends to be unaffected by fluctuations in volume achieved.

Fixed Selling Costs (or overheads): see Fixed Costs.

Flexible Budget: a budget which, through recognition of the difference in behaviour between fixed and variable costs as activity levels fluctuate, can be revised so that the actual costs at any particular activity level can be properly compared with the costs which should have been incurred at that actual activity level.

Gross Capacity: maximum possible productive capacity, in hours or in production unit terms, eg, '1,000 tonnes per week'. *Practical* capacity is usually based on gross capacity less substantial deductions: for example, gross capacity might be 7 days × 24 hours = 168 hours per week and practical capacity might be 5 days × 8 hours = 40 hours per week if extra shift and weekend working were considered impracticable. Budgeted output in standard hours might be based on a further reduction from 40 hours to allow for downtime, waiting time, etc, so that the budgeted output might be based on 36 hours of actual operations (or net practical capacity or activity).

Indirect Costs: costs which cannot be traced directly to specific products, jobs or processes. The term may also be used to describe costs which cannot be traced directly to a particular cost centre; for example, a share of a works canteen total deficit would be an indirect cost to particular manufacturing cost centres whose employees used the canteen. At product level, the salary of a works foreman who did not charge his time to specific products would be an indirect cost to be included in product costs as part of overheads.

Non-Controllable Variances: Variances which occur as a result of events, circumstances or conditions outside the authority and spheres of influence of the management of an organisation, eg, general inflation within the economy or political events overseas. However a particular variance within an organisation may be assessed as controllable by one level of management and non-controllable by others.

Operating Statement: 'A summary of the operating costs (and where appropriate, of the income and profit margins) of the whole or part of the activities of an undertaking for a specified period. Note: where variance accounting is applied, operating statements will usually provide information regarding the units produced in the period, the comparison of actual and standard or budgeted costs, income and profit margins, and an analysis of the variances.'[1]

Prime Cost: the total cost of direct materials, wages and expenses. The term normally includes only production costs.

Product Cost: the total of those categories of cost which form part of stock valuation. Such costs can therefore be removed from the time period in which they were actually incurred, provided there is a closing stock of the product concerned which is expected to be saleable for at least the total of those costs, ie provided the costs are realisable in due course.

Production Volume Ratio: the relationship between budgeted output and actual output achieved, expressed as a percentage. When actual output exceeds budgeted output the ratio will be greater than 100%, and therefore favourable. Unless this ratio is to be analysed further, it is not necessary to convert budgeted and actual output to standard hours.

Production Yield Variance: see Yield Variance.

Productivity (or Efficiency) Ratio: the relationship between actual direct hours worked and standard hours' worth of output achieved. If the output hours exceed actual hours, the ratio will be greater than 100%, and therefore favourable.

Profit and Loss Account: 'A financial statement which shows the net profit or loss of a business for a given accounting period. A detailed profit and loss account will normally show the gross profit ... and the various expenses incurred in selling goods or services, and in administering and financing the business.'[1]

Profit Variance: a variance which is a constituent part of the total difference between an originally budgeted and an actual profit. The sum of all individual profit variances which are caused by deviations between actual and budgeted sales and expenditures is called the total profit variance.

Raw Material Variance: see Direct Material Variances.

Sales Price Variance: that part of a total variance between actual profit and what that profit should have been (according to standards) at that actual activity level, which is brought about by changing unit selling prices from standard to actual. The actual sales quantity is multiplied by the difference between the actual and standard selling prices

Sales Volume Variance: the difference between an originally, budgeted profit and an actual profit which is caused by selling more or fewer units than budgeted. The physical quantity difference is multiplied by the standard profit per unit, except when marginal costing is used, when the standard contribution per unit is used.

Sales Volume Variance: Mix: the actual sales quantities achieved, split between products in the proportions of the standard mix, and evaluated at standard profit per unit (or contribution per unit when marginal costing applies), *less* the actual sales quantities achieved in actual mix proportions, evaluated at standard profit per unit (or contribution per unit when marginal costing applies). When the latter half of the comparison is the greater, the variance is favourable.

Sales Volume Variance: Bulk: the budgeted bulk quantity evaluated at standard profit per unit (or contribution per unit when marginal costing applies) less the actual bulk quantity achieved, split between products in the proportions of the standard mix, evaluated at standard profit per unit (or contribution per unit when marginal costing applies). When the latter half of the comparison is the greater, the variance is favourable.

Scrap Ratio: that proportion of total production output which fails to reach the finished goods stock stage or the next production department. The total of the scrap ratio and the production yield ratio should be 100%. Alternatively, a scrap ratio may be a simple percentage of the total raw material input to production.

Standard Cost: 'A carefully predetermined cost that should be attained; usually expressed per unit.'[3]

Standard Costing: 'The preparation of standard costs of products and services.'[1] 'Product costing using standard costs rather than actual costs; may be based on either absorption or (marginal) costing principles.'[2]

Standard Hour: 'A hypothetical unit pre-established to represent the amount of work which should be performed in one hour at standard performance.'[1] Thus, if a factory produces 600 toy tricycles in a given period and ought to have taken 20 minutes of directly charged time per tricycle, 200 standard hours of output have been achieved. If, say, 180 hours are actually charged directly through direct labour analyses, there is a variance between *input* hours (180) and output achieved (200 standard hours) and when given a monetary evaluation, the difference leads to certain standard costing variances such as a direct labour efficiency variance.

Standard Performance: 'The rate of output which qualified workers can achieve without over-exertion as an average over the working day or shift provided they adhere to the specified method and provided they are motivated to apply themselves to their work.' (Term No. 51004 in BS 3138, by kind permission of the British Standards Institution.)

Standard product specification sheet (SPSS) or Standard Produt Cost Sheet (SPCS): 'A document which provides for the assembly of the detailed standard cost of a unit or batch of product. The selling price and the contribution or profit may also be shown.'[1]

Substitution Variance: that part of a direct labour cost variance which is caused by using a grade of labour which is at variance with the predetermined (standard) grade for the job, product or process concerned. The calculation of a substitution variance takes place on the assumption that the standard rate appropriate to the 'wrong' grade used is actually being paid: if it is not, a *rate* variance also applies. The formula is: actual hours charged times the standard rate for standard operative(s); *less* actual hours charged times the standard rate for actual operative(s) used. If the latter is greater, an unfavourable variance results.

Total Profit Variance: see Profit Variance.

Variable Costs: those categories of cost which vary in total with changes in activity levels, eg, direct materials.

Variance: a deviation of actual results from expected or budgeted results: a specific variance arises from comparing actual costs of a particular category with standard cost, or actual sales with budgeted sales.

Variable Selling Costs (or overhead): a cost related to selling which tends to vary in amount in direct proportion to changes in the volume of units sold. Alternatively, a variable selling cost budget may occasionally be flexed to take account of deviations between budgeted and actually monetary sales turnover, although this approach can be faulty if, for example, sales price increases are approved which cause a turnover rise but which do not necessitate any selling cost increases.

Variable Works (or Production) Cost: 'The sum of prime cost (direct materials, direct wages and direct manufacturing expenses) and variable production overhead (overhead cost related to production which, in the aggregate, tends to vary in direct proportion to changes in the volume of output).'[1]

Variable Works (or Production) Overhead: see Variable Works (or production) Cost.

Work in Progress: 'Materials, components, or products in various stages of completion during a manufacturing process.The term also applies to partly completed contracts.'[1]

Work in Progress Control Account: see Control Accounts.

Yield Ratio: may either by the relationship of good output weight of saleable commodity to the weight of input entering a process (expressed as a percentage), or the proportion (as a percentage) of total production (in units) which passes inspection and proceeds to finished goods account in the nominal ledger as saleable, or to the next production department.

Yield Variance: this variance may be that part of a Direct Material Usage Variance which is caused by using excess or short measure of input bulk of mixed ingredients in a manufacturing process (as compared with standard total bulk allowed for the given production activity level). However when there is only one raw material ingredient, the Direct Material Yield Variance is the same as the Direct Material Usage Variance, in which case the latter expression is preferred. Again, this variance may be the standard output cost of those finished units which were unexpectedly scrapped (unfavourable variance) or of those which were expected to be scrapped from the total activity level achieved, but which survived (favourable variance): in such cases, a Production Yield Variance is involved.

1. 'Terminology of Management and Financial Accountancy' published by The Institute of Cost and Management Accountants, 63 Portland Place, London, W1N 4AB.
2. 'Managerial Accounting:an Introduction to Concepts, Methods and Uses', by Davidson, Schindler, Stickney and Weil (The Dryden Press, Illinois).
3. 'Cost Accounting: a Managerial Emphasis', by C. T. Horngren (3rd Edition) (Prentice/Hall International).

FURTHER READING

Terminology of Management and Financial Accountancy (The Institute of Cost and Management Accountants (ICMA)).

Cost and Management Accountancy for Students (ICMA: Heinemann).

Bigg's Cost and Management Accounts (Tenth Edition), Volume One: Cost Accounts (Macdonald & Evans).

Wheldon's Cost Accounting and Costing Methods, 14th Edition, L. W. J. Owler & J. L. Brown (Macdonald & Evans).

Cost Accounting: A Managerial Emphasis, by C. T. Horngren, Fourth Edition (Prentice/Hall International Inc, London).

Understanding Management Accounting, by T. M. Walker (Gee & Co).

Management Accounting, by Norman Thornton (Heinemann Accountancy and Administration series).

Standard Costing, by J. Batty, Fourth Edition (Macdonald & Evans).

Variance Accountancy, by E. Laidler (ICMA: Macmillan).

SELECTED EXAMINATION QUESTIONS

(1) (a) Explain briefly:
    (i) how standards are compiled for material and labour costs for a product;
    (ii) the nature and purpose of material and labour variances.
  (b) Calculate the material and labour variances from the data set out below and present your answers in the form of a statement for presentation to management.

	Standard
Weight to produce one unit	12 kilograms
Price, per kilogram	£9
Hours to produce one unit	10
Wages rate, per hour	£2

Actual production and costs for week ended 12th November, 1977:

Units produced	240
Material used	2,640 kilograms
Material cost	£26,400
Hours worked	2,520
Wages paid	£5,544

(The Institute of Cost and Management
Accountants (ICMA), Cost Accounting 1,
November 1977).   (25 marks)

(2) You are required, as assistant management accountant of Ayebee Limited, to prepare a profit and loss statement for the month of April 1978. The format of the statement and the relevant data are given below:

Information taken from the standard costs and budgets for the company's two products are:

Per Article:	Price per unit £	Product Aye units	Product Bee units
Direct material: W	4.3	4	—
X	6.0	5	—
Y	2.0	—	10
Z	2.2	—	4
	Rate per hour £	hours	hours
Direct wages, grade: I	2.2	8	4
II	1.8	4	8
Budgeted:			
Output per month, articles	320	400	

Overhead for the month is
£34,560, absorbed on an
hourly rate basis.
Profit, 20% of selling price.

Actual data for April 1978 were as follows:

	units	price per unit £
Used, direct material: W	1,280	4.2
X	1,600	6.2
Y	4,000	2.1
Z	1,580	2.0

	Product Aye	Product Bee
Output, articles	315	390

	£
Overhead incurred	33,400

Direct wages paid:

	Rate per hour £	Hours
Grade: I	2.0	3,960
II	1.7	4,260

There was no stock at the beginning or end of the month.

Format of:

Profit and Loss Statement
for month ended 30th April, 1978

	Product Aye £	Product Bee £	Total £
Sales, actual quantity at standard price	___	___	___
Standard cost of sales:			
Direct material			
Direct wages			
Overhead	___	___	___
Total	___	___	___
Standard profit on actual sales	___	___	___
Variances:			
Direct materials: price			
usage			
cost			___
Direct wages: rate			___
efficiency			
cost			___
Overhead: expenditure			
productivity			
capacity			
cost			___
Total			___
Actual Profit			___

(ICMA, Cost Accounting 2, May 1978).   (40 marks)

(3) (a) Discuss the factors that a management accountant should consider when deciding whether or not to investigate variances disclosed in reporting on standard costing or budgetary control systems.

(b) Outline briefly what approaches the management accountant might take to develop a routine to assist in this area of decision-making.

(20 marks)

(ICMA, Management Accounting I, November 1977)

(4) Suckers Limited produces vacuum cleaners. An integrated system of standard costing and budgetary control is operated.

The undernoted data relating to the budgeted and actual production and sales for the four weeks ending 28th January 1979 is available.

	1979 £
Budget sales value per unit	80.00
Standard production cost per unit –	
Material	40.00
Labour	15.00
Production overhead – fixed	3.00
– variable 5 hrs per unit	5.00
	63.00
Budgeted labour rate per hour	£3.00
Production in units – budget	175
– actual	170
Sales in units – budget	180
– actual	200
Actual labour – hours	680
Actual labour rate per hour	£4.00
	£
Budgeted selling expenses – fixed	360
– variable	900
Actual sales	15,600
Materials issued at standard price	6,760
Actual production overheads – fixed	550
– variable	875
Actual selling expenses – fixed	350
– variable	900

Required
Prepare an operating statement for the period to 28th January 1979 showing the appropriate budget, actual and variance figures.

(The Institute of Chartered Accountants of Scotland, August 1979)

(5) Slyme Limited manufactures a commercial cleaning concentrate from two ingredients, X and Y. A standard absorption costing system is in use. Shown below are certain balances in the company's cost records at 30th September 1977 after twelve months' trading:

	Dr £	Cr £
Standard cost of goods sold	273,000	
Variances:		
Direct material usage	500	
Labour efficiency		3,500
Labour rate	3,100	
Unapplied overhead	2,000	

Material price variances are taken on purchase. The balance on the direct material price variance account is zero, but analysis reveals a debit balance of £3,000 in respect of X and a credit balance of £3,000 in respect of Y.

The standard mix of ingredients per standard unit of output is 10 gallons of X to 3 gallons of Y. Actual consumption of X during the course of the year was 2,000 gallons less than standard while actual consumption of Y exceeded standard by 2,000 gallons. There are no opening stocks. Physical closing stocks were as follows:

	Quantity	Original purchase cost
Material X	22,000 gallons	£17,160
Material Y	4,000 gallons	£3,600
Finished stock	2,000 standard units	—

Labour costs exceed standard by 10p per hour. Actual overhead expenditure was £170,000. Overhead is applied at 150% of direct labour hour costs. 6,000 standard units were sold during the period.

No overhead efficiency variance has been taken out.

You are required to prepare a table showing the total standard cost of a unit of output and the various cost elements per unit of output in standard quantity and standard value.

(The Institute of Chartered Accountants
in England and Wales (ICAEW), December 1977)

(6) A furniture manufacturer has established standard costs in the joinery department, in which one size of a particularly styled kitchen cabinet is produced. The standard costs of producing one of these cabinets are shown below:

KITCHEN CABINET STYLE 1200/01

		£
Materials:	Timber 50 ft of board at 10p per ft	5.00
Direct Labour:	3 hours at £3 per hour	9.00
Indirect costs:		
	Variable charges – 3 hours at 50p	1.50
	Fixed Charges – 3 hours at 25p	.75
		16.25

The cost of operations to produce 400 of these cabinets during October are stated below. There were no opening stocks.

		£
Materials purchased:	25,000 ft of board at 11p	2,750
Materials used:	19,000 ft of board	
Direct labour:	1,100 hours at £2.95	3,245
Indirect costs:		
	Variable charges	650
	Fixed charges	355

The flexible budget for this department called for 1,400 direct labour hours of operation at the monthly activity level used to set the fixed overhead rate.

You are required to compute the following variances from standard cost, identifying them as favourable (F) or unfavourable (U):

(a) material purchase price
(b) material usage
(c) (i) direct rate
      (ii) direct labour efficiency variance
(d) (i) variable overhead total variance
      (ii) fixed overhead budget variance (expenditure variance)
      (iii) fixed overhead volume variance
(e) (i) variable overhead expenditure variance (rate or price variance)
      (ii) variable overhead efficiency variance.

(23 marks)

(ICAEW, December 1975)

(7) A chemical company has the following standards for manufacturing a machine lubricant:

	£
5 gallons of material P at £0.70 per gallon	3.50
5 gallons of material Q at £0.92 per gallon	4.60
10	**8.10***

*Cost of 10 gallons of standard mix which should produce 9 gallons of finished product at a standard cost of £0.90 (£8.10 ÷ 9) a gallon.

No stocks of raw materials are kept. Purchases are made as needed so that all price variances relate to materials used. Actual results showed that 100,000 gallons of material were used during a particular period as follows:

	£
45,000 gallons of material P at an actual cost per gallon used of £0.80	36,000
55,000 gallons of material Q at an actual cost per gallon used of £0.97	53,350
100,000	**89,350**

Good output:

		£
92,070	gallons at a standard cost of £0.90 per gallon produced	82,863
	Total unfavourable material variance	6,487

You are required to:
(a) analyse
    (i) the total material variance in terms of price and usage variances,
    (ii) the usage variance in terms of mix and yield variances and
(b) explain the circumstances under which a material mix variance is relevant to managerial control.

(ICAEW, July 1975)

(8) KC Chemicals Ltd produce an industrial purifying agent known as Kleenchem, the budgeted weekly output/sales of which is 10,000 litres, the standard cost per 100 litres being:

Material	250 kg costing 50p per kg
Labour	4 hours at £1.25 per hour
Overhead	£5 (budgeted absorption of fixed cost)

The standard selling price is £1.50 per one-litre container.

During week ended 26th November the output of Kleenchem was 9,860 litres all of which was sold, the invoiced value being £14,750. The material input was 24,720 kg, which cost £12,300. Production employees booked 380 hours to the process and were paid £490. Overhead amounted to £525.

You are required to use the foregoing information to produce the operating statement for the week ended 26th November in standard costing format.

(26 marks)
(The Association of Certified Accountants,
Accounting 2: Costing (December 1976)

INDEX

Abnormal scrap, units of production, 73, 74-78, 79, 119, 120, 121
Abnormal Scrapped Production Variance, see Production Yield Variance
Abnormal stock loss variance account, 172 (see also Production yield variance account)
Absorption costing, 101, 117, 125, 136, 142
Absorption rate (or application, conversion, or recovery rates), 5, 43, 96, 101, 106, 108, 110, 113, 172
Actual Gross Profit, 44
Actual Profit, 16, 17, 18, 19, 20, 22, 24, 34, 35, 42, 44, 47, 51, etc, etc
Adjusted capacity variance, 111
Administration overhead, as a category, 25, 112
Administration overhead volume variance, 113
Administration overheads, book-keeping, 27, 112
Administration overheads expenditure variance, 112, 113
Administration overheads volume variance, 142

Balance Sheet, treatment of variances, 3, 4, 11, 16, 17, 18, 20, 21, 22, 34, 35, 44, 45, 46, 51, 57, 76, 84, 89, 98, 100, 103, 104
Balances on stock accounts, brought forward from earlier period, 23
Budgeted contribution per unit of key factor, 118
Budgeted output: compilation of, 112
Budgeted profit, 16, 17, 18, 19, 20, 22, 23, 44, 47, 51, etc, etc
Budgets at subsidiary account level, 95, 96

Calendar variances, 109, 110, 111
Canteen account, 97
Capacity available, 112
Capacity ratio, 106, 115, 116, 117, 122, 123
Capital employed, 16
Categories of cost, 25, 49
Contribution per hour, 118, 119
Contribution per product, 129
Control accounts, 7, 25, 29, 30, 38, 39, 77, 95, 96, 97, 101, 138, 142
Control of costs, 6, 10, 12, 13
Cost of Production, at standard, 101
Cost of Sales at Standard Account, General book-keeping, 30, 31, 33, 39, 42, 101, 102, 138, 172
(Costing), Profit and Loss Account, see Profit and Loss Account
Conversion rate, see absorption rate
Criteria for investigating variances, 178-179

Departmental accounts, general use of, 96, 151
Depreciation, 43
Direct expenses, as a category 25
Direct Labour Cost Variance Account, 29, 32, 81, 82, 83, 84, 86, 87, 88, 89, 91, 92, 93
Direct Labour Efficiency Variance Account, 29, 38, 41, 81, 83, 84, 86, 88, 90, 91, 92, 93, 143, 144, 145, 176, 189
Direct Labour Rate Variance Account, 29, 38, 41, 81, 83, 84, 86, 87, 88, 89, 90, 91, 92, 93, 109, 143, 144, 145, 176, 189
Direct labour, as a category, 25
Direct labour efficiency ratio, 87, see also, Efficiency Ratio
Direct (raw) materials, as a category, 25

Direct materials usage variance account, see under 'Raw materials'
Direct (raw) materials cost variance, 50, 51, 52, 55, 56, 58, 59, 60, 61, 63, 148
Direct materials price variance, see under 'Raw materials'
Direct (raw) materials Scrap Yield Variance account, 54, 61, 64, 148
Direct (raw) materials scrap price variance account, 55, 62, 64, 148
Distribution overheads, as a category, 25
Downtime, inclusion in standards, 8, 94, 112, 121, 122, 123

Earned surplus account, see Profit and Loss Account
Effectiveness ratio, 124
Efficiency ratio (or rate), 87, 88, 108, 109, 111, 115, 116, 117, 119, 122, 123
Examination instructions, on stock valuation, 20, 113, 142
Exception report, 3

Finished Goods Stores Control Account, 142
Finished Goods Stock Account, General book-keeping, 30, 33, 37, 42, 74, 77
First-in-First-out stock issues, (FIFO), 23, 58
Fixed Administration Overhead Volume Variance, 142
Fixed Production Overhead Volume Ratio, 106, 119, 122, 123
Fixed Production Overhead Volume Variance, 47, 49, 101,103, 104, 105, 106, 107, 108, 109, 110, 111, 142, 143, 144, 145, 176, 177
Fixed Overhead Expenditure Variance, 49, 101, 102, 105, 129, 143, 144, 145, 177
Fixed Production Overhead Capacity Variance, 106, 107, 108, 109, 110, 111, 112, 119
Fixed Production Overhead Capacity Ratio, 106, 122, 123
Fixed Production Overhead Calendar Variances, 109, 110
Fixed Production Overhead Efficiency Variance, 106, 108, 109, 111, 119
Fixed Production Overhead Volume Variance, at departmental level, 107, 108, 115, 118
Fixed Production (Works) Overhead Cost Variance Account, 39, 102, 104, 105
Fixed selling costs, book-keeping, 28, 138
Fixed selling cost expenditure variance, 136, 137
Fixed selling cost volume variance, 136, 137, 143
Fixed selling overhead, as a category, 25
Fixed Works (Production) Overheads, book-keeping, 27, 100
Fixed Works (Production) Overheads, as a category, 25, 100
Flexed standard cost, 97, 118, 136
Forced standardisation, 183

Gross capacity, 122, 123

Idle time, 2, 112
Incomplete work, 94

Interpretative comments, 149, 152, 153, 154, 158, 159, 172, 173
Key factors, 118

Last-in, first out stock issues, (LIFO), 23

Machine Shop Effectiveness Ratio, 124
Managerial variances, 3
Marginal costing, 101, 102, 125
Marketing costs, 135

Normal operating conditions, 85
Normal scrap, units of production, 73, 74-78, 79

Objectives, Management, 1, 6
Achievement of, 2
Opening stock, at standard, 23
Operating statement; see Profit and Loss Account

Piece rate, 85
Practical capacity, 121
Product unit, 95
Production Capacity Ratio, 115, 116
Production cost variance, 22, 23
Production cost ratios, 114
Production departments in subsidiary ledgers, 25, 95, 96, 97
Production Efficiency (or Productivity) Ratio, 115, 116, 122, 123
Production Scrap Ratio, 119
Production Scrap Yield Variance account, 78, 79
Production Volume Ratio, 115, 116, 117, 118, 122, 123
Production Yield Variance, 73, 74, 76, 77, 78, 79, 80, 119, 120, 172, 177
Productivity agreement, 87, 94, 109
Productivity ratio, see Efficiency ratio
Profit and Loss Account (or profit statement), 4, 5, 11, 15, 16, 17, 18, 20, 21, 22, 23, 30, 31, 34, 35, 39, 42, 43, 44, 45, 46, 57, 58, 59, 62, 63, 68, 69, 72, 104, 113, 121, 130, 131, 134, 137, 139, 140, 141, 147, 151, 156, 157, 161, 162, 168, 169
Profit statements, see Profit and Loss Account

Raw (Direct) Material Price Variance Account, 29, 32, 38, 51, 52, 53, 58, 60, 61, 63, 69, 81, 142, 143, 144, 145, 175
Raw (Direct) Material Usage Variance, analysis, 65, 66, 67, 68, 69, 70, 71, 72, 80
Raw (Direct) Materials Cost Variance, 50, 51, 52, 55, 56, 58, 59, 60, 61, 63, 148
Raw Material Stock, book keeping, 29, 32, 37, 40, 52, 77
Raw Material Usage Variance Account, 29, 32, 39, 41, 53, 59, 60, 61, 64, 65, 66, 67, 68, 69, 70, 71, 72, 76, 79, 80, 81, 143, 144, 145, 148, 176
Revision of Standard, 10, 185, 186, 187, 188, 189
Revision variances, 186, 187, 188, 189

Sales Account, 78
Sales price variance, 20, 21, 22, 23, 39, 42, 49, 125, 126, 127, 129, 131, 133, 135, 158
Sales turnover variances, 46, 47, 125
Sales Volume Variance, 19, 22, 23, 44, 49, 125, 126, 127, 128, 131, 133, 135, 142, 158, 178

Sales Volume Variance: bulk quantity deviations, 128, 129, 131, 135, 158, 170, 178
Sales Volume Variance: mix deviations, 128, 131, 135, 158, 170, 178
Scrap, inclusion in standards, 8, 73
Scrap ratio, 119
Scrap yield variance, 120
Selling costs, 43, 135
Selling Cost Variance Account, 43
Selling Cost Variances, 126, 135, 136, 137, 143
Standard cost per unit, 50
Standard cost specification sheet, 7, 8
Standard costing, objectives, 3, 5, 6, 7, 8, 9, 10, 13, 14, 42, 102, 120
Standard costing system, justifying, 11, 180-181
Standard costing system, setting up 180-183
Standard costing system, operating difficulties, 183-186
Standard departmental operating hour, 85
Standard direct labour hour, 85
Standard hour, 85, 107, 108, 109, 115, 122
Standard, improving on, 10
Standard labour hour, 85
Standard machine hour, 85
Standard product specification sheets, 7, 8
Standards, construction of 4, 10, 11, 184
Statement of performance:
   see Profit and Loss Account
Stock losses, treatment of, 170, 171, 172
Stock valuation; treatment of administration overheads in, 112
Stores Control Account (Finished Goods), 142
Stores Control Account (Raw Materials), 142
Subsidiary ledgers for departments, 25, 95, 96, 97
Subsidiary ledgers, general use of, 96, 97
Subsidiary ledgers for stock, 7, 25
Substitution variance, 89, 90
Summary trading (or operating) statement, 161, 162

'T' accounts, 37-39, 42
Technological change, 184
Total profit variance, 3, 16, 21, 31, 45, 46, 91
Total variances, 3, 16, 21, 31
Transfer of stock, 6, 7, 16, 17, 29, 30, 31, 32, 33, 37-39, 41, 42
Trial balances, 100, 103
Turnover variances, 46, 47, 125

Unmeasured work, 94
Unsold stock, 101, 106, 118, 140, 141, 172

Variable selling overhead, as a category, 25, 112
Variable selling overheads, bookkeeping, 28
Variable Works (Production) Overhead Variance Account, 30, 39, 49, 98, 99, 143, 144, 145
Variable Works (Production) Overheads, as a category, 25 . . . book keeping, 26
Variable Works Overhead Efficiency Variance, 98, 99, 100
Variable Works Overhead Rate Variance, 98, 99, 100
Variances, creation of, 3, 5, 11, 13, 15, 16, 31, 32, 33, 34, 35, 37, 38, 39, 40, 41, 42, 45, 54, 56, 57
at departmental level, 95, 96
manageable, 3
total, 3, 4, 5, 16, 45
for balance sheet purposes, 3, 4, 15, 20, 21, 22, 31, 34, 35, 40, 41, 44, 45, 51, 57, 76, 82, 84, 89, 99, 100, 103

causes of, 4, 5, 6, 11, 13, 18, 31, 63, 85, 175-179
   categories, 5, 13, 190
   controllable, 5, 6, 10, 13, 181, 189
   non-controllable, 5, 6, 10, 13, 181, 185, 189
   compensating, 6, 10
   aggregate, 6
   level of detail required, 181, 185
   significant, 6, 10, 13, 42
   temporary and permanent, 10, 11, 13

'non-variances', 45, 46, 47, 125
   (sales) turnover variances, 46, 125
Volume ratio, 106, 115, 116, 117, 118, 119, 123

Wages Control Account, 38, 40
Work in Progress Account, general
   book-keeping, 25-27, 29, 32, 37, 40, 41, 42, 43, 74, 77, 96, 97, 100, 101, 103

Yield Variance, see Production Yield Variance